Thomas Middleton & the New Comedy Tradition

Thomas Middleton

&

the New Comedy Tradition

George E. Rowe, Jr.

University of Nebraska Press ● Lincoln and London

The publication of this book was assisted by a grant from The Andrew W. Mellon Foundation.

Portions of Chapters 3 and 5 have appeared previously in different form as "Prodigal Sons, New Comedy and Middleton's *Michaelmas Term*," *English Literary Renaissance* 7 (1977): 90–107, and "*The Old Law* and Middleton's Comic Vision," *ELH* 42 (1975): 189–202.

UNP

Publishers on the Plains

Library of Congress Cataloging in Publication Data

Rowe, George E   1947–
    Thomas Middleton and the new comedy tradition.

    Includes index.
    1. Middleton, Thomas, d. 1627—Criticism and interpretation.   2. Classical drama (Comedy)—History and criticism.   I. Title.
PR2717.R6   822'.3   79–4289
ISBN 0–8032–3853–3

Manufactured in the United States of America

To my mother,
Selma Schindler Rowe,
and
to the memory of my father,
George Ernest Rowe (1896–1972)

Contents

Acknowledgments

Research grants from the National Endowment for the Humanities and Wichita State University helped make this book possible, and I would like to thank both institutions for their aid. The editors of *ELH* and *English Literary Renaissance* kindly have allowed me to reprint articles which originally appeared there in slightly different form. For permission to quote copyrighted material I wish also to thank the University of Nebraska Press, publishers of *Michaelmas Term*, edited by Richard Levin, *A Mad World, My Masters*, edited by Standish Henning, and *No Wit, No Help Like a Woman's*, edited by Lowell E. Johnson; Ernest Benn, Ltd. and W. W. Norton and Co., Inc., publishers of *A Trick to Catch the Old One*, edited by G. J. Watson; and Manchester University Press and the Johns Hopkins University Press, current publishers of *A Chaste Maid in Cheapside*, edited by R. B. Parker (introduction and apparatus criticus copyright © 1969 by R. B. Parker), *The Changeling*, edited by N. W. Bawcutt (introduction and apparatus criticus copyright © 1958 by N. W. Bawcutt), and *Women Beware Women*, edited by J. R. Mulryne (introduction and apparatus criticus copyright © 1975 by J. R. Mulryne).

Jackson Cope, Alan Dessen, Cyrus Hoy, Arnold Stein, and Donald Wineke all gave of their time to read—and improve—the manuscript, and I am grateful for their help. My greatest debt, however, is to Jackson Cope—as scholar, teacher, and friend. It was he who first introduced me to the pleasures and challenges of Renaissance drama and kindled my interest in

Thomas Middleton. This book could not have been written without his generosity, encouragement, and support. Finally, to Kathy, my wife, I owe my deepest gratitude. She has left her imprint on this study in ways too numerous to mention.

Thomas Middleton & the New Comedy Tradition

1
Introduction

> *No poet, no artist of any art, has his complete meaning*
> *alone. His significance, his appreciation is the apprecia-*
> *tion of his relation to the dead poets and artists.*

In the decades since these words first appeared in T. S. Eliot's "Tradition and the Individual Talent," it has become increasingly evident that the meaning of any single literary work depends not only upon its specific qualities, but also upon its relation to the order of literature as a whole.[1] Every poem, novel, and play is both derivative and unique, at once part of a continuing literary tradition and yet distinct from other works within that tradition. And thus every poem, novel, and play necessarily engages in a dialogue with earlier works, as its author remakes and reinterprets the literary forms and conventions of the past in the light of the historical pressures of the present and his own particular consciousness. This study is an investigation of Thomas Middleton's involvement in that process of reinterpretation, of the ways in which he revised one of

1

the central dramatic traditions available to an English Renaissance playwright, New Comedy, and of the reasons for those
revisions. In the following pages I hope to demonstrate that
Middleton's plays systematically undermine New Comedy
conventions in order to criticize the assumptions and values
which lie behind them and, ultimately, to reject the explanation of existence which the form embodies.

The New Comedy structure which Middleton and his contemporaries inherited is as simple as it was (and is) enduring.
From its origins in Greece through the plays of Plautus and
Terence to the Renaissance, the basic form remained relatively
unchanged. Northrop Frye describes a typical plot as follows:
"What normally happens is that a young man wants a young
woman, that his desire is resisted by some opposition . . . and
that near the end of the play some twist in the plot enables the
hero to have his will." The hero's difficulties form the action of
the comedy, and the resolution of those problems its conclusion. These difficulties usually have their source in the hero's
father or in "someone who partakes of the father's closer
relation to established society: that is, a rival with less youth and
more money." The protagonist's victory often represents the
symbolic overthrow of a harsh, restrictive society by one which
is freer, more accepting, and more inclusive; and as "the final
society reached by comedy is the one that the audience has
recognized all along to be the proper and desirable state of
affairs, an act of communion with the audience is in order."
Indeed, "the resolution of comedy comes, so to speak, from the
audience's side of the stage."[2]

Frye's description of New Comedy is, to be sure, a highly
selective one. Doubtless, no single Roman comedy fits his
model in every detail, and a few do not seem to fit it well at all.[3]
Nor do Frye's comments cover the entire range of elements
present in the plays of Plautus and Terence; they are not
intended to do so. Frye's model is neither prescriptive nor
rigid.[4] It is simply an accurate and illuminating summary of the
kinds of activities we are apt to encounter in plays of this type.
He has isolated the most lasting and, I think, most essential
aspects of the New Comedy tradition, aspects which were re-

peated, expanded, and developed by a great many European dramatists who wrote after Plautus and Terence. He focuses on the central conflict which lies behind New Comedy—a conflict between forces associated with death and sterility and ones associated with life and fertility—and shows how this conflict is *usually* (but not always) embodied in New Comedy plots. Although Middleton and his contemporaries did not have Northrop Frye at their side to describe the essential features of Roman comedy and may, in fact, have spoken of Roman plays in somewhat different but by no means antithetical terms, it was, I believe, precisely the features of New Comedy Frye singles out that they responded to—that most writers within this tradition have responded to—when writing their own comedies.[5] For the most part, they did not imitate a particular Roman play while writing. They imitated and made contemporary something much more general and flexible: a plot structure, or pattern of expectations, assumptions, and values, which was an amalgamation of their experiences of New Comedies written by Italian and English as well as Roman playwrights.

Indeed, a Renaissance dramatist or theatergoer unquestionably would have recognized the main characteristics of the plot which Frye describes—the conflict of generations, the thwarting of young love and its eventual consummation, the audience's approval of that union—as those of traditional comedy. There are several reasons for this. First, even a person of minimal education in the Renaissance would be familiar with New Comedy from his schooling, because, as T. W. Baldwin has exhaustively shown, an intensive study of Terence and, to a lesser extent, Plautus formed an integral part of grammar school curricula in the sixteenth century. Moreover, virtually all critical discussions of comedy written during the sixteenth century analyzed diction, plot, and character in Terence's plays. For the most part, these discussions did not find fault with the Roman dramatist. On the contrary, Terence's plays were frequently advanced as a norm against which all comedy should be measured. Given these tendencies in education and dramatic theory, it is no accident that comedy was one of the first dramatic forms fully to be realized on the Renaissance stage. Nor is it surprising that most English Renaissance comedies have, in Madeleine Doran's words, "identifiable features of Roman comedy in the plotting."[6]

Renaissance dramatists, of course, seldom adopted New Comedy conventions without mingling them with other forms and traditions: the Italian *commedia erudita* and *commedia dell' arte*, medieval romance, satire.[7] But these additions usually do not alter the basic character of Roman comedy in any essential way. The form is expanded and some new concerns are superimposed upon it, but in general these new elements complement rather than contradict themes and values already implicit in comedy. The *commedia erudita* has roots in Roman drama as well as in Boccaccio's prose narratives, and the *commedia dell' arte* also is indebted to the traditions of literary comedy. Characters and events drawn from medieval romance simply reinforce the romantic materials Renaissance theorists had already detected in Terence and Plautus. Similarly, the taste for satire and the depiction of native folly, which led in English Renaissance drama to the development of city comedy, seldom did more than impose apparently realistic and contemporary veneers on what are basically New Comedy plots. Admittedly, there were some dramatists who went further than this type of synthesis. Because the perspective of New Comedy is not easily reconciled with a strict Christian view of society, some writers developed alternative and competing comic forms: the Christian Terence and "comicall satyre" are perhaps the most important. But to most Renaissance dramatists and audiences, comedy meant New Comedy. Theirs was an adulterated and peculiarly Renaissance version of the form, but it still remained recognizably within a dramatic tradition extending back through Roman comedy to Menander and his contemporaries. It is this tradition which lies behind many of Thomas Middleton's plays.[8]

The relationship of Middleton's dramas to conventional comedy is, however, complex and ambiguous. Unlike Shakespeare's comedies, which develop and expand the potential of Roman comedy, or Jonson's, which gradually move away from

Latin models to create a comic world which is uniquely their own, Middleton's plays (both comedies and tragicomedies) often seem to follow New Comedy patterns but, paradoxically, do not affect us in the way that dramas based upon the typical plot structure of Plautus and Terence normally do. They contain characters and events which seem familiar; yet, at the same time, they deny us our familiar responses. Many of Middleton's dramas, in other words, both are and are not New Comedies. It is this ambiguity, I believe, which accounts for so many readers' dissatisfaction with his plays.[9]

A drama's meaning and effect depend in part upon the learned and habitual responses which its audience brings to the theater.[10] Because a play exists in time, we must quickly make certain assumptions about its major themes, characters, and so on, in order to begin organizing and interpreting the events which we see before us. These assumptions are usually generic ones: an audience determines what kind of play it is watching and adjusts its way of responding to the play accordingly. Our notions of genre are derived primarily from our previous experiences in the theater, our encounters with plays which seem similar to the one we are presently watching. The more thoroughly conventional (and thus uniform) a given genre is, the more strongly it controls our expectations and responses. The most stylized aspects of the genre act as signposts, reassuring us that we are on familiar ground and directing our reactions into familiar patterns. Part of our enjoyment consists in this knowledge and in watching a play move toward a conclusion which we already anticipate.

Such is the case with New Comedy, a genre which is highly conventional and thus remarkably consistent in the kinds of characters and events it describes. As complex as the details of comic plots often seem, the overall structure and movement of those plots is totally predictable. Once we realize that the work before us is in the tradition of conventional comedy (and the realization may not be fully conscious), we immediately know that our sympathies should lie with youth and that all will come out well for the protagonists. At the end of the play we applaud a state of affairs which we have recognized since the beginning of the drama to be both beneficial and *inevitable*. Because New Comedy is so stylized and therefore creates strong and specific patterns of expectations, a comic play's failure to fulfill those expectations is usually disturbing. This failure and disturbance are precisely what happen with many of Middleton's dramas. Having assumed that we have entered a New Comedy world and established a certain perspective as a result, we are confronted suddenly by characters and incidents which violate the rules of the generic category we have assigned to the play. Our method of interpreting the drama no longer seems relevant. The play itself no longer appears to have a coherent form. We are left confused, unsatisfied, and perhaps slightly uneasy. The communion between audience and players which should conclude comedy becomes impossible because that communion depends upon the fulfillment of audience expectations.[11]

Middleton's comedies fail to keep the promises implicit in their apparently conventional form because they contain an almost endless variety of virtually irreconcilable elements which resist the normal comic movement toward moderation and harmony.[12] The world of his most typical plays is filled with discord and conflict. Idealism is juxtaposed to cynicism; serious concerns mingle with farcical ones. Plots characterized by radically different tones (*A Trick to Catch the Old One*) or by opposing values (*Michaelmas Term*) are placed side by side within a play without any apparent attempt to unify them. At times, the events in the plays seem on the verge of tragedy, as the characters' actions go far beyond the normal boundaries of comic folly (Philip's failure to ransom his mother and sister in *No Wit, No Help Like a Woman's*, Whorehound's repentance in *A Chaste Maid in Cheapside*, and the pregnant Page's dance in *More Dissemblers Besides Women*, for example). The characters themselves sometimes behave so mechanically and excessively that they seem to belong in allegory rather than comedy. Overwhelmed by his own particular obsession, a figure such as Tangle (*The Phoenix*), Harry Dampit (*A Trick to Catch the Old One*), or Tim (*A Chaste Maid in Cheapside*) becomes totally alienated from his fellows and so cannot interact meaningfully with them. Moreover, human personalities are remarkably fluid and inconstant in Middleton's plays; the characters often move quickly and implausibly from one form of extreme behavior to another. At the end of *The Phoenix*, Tangle suddenly rejects his mad interest in law and adopts a peaceful demeanor which contrasts starkly with his previous personality. In *Michaelmas Term*, Quomodo inexplicably loses the cleverness which has brought him success throughout the play, while his foolish victim, Richard Easy, does the opposite and becomes an intelligent man. In *A Mad World, My Masters*, Middleton emphasizes the inconsistency of his characters' personalities by assigning them names which allude to contradictory qualities: *Folly / wit, Penitent / Brothel, Frank / Gullman*.

The society described in Middleton's plays inevitably clashes with such conventional comic values as reconciliation and harmony. By including elements so discordant or so potentially tragic that they cannot easily be accommodated and reconciled within a New Comedy plot, Middleton subverts the apparently traditional comic form of his dramas. Their content (and the responses called for by that content) contradicts their structure (and the very different pattern of expectations and responses implicit in that structure). Despite the fact that their plots and characters are ostensibly familiar, the effect of the plays is finally very different from that of conventional comedy. At the same time that most of Middleton's comedies and some of his tragicomedies encourage our participation in their festivities, they paradoxically make that participation impossible.

The problematic nature of so many of Middleton's plays might, admittedly, be the product of artistic failure rather than intent. The evidence, however, suggests otherwise. There have been many fine analyses of Middleton's uneasy mixtures of contrasting elements (especially comic and tragic ones), but no one, I believe, has fully realized how systematic and self-conscious those mixtures are.[13] The discords are intentional, a fact Middleton himself makes explicit in at least two instances. The first occurs at the end of act 2 scene 1, in *A Trick to Catch the Old One*. Mistress Lucre enters and angrily vows to punish her husband for insulting her. Her son, Sam Freedom, is eager to

know the kind of revenge she contemplates and asks: "Is it a
tragedy plot, or a comedy plot, good mother?" (l.349).[14] She
replies that it is neither, that it cannot be so easily and conventionally categorized: " 'Tis a plot shall vex him," she says
(l.350). The answer is a surprising but important one, for
Mistress Lucre is talking about the nature and effect of Middleton's plot as well.

A similar and perhaps more illuminating passage occurs in
Hengist, King of Kent, a play whose generic affiliations have
been in question since its initial publication under the rubric of
comedy with the title *The Mayor of Queenborough*. For whereas
the main plot of *Hengist* is a chronicle play dealing with ambi-
tion and the relationship of sexuality and power, the subplot
depicts the career of a clownish tradesman named Simon. A
fool who burlesques the middle class heroes of Dekker and
Deloney, Simon is an ambitious man. He is elected mayor of
Queenborough, withstands the "revolt" of a Puritan named
Oliver, and orders that his adversary be punished by watching
a play. The scene of Oliver's ordeal, like a similar scene at the
end of *A Mad World, My Masters*, functions on several levels at
once. Many of the speeches have a double and sometimes a
triple significance: for Simon's play, for *Hengist, King of Kent*,
and for the world of Middleton's audience. In the midst of the
festivities Simon is robbed by the players, and his reaction is
crucial to a full understanding both of the drama in which he
appears and, more generally, of Middleton's art. Momentarily
blinded by the meal which the actors have thrown in his face,
the tradesman exlaims: "A pox on your new additions! they
spoil all the plays that ever they come in: the old way had no
such roguery in it. Call you this a merry comedy, when a man's
eyes are put out in't?" (5.1.232–35).

By calling attention to the discord at the heart of the merry
comedy he had hoped to enjoy, Simon points to the effect of his
own actions on *Hengist, King of Kent*. The foolish tanner is out
of place in this drama. The low comedy scenes in which he
appears make no important thematic contribution to the main
plot. Thus, when shortly after the robbery Hengist dismisses
Simon's attempt to tell him the "jest" (l.301) by attacking the

clown's "unseasonable folly" (l.302), his words might also be applied to the entire subplot.[15] Simon's presence here and throughout the drama disrupts the tone of the play's more serious elements. The subplot is "unseasonable" and indecorous. But significantly, Middleton does not attempt to obscure this disunity. Rather, through Simon's comment on the play-within-the-play, Middleton calls our attention to the clash of uncongenial materials in his own drama, to the farce he juxtaposes to tragedy, and to the disharmony which results.

Clearly, Middleton did not endeavor to write plays with tightly structured plots and consistent tones. Instead, he created dramas which are intentionally ambiguous and unsettling. The confusing surface of Middleton's plays is a perfect analogue of the disordered world they portray. Middleton's audience, like the characters it watches onstage, is continually reminded that its ability to understand and interpret events is very limited. We remain uncertain in our judgments because there is no certainty or order in Middleton's world. But Middleton's deliberate use of characters and events which cannot easily be accommodated into conventional comedy at the same time that he retains the outward appearance of comic form does more than simply upset audience expectations. By undermining the usual effect of the conventions he is employing, Middleton calls attention to those conventions. We become at least as aware of the plays' form as of their content.

As a result, the subject of Middleton's dramas often becomes the assumptions and values which underlie the form and conventions of New Comedy. Middleton seems to have realized very early in his career that literary form is not simply a matter of empty patterns and techniques, but that genres and conventions subtly express value judgments and present methods of ordering and interpreting reality. Thus a genre endures, as Claudio Guillèn has argued, "insofar as it continues to be a problem-solving model," a way of giving coherence to the reality an author perceives.[16] Because Middleton felt that New Comedy no longer performed this function, he used his plays—the tragedies and tragicomedies as well as the comedies—to provide an extended commentary on the inadequacies of the genre. In essence, Middleton is testing the view of reality which is implicit in comedy; he is examining its method of explaining human existence.

In doing so, Middleton questions almost all important comic values and assumptions, but he reserves special emphasis for two: New Comedy's affirmation of a unified human community and the form's celebration of man's ability to renew himself and his society. The most obvious sign of Middleton's disbelief in the former is the extremism which typifies the personalities and actions of the individuals in his plays and so alienates them from one another. A second indication concerns the resolutions of his dramas. Because of its inclusiveness and festivity, the conventional comic resolution is the genre's most striking way of asserting the possibility of constructing a homogeneous community of man and proclaiming the belief that all men are one, both in wisdom and in folly. The conclusions of Middleton's comedies, however, are usually problematic and at times patently unconventional. As a result, they frequently subvert the very values and beliefs they should emphasize. In order to accept the apparently harmonious outcome of *Michaelmas Term*, for example, we must forget much that has occurred in the preceding scenes: Easy's foolishness, Quomodo's brilliant plotting, the disgusting actions of Lethe and the Country Wench. But as we will see, Middleton makes the forgetting very difficult; and instead of participating in the concluding festivities, we tend to remain distanced and even somewhat puzzled by what we have just witnessed onstage. Similarly, we may applaud the reconciliation of Witgood with his uncle and the Courtesan with Hoard at the end of *A Trick to Catch the Old One*, but our joy is inevitably qualified by the continuing presence of the play's anticomic society. *No Wit, No Help Like a Woman's* presents an extensive critique of the comic conclusion itself and demonstrates that it represents an unnatural unity which can be maintained only by ignoring the realities of a disordered world.

The traditional comic movement toward a unified human community is rejected again and again in these plays. The blurring of distinctions between individuals which comic inclusiveness requires presumes a unity which, according to Middleton, no longer exists. Thus, while many of his plays contain references to idealized harmonious societies, those societies always lie forever buried in the past or exist somewhere offstage, a distant symbol of dreams which never can be realized. Likewise, all of the characters who attempt to impose some sort of order on the vagaries of their existence—Tangle in *The Phoenix*, Bounteous Progress and Follywit in *A Mad World, My Masters*, Quomodo in *Michaelmas Term*, Weatherwise in *No Wit, No Help Like a Woman's*, Tim in *A Chaste Maid in Cheapside*—are either amoral tricksters or fools and often both. Their unities—like the unities which New Comedy affirms and which the New Comedy conclusion depicts, Middleton would say—are empty and meaningless. The world of his plays simply cannot be arranged according to the precepts of any abstract system. The dramas are filled with conventional ideas of order, moral and ethical as well as generic, but these codes bear little relation to the events the plays depict.

Middleton denies with equal force comedy's traditional assumption that the victory of young love brings with it a renewal of the human community and thus provides a way of both overcoming the ravages of time and creating order and continuity. Indeed, young love is not always admirable in Middleton's plays. In *Michaelmas Term*, Lethe makes his mother his bawd in the name of love; and in *No Wit, No Help Like a Woman's*, Philip Twilight spends money intended to ransom his mother and sister from captivity on a tavern girl. New Comedy tells us that we should value romantic love over love for family, but in both cases Middleton's handling of the young lovers makes this view rather unattractive. Middleton also complicates our attitude toward youthful desires by employing prodigal son motifs in several plays (*Michaelmas Term*, *A Trick to Catch the Old One*, *No Wit, No Help Like a Woman's*, *The Old Law*). The prodigals' denials of heritage and ancestry irrevocably sever present from both past and future and thereby destroy comedy's age-old assertion that man might live on after death through his offspring. The youths do not renew their families or societies; they destroy them. Middleton's distrust of the promise of rebirth which underlies comic structure is perhaps most evident in *A Chaste Maid in Cheapside*. There he carefully calls our attention to that promise and then slowly rejects it, demonstrating that it has no meaning for the world of the play and, by extension, none for our world either.

Middleton's refusal to accept the traditional comic affirmation of both a unified human community and the regenerative power of young love also destroys the ambivalence with which New Comedy normally views misrule and license. In his plays, misrule and freedom are not good and necessary expressions of human energy which enable the individual and his society to remain vital and creative. Instead, they are aspects of a general disorder which has no positive influence. Freedom usually means irresponsible and self-centered behavior—from the examination of the prodigals in *Michaelmas Term* to the portrayal of Allwit in *A Chaste Maid in Cheapside*. And misrule is often destructive; the dramas are characterized by what R. B. Parker has called a "mood of soiled saturnalia," of festivity somehow gone wrong.[17] At times, misrule even assumes a terrifying aspect—a state of affairs most powerfully explored in *The Old Law*.

The Old Law, of course, is technically a tragicomedy rather than a comedy; but as will be shown in Chapter 5, Middleton's examination of comic conventions and assumptions continues into the tragicomedies, written during the second decade of his career. This is not surprising, because Renaissance tragicomedy is essentially a comic form both in theory and practice (see below, this chapter). And despite the exotic locales, ostensibly tragic conflicts, and idealized characters associated with this dramatic hybrid, the structure of a typical tragicomic plot is often indebted to New Comedy. Indeed, given the tendency of Renaissance theorists and dramatists to emphasize and expand the romance elements present in Roman comedy in their own discussions and versions of the form, it is sometimes difficult to distinguish Renaissance adaptations of New Comedy from Renaissance tragicomedies. *The Old Law* itself might be called a New Comedy *reductio ad absurdum*. When the play opens, the young citizens of Epire pass a law condemning all of their elders to death and so legislatively insure a comic triumph of youth over age. The drama begins where most comedies end and, paradoxically, develops toward a situation similar to that of the normal opening of Roman comedy, a situation in which aged authority restrains youthful desires. In doing so, *The Old Law* transforms festivity into nightmare, as Middleton uses the heightened tensions of tragicomedy to look beneath the traditionally benign surface of New Comedy and reveal the potentially destructive impulses which the form embodies.

Although Middleton's study of comic conventions extends beyond his tragicomedies into his tragedies (see Chapter 6), *The Old Law* is the culmination of his investigation of New Comedy. In many ways the drama is the most striking expression of his comic vision, and by now it should be clear that that vision is in fact a resolutely anticomic one. Middleton's critique of New Comedy is at once thorough and powerful. He does not simply reject the form and invent a new one, nor does he openly satirize or burlesque the conventions he is employing. Middleton's commentary is more subtle and, I think, more disturbing, because he seldom states his intentions explicitly. His plays—most of the comedies, some of the tragicomedies, and to a lesser extent the tragedies—draw heavily upon the New Comedy tradition. Their plots and characters often look familiar, and we expect them to function accordingly. When they don't fulfill our expectations or do so in peculiar ways, we at first are puzzled and then are led to examine the assumptions under which we have been working. As noted above, those assumptions are generic ones, and Middleton thereby brings us to understand the limitations and dangers of the view of reality embedded in the comic genre the plays seem to exemplify.

Northrop Frye has argued that the logical end of comedy is festive, but he adds (speaking of *As You Like It*) that "anyone's attitude to the festivity may be that of Orlando or of Jaques." Shakespeare's comedies demonstrate the views of the former character, Middleton's those of the latter. Frye goes on to state that these two attitudes are present in everyone's response to

comedy: "Part of us . . . if we like the comedy, feels involved in
the new society [at the end of the play] and impelled to participate in it, but part of us will always remain a spectator, on the
outside looking in."[18] Shakespeare emphasizes our involvement, while Middleton increases our alienation, and this is a
crucial difference. If for Shakespeare comedy is "the genuine
form of the world that human life tries to imitate,"[19] for Middleton it is a foolish and potentially terrifying illusion. Indeed,
if Shakespeare's dramas had been written from the perspective
of that strange antagonist of festivity in Arden, the resulting
plays might have been very much like the dramas discussed in
the following chapters.

As striking and as profound as Middleton's revisions of
New Comedy are, however, they are not out of keeping with
the relatively free handling of inherited traditions typical of
English Renaissance writers. For if the artists of that period
tended to measure their achievements against those of the
ancients, they did not attempt to conform to past standards in
every respect. Milton states, after all, that *Paradise Lost* contains
"things unattempted yet in Prose or Rhyme" (1.16); and Jonson, perhaps the most famous English classicist of the period,
was in his own way an advocate of change: "For all the observations of the *Ancients*, wee have our owne experience: which, if
wee will use, and apply, wee have better meanes to pronounce.
It is true they open'd the gates, and made the way, that went
before us; but as Guides, not Commanders." In fact, the age
saw the beginning of what was later to become the "battle of the
ancients and moderns."[20]
    This habit of expanding and attempting to go beyond older
artistic forms accounts for the richness and variety of English
Renaissance literature and for its extraordinary and marvelous
diversity. But although most English Renaissance writers
commonly agreed that inherited traditions might be altered to
reflect their own experience more accurately, they went about
reworking older forms in two different and basically antithetical ways.[21] The first method is a product of what is usually
called the Christian Humanist outlook. It dominates English

literature in the sixteenth century, although it is not confined to that century, and it is the method of the greatest writers of the English Renaissance: Spenser, Shakespeare (for the most part), and Milton. Its overriding tendency is to synthesize, to mold various conventions and genres into a unified whole greater than the sum of the parts. The principle *concordia discors* perhaps best describes this manner of revising artistic traditions. Past forms are not rejected; instead, they are employed within new contexts and mingled with one another in new ways. This use of inherited traditions is therefore conservative in the best sense: it renews and preserves the past by giving it meaning for the present. Thus in good humanist fashion it affirms the belief that the world of literature, like the world at large, is of a piece.

The second method of reworking literary tradition is very different. In the first place, it is not conservative. Authors altering inherited forms in this manner do not expand them; they reject them or proclaim their inadequacy. The mixtures of once distinct genres and conventions found in the works of these writers do not create a *concordia discors* by fusing those genres and conventions into a unified whole. Instead, the mixtures seem disorganized and contradictory and convey a sense of confusion and uncertainty. As such, these works are an artistic corollary of the disillusionment which, in England, accompanied the breakdown of the Christian Humanist world view at the end of the sixteenth century. They reflect a society where, in Douglas Bush's words, "normality consists in incongruity." At a time when the elaborate interrelationships, hierarchies, and idealized systems which form the essence of Christian Humanism were being measured against the realities of a seemingly chaotic world, it is no accident that traditional forms of art were also being tested and in many cases rejected and that new forms or combinations of forms were being developed to express the disorder which many artists saw around them. Herschel Baker has noted that the "compulsion to evolve new methodologies for dealing with new kinds of knowledge was the most generative factor in the thought" of the seventeenth century, and that compulsion was felt not only by philosophers and scientists but also by poets and dramatists, Thomas Middleton among them.[22]

Indeed, the critical analysis of inherited literary forms and the attempt to invent or discover forms which can embody feelings of uncertainty and confusion are present everywhere in the literature of the early seventeenth century.[23] In poetry, these tendencies underlie the unexpected combinations and reversals of Donne's best poems and Marvell's extended discussion of pastoral conventions. In prose, they are reflected in Bacon's use of the essay and in the anti-Ciceronian movement and the general popularity of Senecan style, a style whose asymmetries can be employed, as Stanley Fish has shown, to fool unsuspecting readers in much the same manner that Middleton often misleads the audiences of his plays.[24] And in the drama, this restlessness with inherited forms and the attempt to find more suitable ones find expression in the sophisticated literary self-consciousness of the coterie theaters and in the tonal complexities and strange mixtures we encounter in plays like *The Jew of Malta, Antonio and Mellida, The Knight of the Burning Pestle, The Revenger's Tragedy,* and *The White Devil* —dramas whose uneasy fusions of disparate materials convey an impression of a world in pieces and testify (sometimes explicitly, sometimes implicitly) to the inability of traditional dramatic genres to deal with that world. Shakespeare himself displays a similar attitude at times, most notably in the systematic deflations of heroic and tragic ideals in *Troilus and Cressida* and in the ambiguities of *Hamlet*—the tragedy, according to one critic, of "an audience that cannot make up its mind."[25] These writers (and others like them) may employ new literary kinds (Bacon), adopt or develop styles more amenable to their world view (Webster), parody and satirize older forms (Beaumont), reject the assumptions of a particular form while using it (Marvell), or do a number of these simultaneously (Donne). But whatever technique or techniques they employ and whatever differences they may have in other areas, all of these writers share a common distrust of older forms and a reluctance to accept the notions of hierarchy and order which lie behind traditional genre systems.

Clearly, Middleton's examination of New Comedy is the product of the same distrust of inherited conventions and of the same unwillingness to accept the literary kinds handed down from antiquity. Like so many of his contemporaries, Middleton does not revise tradition in order to create new syntheses which express the marvellous unity in diversity of the world. He revises it in order to reject it. Moreover, the same historical pressures which gave impetus to the general shift in the attitudes toward and uses of literary tradition traced above provided a particularly favorable context for the questioning of comic values present in Middleton's dramas. For while Middleton's may be the most extensive attack on comic assumptions in the English Renaissance, it is not the only one: Jonson, Marston, and even Shakespeare (in a few instances) variously question the genre.[26] The fact that four rather dissimilar writers explore (admittedly to different degrees) the inadequacies of New Comedy suggests that their interest in the genre has external as well as internal causes and that historical conditions at the end of the sixteenth century made comedy especially ripe for examination.

Indeed, the pervasive influence of Plautus and Terence in the sixteenth century is attributable in part to the compatibility of certain basic comic values—moderation, reconciliation, and the unity of human and natural realms—with ideas emphasized by the early Christian Humanists: the *via media*, the unity of classical and Christian beliefs, and the importance of natural law. As has been implied above, the Christian Humanist mind is comic in the broadest sense. Like the heroes of New Comedy, the humanist revolts against a moribund and rigid tradition (the "Dark Ages"). And, as in Roman comedy, this revolt does not attempt to destroy the older tradition or even to create something totally new, but to return to the values of a freer, more humane era—the religion of early Christianity, the learning of classical antiquity—which existed prior to the dominance of that overly restrictive order. Thus the humanist, like his comic counterpart, is at once progressive and conservative. He modifies tradition in order to broaden tradition, a goal clearly shown by the generic mixtures which a

typical humanist produced when he turned to literature, mixtures whose tendency toward *concordia discors* is itself indicative
of a comic viewpoint. In a sense, then, to reject the ideals of
Christian Humanism is to reject some of comedy's most important values, and the waning of the humanist tradition
undoubtedly encouraged writers who were aware of its decline
to question a literary form whose interpretation of reality
closely coincided with the beliefs of that tradition. Just as the
similarity between Christian Humanist and comic attitudes
made the sixteenth century an especially fertile breeding
ground for New Comedy, so the new and very different views
of the world which came to the fore at the beginning of the
seventeenth century made it increasingly difficult for artists to
accept comic assumptions and ideals.

The historical developments which encouraged Middleton
and other writers critically to examine New Comedy also help
explain why his dramas—whatever their generic labels—
should be distinguished carefully from a kind of drama they at
first seem to have much in common with, Renaissance
tragicomedy. This distinction is necessary whether we compare them to the genre as described in Giambattista Guarini's
treatises or as popularized on the English stage by Beaumont
and Fletcher. The tragicomic form which Guarini envisioned is
remarkably optimistic.[27] Closely allied to the *felix culpa* pattern
which Christians see everywhere in history and in their own
lives, it was a new and better genre for a new and better age.[28]
"What need have we today to purge terror and pity with tragic
sights, since we have the precepts of our most holy religion,
which teaches us the word of the gospel?" Guarini asks. But
despite this apparent modernism, Guarini's ultimate aim was
conservative. He hoped "to raise comic poetry from . . . a state
of disgrace . . . [so that] it may be able to please the unwilling
ears of a modern audience." This could be done by mingling
"with the pleasing parts of comedy those parts of tragedy that
can suitably accompany comic scenes." The key phrase here is
suitably accompany, for tragicomedy is not simply a crude combination of comic and tragic conventions. A true tragicomedy
joins only those aspects of comedy and tragedy "that can

coexist in verisimilitude and decorum" and so creates a new and perfectly unified third form: "Nothing can be mixed if . . . its parts are not so mingled that one cannot be independently recognized or separated from the other," Guarini warns. Such mixtures are found everywhere in nature, and tragicomedy is thus a natural and harmonious genre. Above all it is a temperate genre, a golden mean which avoids the faulty extremes of both comedy and tragedy: it "does not inflict on us atrocious events and horrible and inhumane sights, such as blood and deaths, and . . . on the other hand, does not cause us to be so relaxed in laughter that we sin against the modesty and decorum of a well-bred man."[29]

Middleton's comic plays—tragicomedies as well as comedies—violate nearly all of Guarini's precepts. They are not harmonious mixtures; they do not mingle only those parts of tragedy and comedy which can exist together in verisimilitude. Their effect is very different from the decorous and controlled delight Guarini praised so highly. As critical responses to his dramas amply demonstrate, Middleton's mixtures of diverse elements are almost always disturbing, and Guarini himself warned that in contrast to the perfect unity of true tragicomedy such combinations compose "an unseemly and monstrous story."[30]

That Middleton's plays might seem so to the Italian playwright is to be expected. Guarini's ideal is the product of a mind consistent with the humanist tradition. His theory provides further evidence of the humanist desire to find a *via media*, a moderate, flexible, inclusive, and harmonious reconciliation of as many apparently dissimilar materials as possible. Unlike Middleton, Guarini does not juxtapose different moods or conventions to create an impression of disorder. His synthesis of comic and tragic is another version of the unity in variety so important to the Christian Humanists, and so it is essentially comic in its assumptions and in its overall perspective. Not only does tragicomedy often employ a comic plot as its starting point, but the vision of the form—its emphasis on the fortunate fall, on harmony, and on moderation—is also an exalted and (in Guarini's eyes) more respectable relative of the vision of New Comedy. Moreover, tragicomedy's origins in comic and humanist ideals made the genre somewhat anachronistic. It was a "new" dramatic form paradoxically based upon beliefs which were being questioned with great insistence at the very time the genre became popular. To Middleton and to others involved in that questioning, tragicomedy could seem only the embodiment of an idealized world which, like the world of New Comedy it closely resembles, had little meaning for Jacobean England.

The tragicomedies of Beaumont and Fletcher, although less tied to a providential view of existence than Guarini's, are equally alien to Middleton's outlook and concerns. At first glance, many aspects of their plays—the clashes of absolutes, the juxtapositions of opposing moods, the rapid reversals of personality, the playing with audience expectations—seem parallel to important characteristics of Middleton's dramas. And indeed they are. But they affect us in totally different ways. As Philip Edwards states, "It is the freshness of invention and the sparkle of the wit that count" in these plays.[31] Each drama is an artistic tour de force and continually calls attention to the elaborate and dazzling manner in which the authors manipulate characters and events. Middleton, as we have already seen, is not interested in rhetorical displays of this sort. He seeks to disturb his audience rather than delight it. In fact, Renaissance theatergoers who responded enthusiastically to the skill of Beaumont and Fletcher probably did not find the experience of Middleton's plays a very pleasant one.[32]

Middleton's dramas clearly do not fall within the generic boundaries of Renaissance tragicomedy, either as defined by Guarini or as practiced by Beaumont and Fletcher. The precepts of the Italian theorist and the works of the English dramatists can tell us a great deal about what Middleton's plays are not, but they cannot tell us more than that. The sixteenth-century critical controversy over this dramatic hybrid, however, does point toward what might be a more satisfactory contemporary description of the qualities and effect of Middleton's dramas. One of the central issues in the debate concerned the relationship between tragicomic form and the natural world. For example, Guarini's chief antagonist, Giason Denores, argued that the genre is an unnatural union of characters and events which should remain separate. The new form sins against nature and so is a "monstrous and disproportionate composition, a mixture of two contrary actions and qualities of persons." In a similar vein Sir Philip Sidney complained that English drama was being contaminated by the presence of "mongrel tragicomedy." On the other hand, Guarini, as noted above, pointed to the natural mixtures which he found comparable to those of his new invention, notably the mixture of the four humors within the body.[33] And he endeavored to distinguish his natural and reasonable combinations from ones which depict "an unseemly and monstrous story."

Despite their contrasting views of tragicomedy, Guarini, Denores, and Sidney are unanimous in condemning discordant or monstrous forms of art; they differ only in how such forms are to be defined. In this matter all three authors demonstrate a humanist viewpoint: they believe that a harmonious interrelationship of elements is an important quality of all good art. But writers who could no longer fully accept the Christian Humanist interpretation of reality took, as we have seen, a very different attitude toward literature and produced very different kinds of literary works. To them the artistic "monstrosity" that Guarini, Denores, and Sidney found so abhorrent was not necessarily undesirable. At approximately the same time that Denores and Guarini were arguing over the merits of a hybrid drama, Michel de Montaigne began writing the essays which have had such an enormous influence on European thought. Like Guarini's new form, these essays also contain apparently contradictory elements; but, unlike Guarini, Montaigne makes no attempt to convince his readers that his creations are harmonious and orderly mixtures. He does the opposite. Montaigne compares his writings to "antike Boscage or Crotesko works: which are fantasticall pictures, having no grace, but in the variety and strangenesse of them," and goes on to ask: "And what are these my compositions in truth, other than antike workes, and monstrous bodies, patched and hudled up together of divers members, without any certaine or well ordered figure, having neither order, dependencie or proportion, but casuall and framed by chance?"[34]

Montaigne is the first author to apply the stylistic description *grotesque* ("Crotesko") to literature. For him the term does not seem to carry with it the strong sense of fear it does in more modern usages, but his association of the word *grotesque* with unstable, contradictory, and incongruous combinations of "divers members" is one which is basic to all definitions of the term.[35] More important, Montaigne's description of his essays might easily be a description of Middleton's plays (and, in fact, of the dramas of writers like Marston, Tourneur, and Webster). At times Middleton's plays also appear to be "patched and hudled up of divers members, without any certaine or well ordered figure." And although Middleton's dramas, like Montaigne's essays, are carefully contrived and controlled by their author, they likewise sometimes seem as if they were "framed by chance." By presenting us with a story (that of New Comedy) which seems familiar and simultaneously denying us our familiar responses, many of Middleton's plays convey an impression of incongruity which is in essence grotesque. Because he does not reconcile the content of his plays with their apparently conventional structure, Middleton literally turns the dramas into grotesque hybrids or, to borrow a phrase from *The Old Law*, into examples of "mixed monstrousness." And this incoherent monstrosity, like that of Montaigne's essays, perfectly mirrors the disorder which Middleton, like the French essayist, saw in the world around him.

The following chapters attempt to support and clarify the ideas outlined in this introduction by analyzing in detail nine of Middleton's plays—seven comedies and two tragicomedies—and by examining briefly some parallels between his tragedies and the comic plays which are the primary interest here. I do not contend that Middleton's critique of New Comedy is present in all of his dramas. Indeed, it is not. *Your Five Gallants*, *A Fair Quarrel*, and *The Witch*, for instance, do not seem concerned with comic conventions and assumptions in a significant way. The same is also true of Middleton's famous political allegory, *A Game of Chess*. Nor am I suggesting that the analyses of the plays discussed below deal with everything of importance in those plays. But it is my belief that the subject of this study is central to Middleton's art from its earliest stages through the late tragedies. If comedy is not the single most important concern in the Middleton canon, it is certainly one of the most important ones.

I have avoided dramas whose authorship is still debated (*Blurt, Master Constable*, *The Puritan*, *The Revenger's Tragedy*, *The Spanish Gipsy*), although some of these plays might have provided additional support for the thesis argued here. Likewise, I have not examined plays that contain Middleton's work but predominantly reflect the vision of another author (*One Honest Whore* and *The Roaring Girl*, for example). Of the dramas extensively dealt with below, only *The Family of Love* and *The Old Law* may contain the hand of an author besides Middleton, and in both of these plays Middleton's is clearly the controlling imagination. The dramas themselves are treated in a roughly chronological sequence.[36] When the chronological relationship between two plays is still uncertain—*The Phoenix* and *The Family of Love*, *A Mad World, My Masters* and *A Trick to Catch the Old One*—I have arranged them in the most convenient order. In general, however, the plays analyzed in Chapter 2 were written before those analyzed in Chapter 3, those in Chapter 3 before those in Chapter 4, and so on. In no case is the reading of a play dependent upon its date of composition or its chronological relationship to other plays in the canon.

The rest of this study is divided into five sections. Chapter 2 proceeds inductively and examines two early comedies: *The Phoenix*, an estates morality play, and *The Family of Love*, the most conventional comedy that Middleton wrote. Both plays are apprentice works, and neither one fully illustrates the major thesis of this book. But both dramas tell us a great deal about two basic chracteristics of Middleton's art: the presence of a world in which such comic values as moderation and reconciliation have no place, and the tendency to push comic conventions to extremes. In essence, Middleton's later com-

edies are a composite of elements present in these early works:
he often imposes a New Comedy structure like that of *The
Family of Love* on a society similar to that of *The Phoenix*, a society
which denies almost all important comic values.

Chapter 3 focuses on *Michaelmas Term* and *A Trick to Catch
the Old One*, plays which undermine their New Comedy form by
containing opposing qualities so extreme that they interfere
with the traditional comic movement toward reconciliation. In
the former play, Middleton subverts the drama's New Comedy
structure by juxtaposing it to a prodigal son pattern which
requires different responses and supports contrary values. In
the latter, Middleton harmoniously merges the prodigal son
parable into comedy, only to create new problems by including
a distinctly uncomic subplot.

Chapter 4 treats three plays which reveal the inadequacies
of basic comic conventions. *A Mad World, My Masters* portrays a
flawed symbol of festivity and generosity, Sir Bounteous Progress, and demonstrates that these comic values have no validity
either in the play itself or in the world outside of the theater. In
No Wit, No Help Like a Woman's Middleton suggests that the
harmonious conclusion toward which comedy develops is an
unnatural and unreal fiction, and in *A Chaste Maid in Cheapside*
he denies that a meaningful relationship exists between comic
form and patterns of natural and spiritual rebirth.

In Chapter 5 I attempt to show how Middleton's analysis of
New Comedy extends into two of his tragicomedies as he
examines the darker impulses and energies which underlie the
normally benign surface of comedy, impulses powerfully expressed by the pregnant Page's strange dance near the end of
More Dissemblers Besides Women and by the terrifying destruc-
tiveness of misrule's triumph in *The Old Law*. Chapter 6 is a
brief afterword which explores relationships between the
critique of New Comedy traced in the preceding chapters and
the nature of Middleton's tragedies.

One additional point needs to be touched on before turning to the plays themselves. Although this study examines the
relationship of Middleton's dramas to the New Comedy tradition, the following chapters contain relatively few references to

specific Roman plays, and intentionally so. Given the almost formulaic quality of Roman comedy, it is nearly impossible to identify a single classical play as the source for an event or character in one of Middleton's dramas. More important, it is my belief that Middleton's indebtedness to the New Comedy tradition, like that of his contemporaries, does not take the form of an indebtedness to a particular play or plays. Very few English Renaissance comedies are based upon a specific Roman play. But Renaissance comedy unquestionably draws upon—is, in large part, a continuation of—the New Comedy tradition. Plautus and Terence gave the Renaissance a highly flexible plot structure and cast of characters which embody certain definable assumptions and values. It was these general features that English Renaissance playwrights repeated, developed, made contemporary, or, in the case of Thomas Middleton, called into question.

2
A World of Extremes

Peace, you're too foul; your crime is in excess.
    The Duke, in *The Phoenix*

Joy not too much; extremes are perilous.
    Lipsalve, in *The Family of Love*

Although we seldom think of Thomas Middleton in a role
other than that of playwright, he began his literary career
writing satiric and didactic verse. His earliest published work,
The Wisdom of Solomon Paraphrased, is a long moralistic poem
based upon Old Testament Apocrypha, while *Micro-cynicon*
dissects the vices of Middleton's day in the manner of Hall or
Marston. Given this apprenticeship, it is not surprising that
some of his early dramas are themselves strongly satiric and
didactic. This is especially true of *The Phoenix*, a play which is a
dramatic version of the two earlier poetic works, at once a
handbook containing advice on how to rule wisely and an
anatomy of corruption at all levels of society.[1]

Middleton is able to accommodate both political and social
commentary in the drama by centering his plot around the

convention of the disguised magistrate.² As the play opens, we see the old Duke of Ferrara surrounded by evil courtiers—Proditor, Lussurioso, and Infesto—whose presence is symbolic of the corruption in the kingdom at large. At the courtiers' bidding, the Duke sends his noble son Phoenix abroad, hoping that the experiences gained while travelling will make the prince more fit to rule. Proditor, on the other hand, sees the decision as a chance to murder Phoenix and usurp the throne. Suspecting that all is not well, Phoenix disguises himself and, accompanied by his servant Fidelio, roots out the evil that lies hidden throughout Ferrara. He saves Fidelio's mother, Castiza, from being sold to Proditor by her husband, the Captain, and exposes a corrupt judge named Falso and a devious lawyer called Tangle. At the end of the play Phoenix strips away his disguise, banishes Proditor, and, with the help of a reformed lawyer named Quieto, sluices Tangle's veins to save the old man from going mad. The victory of good over evil is absolute, and Ferrara is freed of the corruption under which it had suffered for many years. The kingdom is reborn.

The rebirth, however, is not an easy one. At the beginning of *The Phoenix*, Ferrara is a fallen world of mists and darkness. Here chaos results from the failure of things to be separate and distinct from one another, to be what they appear or, rather, to appear what they are. Like Fitzgrave in *Your Five Gallants*, Phoenix immerses himself in this world of mutability and uncertainty in order to combat the masks and inconstancy of evil. Ideals have been defiled. The law, once a bright sun, is hidden by dross and clouds "that get between thy glory and their praise, / That make the visible and foul eclipse" (1.4.209–10).³ Evil lurks in a "blind parlour" (4.1.214), and even Justice Falso can fall prey to the confusion he has helped create, mistaking a knight for a gentleman (1.6.150–51), or not recognizing one of his own thieves (3.1.).

The major cause of this confusion is the tendency of evil to mimic or parody good and so to become indistinct from it. The evil characters in the play usually echo the statements and actions of the virtuous ones in ways that completely subvert their original intentions. The most common inversions concern familial relationships. The Knight, for example, reminds us of the old Duke's joy that Phoenix is more than worthy of his birth (1.1.30–34) when he tells his mistress, the Jeweller's Wife, "I love thee better for thy birth" (1.5.21). Falso's arguments that his niece commit incest with him (2.3.33–34) simply push to an extreme all of the pieties about filial affection that we have been hearing from Fidelio. Likewise, the Jeweller's Wife excuses her adultery with the Knight on the grounds that the Knight is, after all, her brother-in-law and thus duty demands that she love him. Evil imitates in other ways as well. The Captain parodies the many discussions of judgment and temperance in the play when he ironically misapplies these concepts while lamenting his marriage to the virtuous Castiza: "What lustful passion came aboard of me, that I should marry? was I drunk? . . . That a man is in danger every minute to be cast away, without he have an extraordinary pilot that can perform more than a man can do!" (1.2.43–48). Falso and Proditor, like Quieto, value peace of mind (1.6.10–13; 1.3.136–37), although the former hopes to gain it by not prosecuting thieves, and the latter finds his solace in thoughts of murdering Phoenix. The mad lawyer Tangle equates pleasure with vexation, and if Phoenix's name symbolically associates the prince with rebirth, Tangle outdoes the drama's most virtuous character by undergoing countless resurrections: "I ha' been at least sixteen times beggared, and got up again; and in the mire again, that I have stunk again, and yet got up again." In the face of such energetic imitation Phoenix can only muse, "And so clean and handsome now?" (1.4.125–28).

The failure of language to communicate clearly and accurately is another source of disorder in the play. Throughout much of the drama, words simply do not mean the same things to all the characters. Normal meanings are perverted or ignored, and responses often bear little relationship to what is being responded to. Phoenix's difficulties with Justice Falso, for instance, directly result from the fact that the two men speak a different language. Having caught one of Falso's cronies stealing, Phoenix brings him to the judge and addresses Falso:

PHOENIX: Sir, we understand you to be the only uprightness of
   this place.
FALSO: But I scarce understand you, sir.
PHOENIX: Why, then, you understand not yourself, sir.
FALSO: Such another word, and you shall change places with
   the thief.   [3.1.83–88]

Falso quickly goes on to praise the speeches of the newly
apprehended thief, to the prince's utter astonishment. Clearly,
justice is impossible in a society where the speech of thieves is
preferred to that of virtuous men and where the denotation of
uprightness is debatable. Because there is no common language,
there is no common ground for judgment, and words can no
longer be counted upon to provide a clear and accurate description of what is and is not.

The lawyer Tangle is an even more striking source of
linguistic confusion than the judge; for Tangle does not simply
alter or ignore normal meanings, he imposes a special and
nearly impenetrable language on reality. Because he is able to
see and to speak only through the labyrinthine obscurities of
law, he hopelessly confounds everyone he comes in contact
with. Phoenix and Fidelio first learn of this strange old man
from the Groom at an inn where they are lodging, but the two
young men (and by extension the audience) are scarcely prepared for the peculiarities of his special world. When Tangle
orders a piece of toast, the Groom asks: "Will you have no
drink to't sir?" Tangle's response violates every principle of
understanding and communication: "Is that a question in
law?" (1.4.48–49). Tangle's obsession leads him to reduce all of
existence to the categories of his profession. The discord that
he causes arises from his attempt to impose absolute unity and
order on a world containing clear and irreconcilable differences, tangling everything up, as it were. Out of Tangle's false
unity springs chaos. Whenever he appears, we hear "the dizzy
murmur of the law" (4.1.39).

At times, Tangle's extraordinary actions border on the
demonic.[4] He linguistically creates an unnatural unity which is
on the verge of exploding as mutually antagonistic elements
strive to escape from one another. The explosion never occurs,

but only because Quieto arrives in time to sluice Tangle's veins at the end of the play in a scene which recalls Jonson's *Poetaster*. What comes out is, fittingly enough, the jargon of law: "O, an extent, a proclamation, a summons, a recognisance, a tachment, and injunction! a writ, a seizure, a writ of 'praisement, an absolution, a *quietus est!*" (5.1.309–11). The first sign of Tangle's reformation is also linguistic. His encomium to "sacred patience" recalls the other passages in the play which praise ideals and firmly aligns him on the side of good. In a sense, Tangle has become Quieto, his opposite, and the language of law has disappeared. His speech has been purified and clarified, leaving only, as he states, "truth in my words" (1.340).

Throughout *The Phoenix*, then, evil characters blur distinctions of all kinds, both by parodying the actions of virtuous individuals and by subverting language's normal communicative function. But the confusion that these characters cause is only temporary, and the play depicts a gradual movement away from a world of obscurity and darkness to one of clarity and light. In *The Phoenix* the defeat of evil brings a new day, as Phoenix remarks after the Captain has been banished: "The scene is cleared, the bane of brightness fled" (2.2.343). Likewise, the highest praise, the Duke tells his son, is an acknowledgment that one can see well:

> To thee let reverence all her powers engage,
> That art in youth a miracle to age!
> State is but blindness; thou hadst piercing art:
> We only saw the knee, but thou the heart.
>   [5.1.176–79]

And in the new day that slowly dawns as the drama progresses, good and evil, justice and injustice, are no longer indistinct from one another. The false and confusing unities created by Proditor, Falso, and Tangle suddenly dissolve under the light of truth; and, as in *Your Five Gallants*, good and evil appear as irreconcilable extremes between which there can be no middle ground. This is the reason why the play is composed of contradictory moods—idealism and cynicism, seriousness and farce—a combination which Samuel Schoenbaum, among others, finds "an odd mixture." But these juxtapositions seem less troublesome once we recognize the play's allegorical framework and accept Middleton's purpose of clarifying the relation between good and evil by defining their differences with increasing accuracy.[5]

Indeed, vice usually moves down the chain of being toward monstrosity and deformity. The Captain is "an ugly land and sea monster" (2.1.15). Proditor associates himself with the devil: "Tread me to dust, thou [Phoenix] in whom wonder keeps! / Behold the serpent on his belly creeps" (5.1.165–66). Virtue, as might be expected, moves upward toward the divine. The ideal resides above, while corruption dominates the sublunar world. Thus Phoenix finds law in its upper parts "sacred, pure, / And incorruptible," but it is "dross" below (1.4.206–8). Similarly, Tangle daily plunges himself above the chin in his work (1.4.265–66). The end of evil is a fall (like Tangle's) into the mire (1.4.125-27, 265–66), or a descent (like the Captain's) into oblivion, as Phoenix notes: "Thou hateful villain! thou shouldst choose to sink, / To keep thy baseness shrouded" (2.2.294–95).

Because the ideal resides in heaven, it is most often associated with the sun, which, until the play's conclusion, is obscured by clouds of evil. Like so many didactic Christian works—Book 1 of *The Faerie Queene* and *Paradise Lost* come immediately to mind—*The Phoenix* contains two basic image patterns: a visual one which opposes light and dark, sight and blindness; and a spatial one which contrasts a fallen sublunar world with an ideal celestial existence. The sun, as a result of its clarifying light and its position beyond the world of mutability, is the focal point of both patterns. It is symbolic of everything that is worthwhile in the play. Significantly, Phoenix is closely linked with the sun, both by his name and by several references in the play. When the old Duke greets his son's return by saying, "Our joy breaks at our eyes" (5.1.56), he is in one sense referring to his own heartfelt tears of gladness; but, more importantly, he is figuratively describing a sunrise. Phoenix wanders through a dark and murky world of confusion and evil to lend his brightness to the aid of good. As he tells Fidelio early in the play, his disguise is simply a necessary preliminary

to the time when he will expose the kingdom's corruptions to
the sunlight of truth: "I hold it a safer stern, upon this lucky
advantage, since my father is near his setting, and I upon the
eastern hill to take my rise, to look into the heart and bowels of
this dukedom, and, in disguise, mark all abuses ready for
reformation or punishment" (1.1.98–102). Furthermore,
Phoenix's disguise is itself a symbolic descent because, by
choosing to reform Ferrara, he leaves an ideal world of study
for the fallen world of experience and reality. Phoenix's virtue
is active rather than contemplative, and thus after encountering Tangle for the first time, he notes the wisdom of his
immersion in an imperfect and mutable society: "They least
know / That are above the tedious steps below: / I thank my
time, I do" (1.4.225–27). Phoenix's descent is the incarnation
of an ideal or, perhaps more accurately, of a god. His unmask-
ings strip away the veil of clouds which usually surrounds
divinity in its relations with man and which has obscured all
ideals throughout the play. We suddenly see the god face to
face.

The aura of divinity that surrounds Phoenix seems to stem
partly from the tradition of disguised magistrate to which he
belongs. J. W. Lever has traced this tradition to folklore and
stories about disguised monarchs, notably the Roman emperor
Alexander Severus. But the tradition also includes stories
about gods who travel secretly in their kingdoms—a mode of
behavior particularly attractive to the Olympic pantheon. As a
result, the ruler's casting off of his disguise often seems to be a
kind of revelation, as, for example, is true of Vincentio's unmasking in *Measure for Measure*. Middleton, however, is not
content to let literary convention point to the divine nature of
his protagonist. Phoenix's name inevitably associates him with
Christ.[6] Proditor's envious reaction to the Duke's praise of
Phoenix in the first scene parallels Satan's jealous hatred of the
Son, and Phoenix's travels recall Christ wandering in the wilderness, because the purpose of Phoenix's intended journey is
"the better to approve you to yourself" (1.1.38). We might also
note that Phoenix is accompanied by faith (Fidelio), and
spends most of his time defending chastity (Castiza) and re-

deeming the manifold corruptions of the law (Falso and Tangle).

Thus, as the society of *The Phoenix* gradually emerges from the mists which symbolized the confusion of evil and the difficulty of discerning truth, the society becomes increasingly polarized. The play moves, like most allegories, toward irreconcilable extremes, toward, in Angus Fletcher's words, "the radical opposition of two independent, mutually irreducible, mutually antagonistic substances . . . Absolute Good and Absolute Evil."[7] In Middleton's play this opposition is embodied in a symbolic struggle between the Christlike Phoenix and the Satanic Proditor, and all aspects of good and evil in the drama are subsumed under one or the other. There is no middle ground. Only the total victory of one extreme or the withdrawal of the other is possible. Paradoxically, the very clarity which finally characterizes the play-society works against the possibility of unity or reconciliation at the play's conclusion, because reconciliation involves blurring distinctions and modifying absolutes, seeking and emphasizing likenesses while overlooking or minimizing differences.

As we have seen, Middleton's drama develops in precisely the opposite manner. Characters in *The Phoenix* who ignore distinctions and create false unities, whether by parody, imitation, or the imposition of a single language on all of existence, are evil rather than virtuous. In this drama, to see through appearances, to see things as they really are, is to isolate and alienate them from one another. Thus the two truly evil characters in the play, the Captain and Proditor, cannot repent and must be banished, cursing as they go. Likewise, Tangle's cure is the destruction of his former self. By sluicing Tangle's veins, Quieto does not simply modify the lawyer's behavior; rather, he totally transforms it as Tangle moves from one extreme to another, from acting with a mad, frenetic energy to patiently accepting whatever life brings him. Ultimately, the conclusion of *The Phoenix* portrays a world so pure, so completely black and white, that it bears little resemblance to the postlapsarian world we inhabit. But this is understandable. The Ferrara that we see at the end of the play, ruled over by the

Christlike Phoenix and free of the corruptions which had earlier beset all levels of society, is not our world. It is a vision of an existence which in Christian terms will never be attained until Christ once again returns to overthrow finally the forces of darkness and confusion.

At first glance the title of *The Family of Love*, which refers to a Puritan sect, implies that Middleton's primary interest here, as in *The Phoenix*, is satiric and didactic.[8] As a result, many readers have treated the play solely as an attack on a religious group which had acquired a great deal of notoriety during the period immediately preceding the performance of Middleton's play.[9] But although the drama in places does satirize Puritanism, the overall focus of *The Family of Love* is not really satiric, and the play's title refers not only to the members of a religious sect but to all the characters in the comedy and, ultimately, to all of humanity. In fact, *The Family of Love* is the most conventional New Comedy in the Middleton canon, as a brief outline of the plot will indicate.

When the play begins, a young man named Gerardine is in love with a beautiful young woman named Maria, but his affections are opposed by her uncle, Doctor Glister. A secondary conflict concerns Glister's rivalry with two gallants called Lipsalve and Gudgeon for the favors of Mistress Purge, a rather free and sensual middle class wife who is also a member of the Family of Love. But the Gerardine–Maria–Glister conflict is clearly the most important. Feigning a sea voyage, Gerardine manages to have a trunk in which he has hidden himself conveyed into Maria's room. The lovers' troubles seem over, until they discover that Maria is pregnant. Undaunted, Gerardine tricks Glister a second time by having the doctor brought to trial for causing his niece's obvious misfortune. Gerardine disguises himself and plays the role of judge. Fearful that he will be imprisoned, Glister agrees to sanction Maria's marriage to her apparently departed lover, and Gerardine suddenly unmasks. The young lovers are brought together with universal approval, and the play ends happily.

In keeping with its basic comic structure, *The Family of Love* begins with an argument between youth and age over the value of love: Maria bridles at the rejection by Glister and his wife of Gerardine's suit. Essentially, the play's two opening scenes introduce the drama's central conflict by presenting a series of hypothetical definitions of love. These definitions are of two types: the first cynical and worldly, the second idealistic and sentimental. For Glister, love is not only made of "tricks and shows," it is "a cold heat, a bitter sweet, a pleasure full of pain, a huge loss and no gain," in short, "an idle fantasy" (1.1.1, 11–13, 23). For his wife, "love is like fasting-days, but the body is like flesh-days" (1.43–44). In a similar vein the gallant Lipsalve provides a pitiful "hieroglyphic" of a true lover (1.2.19). On the other hand, as Richard Levin notes, the statements of Gerardine and Maria express, "particularly in the early scenes, an exalted sentimentality that is deliberately marked off from the much more realistic perspective of the subplot."[10] No one gains the upper hand in these early debates; but the prevalence of definitions of love in the first two scenes, and in fact throughout *The Family of Love*, implies that Middleton is attempting to present a detailed analysis of that emotion.

One key to understanding this examination is the title of the play. Levin restricts the meaning of the title to Gerardine and Maria. According to his reading of the comedy, genuine love is neither the animalistic love of the gallants nor the hypocritical spirituality of Mistress Purge, but something altogether different. And so the young lovers constitute "the only real 'family of love' in a hostile world incapable of achieving or even appreciating it."[11] Gerardine himself lends support to this view by echoing the traditional contrast between the two Venuses as he prays for his love's success:

> Celestial Venus, born without a mother,
> Be thou propitious! thee do I implore,
> Not vulgar Venus, heaven's scorn and Mars his whore.
> [4.2.98–100]

In so praying, Gerardine intimates that his love is radically different from that of a Lipsalve or a Mistress Purge, and initially the society of *The Family of Love* thus seems remarkably similar to that of *The Phoenix*. The vivid contrast between the

young lovers and the other characters, and between their view
of love and that of their fellows, is reminiscent of the absolute
dichotomies toward which *The Phoenix* steadily moves. Both
plays seem to depict the opposition of polar extremes.

Yet a moment's reflection on *The Family of Love* as a whole
suggests that the differences between Maria and Gerardine
and the other characters are not as great as Gerardine would
have us believe. In fact, *The Family of Love* develops in precisely
the opposite direction from that of *The Phoenix*. Instead of
progressing from a world of experience toward one which is
increasingly ideal and abstract, *The Family of Love* progresses
toward the real and the physical. And whereas Middleton
emphasizes distinctions between characters and values in *The
Phoenix*, in *The Family of Love* he focuses on similarities. Unlike
allegory and like most conventional comedies, the plot of *The
Family of Love* moves away from extremes, seeking a moderate
middle ground that can accommodate as large a cross section
of the play's society as possible. As a result, the comedy begins
where *The Phoenix* concludes—with clear and apparently irreconcilable differences—and develops toward a conclusion
which is reminiscent of the mists and blurred distinctions at the
beginning of Middleton's allegorical drama. The ending of *The
Family of Love*, unlike that of *The Phoenix*, is inclusive rather
than exclusive. No characters are permanently banished from
the world of this play (like Proditor and the Captain), and no
one is totally transformed from his former self (like Tangle).
Humors are purged, of course, but only so far as is necessary to
admit everyone into the play's concluding festivities. And as I
hope to show, no character in the play is excluded from a
symbolic Family of Love that is closely tied to the desires of the
flesh. Although all virtuous individuals in *The Phoenix* would
surely prefer a spiritual love to an earthly one, no one in *The
Family of Love* finally chooses Celestial Venus over Vulgar
Venus.[12]

The extent of the contrast between the young lovers and
their antagonists is modified as early as act 1, scene 2. Gerardine's dialogue with Maria may be intended as a parody of the
famous balcony scene in *Romeo and Juliet*, and both lovers

display a surprising degree of practicality and a keen interest in physical matters.[13] For example, in fewer than seventy lines, the content of Maria's speeches changes from lofty idealism to bawdy joking—"He that, to get up to a fair woman, will stick to vow and swear, may be accounted no man" (ll.108–9)—and realistic advice about the problems of getting through a narrow chamber window (ll.136–39). Shortly afterward we learn that Maria conceives of paradise in physical terms (2.4.36–41), as she defends her love which is "as far from show of niceness as from that / Of impure thoughts" (ll.14–15).

A similar and even more surprising alteration of our understanding of Gerardine and Maria occurs at the beginning of act 3. At first we encounter the same kind of sentimentality that we have been led to associate with the two lovers. Gerardine compares his affections to the spheres, and Maria complains about the powers of "erring sense" (l.21). However, her lament ironically is borne out as Gerardine quickly forgets his allegiance to Celestial Venus and exclaims: "O, my blood's on fire! / Sweet, let me give more scope to true desire" (ll.39–40). The distance which seemed to separate him from men like Lipsalve and Glister becomes smaller and smaller as he emphasizes body over spirit, action over expression: "Tut, words are wind; thought unreduct to act / Is but an embryon in the truest sense" (ll.42–43). In fact, Gerardine's new interests provide support for both Glister's opening judgment on young lover's vows ("tricks and shows") and Mistress Glister's observations on the penchant of youth for feasting days over fasting days. His bawdy wordplay (ll.46–55) echoes the gallants' speeches throughout the work. Like all of the other characters, Gerardine is obviously a victim of "erring sense," and his metaphoric reference to conception ("embryon") soon proves prophetic.

The Family of Love may begin with what seems to be a clear opposition between virtuous and unvirtuous love, or between idealism and cynicism; but as the play progresses, this opposition becomes much less definite. Gerardine and Maria are superior to the other characters in the play, and their view of love is certainly more admirable. But these are differences of

degree, not kind, and it is easy to exaggerate them or to accept
Gerardine's comment on the two Venuses at face value.[14]
When Dryfat expresses the hope that Gerardine will become a
member of the Family, Gerardine's sarcastic reply—"That's
most likely, for I hold most of their principles already"
(4.2.70–71)—contains more truth than he knows. It is no accident that Gerardine is related to Mistress Purge. And when
Lipsalve and Shrimp talk midway in the play about the
former's undying desire for Maria, they are talking about
Gerardine and Maria as well:

> SHRIMP: But, lord, sir, how you hunt this chase of love! are you
> not weary?
> LIPSALVE: Indefatigable, boy, indefatigable.   [3.2.19–21]

The youths' brief interchange might indeed provide an
epigraph for *The Family of Love*, because the inexhaustible
pursuit of sexual satisfaction that Lipsalve describes is characteristic of most of the play's major figures. The characters'
spiritual concerns are usually subservient to their physical
needs, and the play is full of incurably literal-minded individuals. The Puritan sect called the Family of Love is guilty, after
all, only of taking the doctrine of charity absolutely literally by
engaging in orgies. Similarly, Mistress Purge divests *unclean*
and *way* of their metaphorical meanings and thus of their
spiritual overtones when she complains that her servant Club
has soiled her clothing: "Fie, fie, Club, go a' t'other side the
way, thou collowest me and my ruff; thou wilt make me an
unclean member i' the congregation" (3.3.1–3). Her conversation with the merchant Dryfat shortly afterward comically
exposes the confusion that attends a woman who cannot dis-
criminate between the letter and the spirit. Lipsalve and Gudgeon have the same problem.

This emphasis on the physical side of human nature lies
behind the many references to physical release in the comedy.
According to the Bellows Mender's Wife, man's essential nature has much in common with her husband's source of liveli-
hood: "And what were men and women but bellows, for they
take wind in at one place and do evaporate at another"
(4.1.20–22). And in this play, at least, she is right. The actions

of taking in and letting out—of eating, defecating, and copulating—dominate the various characters' lives. Almost everyone in the play expends the bulk of his energy procuring food, getting into bed, or ensuring that his trips to the privy will be successful. Furthermore, there is one other kind of release which is also worth noting. For Glister, laughter is an explosion of pent-up energy. Having tricked Lipsalve and Gudgeon into beating one another, the doctor exclaims: "Ha, ha, ha! O, for one of the hoops of my Cornelius' tub! I needs must be gone, I shall burst myself with laughing else" (3.6.31–33). Presumably the audience of Middleton's play should react to its pleasantries in the same manner.

The word most commonly associated with physical release in the drama is *purgation*, and purgation is the business of two of the play's primary characters, Glister and Purge.[15] More important, purgation is also the business of the dramatist, and it is the role of dramatist that Gerardine accepts at the end of the play. Just as Glister manipulated Lipsalve and Gudgeon to a comic confrontation ending in the powerful release of the doctor's own laughter, so Gerardine, as he tells Maria, forges "a mirthful plot / To celebrate our wish'd conjunction" (5.2.33–34), in which his enemies "may happily prove particles in our sport, and fit subjects for laughter" (ll.49–50). Thus the final scene of the comedy—now both Gerardine's and Middleton's—opens with Dryfat shouting, "Come, Club, come, there's a merry fray towards; we shall see the death of melancholy" (5.3.1–2) and preparing to call defendants to trial "upon thy purgation" (l.183).

References to physical purgation are common in Renaissance satire and satiric comedy and have their source both in the physiological theory of humors prevalent during the period and in Renaissance commentaries on the medical analogy present in the Aristotelian concept of catharsis. The words *purge* and *purgation*, which English writers used in connection with both the theory of humors and Aristotle's doctrine, had, as a result, an extraordinarily wide range of meaning.[16] In Jacobean England to *purge* was (among other things) to make physically pure or clean, to empty the bowels by means of evacuation, to make free from moral defilement (*OED*).

All three definitions are relevant to *The Family of Love*. For if we keep the various senses of *catharsis* or *purgation* in mind, the relation of Mistress Glister's incredible fastidiousness to the rest of the play becomes clear. The poor woman never appears without complaining about dirty feet, spitting, or bad breath. Likewise, when Gerardine encounters the "rank scent of knavery" (3.1.61), or Lipsalve vows to Gudgeon that "the wind shall not take the breath of our gross abuse" (3.6.51–52), they are not simply making tasteless jokes. The play is filled with olfactory imagery (2.3.25, 50–51; 2.4.128–29; 3.7.30–31; 4.1.57–59, 107–9), and with references to defecation which would otherwise be gratuitous: in his will Gerardine leaves Mistress Purge "a fair large standing cup, with a close-stool [chamber pot]" (1.3.147), and Gudgeon speaks of the "close-stool" (3.5.7) of his mind, for example. At the same time, this very specific kind of physical purgation is intimately linked with the characters' sexual desires. Glister tells Lipsalve that women are most apt to succumb "after the receipt of a purgation, for then are their pores most open" (2.4.118–19). Mistress Purge is Glister's "vessel of ease" (2.4.145) and Lipsalve's "cordial of a Familist" (3.4.89). For Gudgeon the end result of love is, like that of any good cathartic, cleansing: "O the naked pastimes of love, the scourge of dulness, the purifier of uncleanliness, and the hothouse of humanity! I have taken physic of master Purge any time this twelvemonths to purge my humour upon's wife" (3.5.1–4).

The characters in the play can also be purged spiritually. Thus Maria finds her "thoughts refin'd in flames of true desire" (3.7.29). The Puritan sect called the Family of Love is concerned, on the surface at least, with this type of cleansing; and Glister's reputation as a magician implies that he can purge the spirit as well as the body. For Mistress Purge a trip to the Family and a visit to her doctor seem to be two sides of the same coin: "In troth, la, I am not well: I had thought to have spent the morning at the Family, but now I am resolved to take pills, and therefore, I pray thee, desire doctor Glister that'a would minister to me in the morning" (1.3.58–61). Such confusion is not surprising from Mistress Purge, who believes that *unclean* means "dirty" and who goes to church for the same reason she sees Glister—to "fructify" (3.3.22). But her statements and actions also reflect the proximity between medical and spiritual senses of purgation in the play. Indeed, all of the different forms of purgation tend to be conflated throughout the comedy, a fact perhaps best demonstrated by Lipsalve and Gudgeon's discussion of the latter's desire for Purge's wife:

> GUDGEON: I am sure she is ominous to me; she makes civil wars and insurrections in the state of my stomach: I had thought to have bound myself from love, but her purging comfits makes me loose-bodied still.
> LIPSALVE: What, has she minstered to thee then?
> GUDGEON: Faith, some lectuary or so.
> LIPSALVE: Ay, I fear she takes too much of that lectuary to stoop to love; it keeps her body soluble from sin: she is not troubled with carnal crudities nor the binding of the flesh.
>
> [2.3.57–66]

Gudgeon's desire for Mistress Purge is here described as a digestive disorder. Frustrated in his attempts to purge himself sexually, he has endeavored to deny his impulses. This denial is explicitly linked to constipation (to *bind* is to hinder the natural flux of the bowels—*OED*), but Gudgeon's efforts have been for naught. His stomach rebels, and Mistress Purge's comfits create desires in him which constitute a kind of metaphoric diarrhea ("loose-bodied"). The "lectuary" that the Puritan wife administers to Gudgeon seems to be both a spiritual aid for salvation and a medicinal paste (*OED*), which acting as a laxative ("soluble"—*OED*) keeps Mistress Purge herself free from sin (itself evidently a kind of constipation). Therefore, according to Lipsalve, Mistress Purge does not suffer from "carnal crudities" (both sinful physical desires and imperfectly digested food—*OED*), nor the "binding of the flesh"—a phrase which now refers to both sinful impulses and digestive difficulties. Lipsalve is, typically, wrong in his assessment of Mistress Purge's interest in love, but the gallants' conversation clearly exemplifies the manner in which the various meanings of purgation overlap in Middleton's drama.[17]

The character in the play most obviously associated with
sexual matters, physical cleanliness, and the spiritual world is
Glister. As noted above, his name and occupation link him to
physical purgation and specifically to defecation. During the
course of the play Glister first purges the gallants
figuratively—"He has given our loves a suppositor with a *re-
cumbentibus*" (3.6.48–49)—and then literally. At the end of the
drama Lipsalve and Gudgeon "depart to the close-stool
whence they came" (5.3.257). Seeking one kind of release, they
have found another, less desirable one. A secondary meaning
of Glister's name—the pipe or syringe used in injecting
enemas, a clyster-pipe (*OED*)—points to the doctor's sexual
proclivities by indicating the potentially phallic nature of much
of his ware. After all, neither the audience nor Purge is really
sure what kind of purgative he administers to the apothecary's
wife in order to make her pregnant. The doctor is also linked to
the spiritual meaning of purgation through his reputation as a
magician. Both Lipsalve and Gudgeon ask him to aid them
magically in their efforts to gain Mistress Purge's love, and the
doctor takes full advantage of their belief. Finally, when Mistress Glister angrily accuses her husband late in the play of
committing adultery, she rightly (if a bit obscenely) associates
Glister's supposed infidelity with his ability to purge others
both physically and spiritually: "No, thou hast been all this
while in an urinal; thou hast gone out of thy compass in
women's waters: you're a conjuror, forsooth, and can rouse
your spirits into circles" (5.1.9–12).

In his dual roles as doctor and magician, Glister's traditional function is to promote fertility and freedom from sterile
and life-denying restrictions.[18] These are the functions which
he presumably undertakes in attempting to make Mistress
Purge pregnant and which Lipsalve and Gudgeon address
when they ask him to help them gain Mistress Purge's love. But
from the perspective of the main plot, Glister fails to fulfill
both roles, because he opposes Gerardine's desire to marry
Maria. In reality, most of the doctor's actions hinder rather
than aid the forces of love and fertility. It is never certain that
Mistress Purge is pregnant, and the doctor's answer to the

gallants' petitions is to thwart the desires of both. Likewise, although Glister believes that Maria's love for Gerardine is a humorous excess, he paradoxically attempts to cleanse that humor through confinement rather than release: he locks her up.

All of the references to purgation in *The Family of Love* provide a vivid parallel to the conventional comic movement from restriction to freedom, from a stultifying moribund society to a fertile and harmonious one. The release associated with purgation is emblematic of the release implicit in the structure of the drama itself. Glister opposes this fundamental comic movement throughout the play: he is a typical New Comedy blocking figure. For this reason the opening scenes of the drama contrast hindrances imposed by the doctor with the unbounded love of Gerardine and Maria. Separated from her lover, Maria defiantly tells her uncle:

> My body you may circumscribe, confine,
> And keep in bounds; but my unlimited love
> Extends beyond all circumscription.
> [1.1.35–37]

Later in the play, Middleton provides a striking visual reinforcement of Maria's words. Gerardine suddenly rises out of the trunk he had managed to have conveyed into her room, enacting a mock rebirth which encapsulates the movement of the entire drama. Glister's attempt to prevent the consummation of his niece's love (and with it the renewal of the play-world) is, on the other hand, a symbolic form of constipation; and, ironically, that is one problem a doctor should remedy rather than cause.

Glister also promotes sterility, because sterility results, Maria tells us, from forced love (3.1.32–33). The doctor is perhaps successful in his attempt to make Mistress Purge pregnant, but we (as well as Purge) are never quite sure whether or not to believe it. In any case, Gerardine's success with Maria vividly contrasts with Glister's dubious achievement. Her progress toward motherhood is evident to all who see her. And whereas Glister employs wit to aid in the sterile multiplication of money (3.2.105–10), Gerardine uses wit as a

means to consummate his love.[19] The close interdependence
of intelligence and love which underlies Gerardine's actions is
made clear by a series of puns which join the two. For both
Maria and Gerardine, "desire's conceit is quick" (1.2.129) both
physically and spiritually, and near the end of the play Gerardine and Dryfat speak of their plot to trick Glister in terms
which suggest natural generation. When Gerardine asks,
"Does our conceit cotton?" the merchant replies, "Full, full: we
are in labour man, and shall die without midwifery" (5.3.30–
34). Indeed, childbirth is the last and most important example
of physical release and the movement from confinement to
freedom in the comedy. The final union of the young lovers
shortly before the birth of their child forms a fitting capstone
to the progression of *The Family of Love* from restriction to
freedom and to Gerardine's machinations in bringing it about
despite the opposition of his future bride's uncle.

In effect, Gerardine takes over the functions which Glister,
as doctor and magician, should fulfill. It is the young lover who
promotes fertility and freedom from life-denying restrictions.
Gerardine, not Glister, finally administers purgation to all of
the characters. And he does so in a role which combines the
qualities of both magic and physic. He becomes, as noted
above, a playwright, and a comic one at that.

The conclusion which Gerardine contrives in his newly
acquired role is remarkable for its emphasis upon reconciliation and for its refusal to make strict moral judgments. It thus
reinforces the comedy's overall development from restriction
to freedom and away from the stark contrasts with which the
drama seems to begin. No one is banished from the play-world,
and no one is really punished. The very name Gerardine
chooses for his disguise anticipates this general acceptance, for
a *stickler* is a moderator, a reconciler of strife (*OED*); and
Gerardine had earlier promised Dryfat that he would act accordingly: "All shall end in merriment, and no disgrace touch
either of their [Mistress Purge's and Glister's] reputations"
(4.2.59–61). In fact, the Club-Law that Gerardine institutes is
essentially a restatement of the basic concerns of comedy: " 'Tis
the law called make-peace: it makes them even when they are at

odds" (5.3.12–13). And in *his* comedy it is Gerardine's duty, Dryfat notes at the end of the play, to "attone them, put 'em together" (5.3.44).

Gerardine cannot really judge his fellows, because he recognizes that they are not very different from himself and because he realizes that all of them are part of the Family of Love, now no longer a Puritan sect but a group which includes a wide cross section of humanity, as the list of defendants Gerardine calls to trial shows:

> Silence! The first that marcheth in this fair rank is Th[r]um the feltmaker, for getting his maid with child, and sending his 'prentice to Bridewell for the fact; Whip the beadle, for letting a punk escape for a night's lodging and bribe of ten groats; Bat the Bellman, for lying with a wench in a tailor's stall at midnight, when a' should be performing his office; and Tipple the tapster for deflowering a virgin in his cellar; doctor Glister, his wife, Maria, mistress Purge: these be the complete number.
> [4.4.170–79]

As individual as all of these people presumably are and as various as their concepts of love must be, Gerardine is not interested in differences but in similarities. All of them have succumbed to one kind of love or another, and it is that common ground which the play emphasizes. Of course, Maria is more noble than Thrum the feltmaker, or Mistress Purge for that matter, but what is truly significant is that Maria, Thrum, and Mistress Purge respond to one of the most basic of all human emotions. And because of this similarity, the differences between them do not seem very important.

The Family of Love thus progresses, like most conventional comedies, toward increasing inclusiveness. Distinctions dissolve as apparently different kinds of persons are closely associated with one another, just as various types of physical release are joined together under the concept of catharsis or purgation. The play begins with what seems to be a marked contrast between Gerardine and Maria on one hand, and Glister, Mistress Purge, and the gallants on the other. But this opposition becomes progressively less well defined as the play develops. Physical desires dominate, and idealism continually

gives way before an amoral vitality. As far as religious matters
go, Dryfat surmises, "Indeed I think we perform those functions best when we are not thrall to the fetters of the body"
(3.3.25–26), but Mistress Purge speaks for all the characters in
the play when she comments a little further on: "Why, then, a
sense let it be,—I say it is that we cannot be without" (ll.41–42).
As Gerardine is quick to point out, love is beyond moral judgment: "Like Jove's, so must thy acts / Endure no question"
(4.2.6–7).[20] The gods' various metamorphoses in the name of
love thus become a justification not only for Gerardine's disguises (4.2.18–19), but also for the conniving of all the characters. If *The Family of Love* comes to any final conclusion concerning love, it is one very similar to Mistress Purge's defense:
"Truly, husband, my love must be free still to God's creatures"
(5.3.425–26). And when Gerardine turns to the audience "for
approbation of our Family" (5.3.455), he is asking the audience
to applaud itself as well.

The Phoenix and *The Family of Love* are both apprentice
works, and at the same time they differ markedly from one
another. Structurally, the plays develop in opposite directions,
each one concluding where the other begins. *The Phoenix*
moves from a world where it is difficult to make distinctions to
one that vividly contrasts characters and values. *The Family of
Love*, on the other hand, progressively modifies the oppositions with which it opens. As different as these two early plays
are, however, they reveal a great deal about Middleton's later
comedies. Specifically, the two dramas have much to say about
extremes, in relation both to comic form and to the technique
of Middleton's plays. And it is to the question of extremism, in
terms both of content and technique, that I would like to turn.

At the end of *The Phoenix*, the Duke rebukes Proditor by
saying, "Peace, you're too foul; your crime is in excess"
(5.1.117). Lussurioso's name links evil to excess, and the need
for moderation is stressed throughout the drama. Early in the
play, for example, the Duke notes that "there's as much disease, though not to th' eye / In too much pity as in tyranny"
(1.1.9–10), and later, Phoenix finds the same fault in Falso's

justice: "So, sir, extremes set off all actions thus, / Either too tame, or else too tyrannous" (3.1.215–16). Quieto is a "wonder for temperance" (5.1.278), and he cures Tangle by pouring "the balsam of a temperate brain" into his veins (5.1.317). These and related passages imply that the conclusion of *The Phoenix* will be analogous to that of Shakespeare's *Measure for Measure*, a play which is structurally similar and which also emphasizes moderation. In Shakespeare's play the finagling of the disguised magistrate finally establishes a tolerable balance between mercy and justice, and lechery and cold-blooded asceticism. But as I have tried to demonstrate, there is no place for compromise in Middleton's drama. Phoenix, a rare "wonder of all princes . . . made of an unusual strain" (1.1.135–36), and Quieto, a "miracle" of a man (4.1.148), are as excessively good as Proditor and the Captain are excessively evil. Although the play says a great deal about the virtues of moderation, it is, finally, a play without a mean.

The *Phoenix*'s world is black and white because it is the world of allegory, a society where there is no possibility of reconciling good and evil and where character alterations, when they occur, are total. Like most allegories, Middleton's play provides little sense of a unified community of man.[21] Thus the society which *The Phoenix* depicts is a profoundly uncomic one in the most fundamental sense. Comic values such as moderation, reconciliation, and inclusiveness have no place here, and in fact are often associated with evil rather than virtuous characters. Freedom is never highly valued in the play, and the love interest is deflected from the protagonist to a lesser figure (Fidelio). More important, youth is not a positive quality. Because Phoenix must deal with a fallen world, experience is preferable to simple innocence, indeed necessary if evil is to be defeated. And because wisdom derives from experience, it is inevitably associated with age throughout the play. Phoenix is praised precisely because he is older in virtue than in years and because "his judgment is a father to his youth" (1.1.18). Youth is equated at best with folly, at worst with evil. It is therefore fitting that Proditor confides his suspicions about Fidelio to the Captain by saying, "All we of the younger house, I can tell you, do doubt him much" (1.3.131–32). If *The Phoenix* were a conventional New Comedy, we would be quick to recognize the statement as one we should sympathize with; but in the Christian allegorical world of this drama, his words are simply another indication of the nobleman's unrelenting evil. In contrast, the world of *The Family of Love* is one of youth, and the play stresses comic values like moderation and reconciliation. *The Family of Love* is Middleton's most conventional treatment of the New Comedy form and, as such, provides a model by which to measure his later development. Gerardine is one of Middleton's most attractive trickster-heroes and is especially notable for employing wit in the service of love. Moreover, the conclusion of *The Family of Love* is one of the most inclusive and festive in the Middleton canon. Because the opening distinctions between the young lovers and the other characters are gradually modified, the play ends with a feeling of genuine reconciliation and affirms the comic belief that the human community is a homogeneous one.

The *Family of Love* is so typical because it focuses on a central characteristic of comic structure, the movement from restriction to freedom, and relates this movement to forms of physical release or purgation. At the same time, the play also (in good comic fashion) closely links this pattern of development with moderation: "Joy not too much," Lipsalve tells Maria, "extremes are perilous" (3.2.43). As a result, Middleton deemphasizes the opposition of virtuous and unvirtuous characters, of the Celestial and the Vulgar Venuses, which at first seems important thematically and which is reminiscent of the allegorical world of *The Phoenix*. Extreme behavior, whether as a result of humor imbalance or excessive virtue, is from a comic viewpoint a form of restriction, because it limits a person's freedom to act in different ways. Humors characters resemble allegorical abstractions in that they act mechanically and compulsively as if they have no freedom of choice.[22] They are always the same. Comedy attempts to purge this obsessive form of behavior in order to make characters more moderate, more human, more everyday, more like one another. As the characters become less extreme, they have greater potential for acting differently in different situations, and the purgation of their humors thus coincides with the larger movement of the play's society from restriction to freedom. Ultimately, the New Comedy world has no place for absolutes or extremes. It cannot tolerate characters who are highly idealized or totally debased. It values the unexceptional in all things. (Terence's *Adelphoe* is perhaps the best classical expression of this viewpoint.) And all of the characters in *The Family of Love* are finally unexceptional, nothing more or less.

Yet *The Family of Love* also contains a warning against this comic movement toward unity and inclusiveness—Dryfat's mocking plea that the court convict Mistress Purge:

> Master doctor, if they be not punished and suppressed by our club-law, each man's copyhold will become freehold, specialities will turn to generalities, and so from unity to parity, from parity to plurality, and from plurality to universality; their wives, the only ornaments of their houses, and of all their wares, goods, and chattel[s], the chief moveables, will be made common.
> [5.3.194–201]

Dryfat, of course, does not take himself seriously, and his plea is rejected by Gerardine; but as an exaggerated comment on the general development of *The Family of Love* and in fact of most comedy, it is accurate enough. Some loss of discrimination is inevitable in any comic resolution—" 'Tis the law called make-peace, it makes them even when they are at odds" (5.3.12–13)—and thus Dryfat's sentiments are of great interest, when viewed from the perspective of Middleton's later work. Although he is merely joking, the merchant makes a connection between comic inclusiveness and the confusions of fallen existence that is only implicit in *The Phoenix*. In his role as prosecuter, Dryfat indirectly suggests that the New Comedy pattern does not trace the emergence of a new fertile and free society from an old stultifying one, but instead represents a distressing movement away from order and stability toward chaos. *The Family of Love* does not support Dryfat's view, but in Middleton's later comedies these fears become a reality.

Moreover, Dryfat's statement is not the only way in which *The Family of Love* qualifies its status as an almost perfectly conventional New Comedy. Despite the play's pervasive emphasis on moderation in all things, the drama contains a radical and extreme treatment of the concept of purgation or catharsis, a treatment which is notable not only for its pervasiveness, but also for its focus on the literal and physical origins of the concept. The density of references to purgation in the play recalls Tangle's obsessive legal jargon in *The Phoenix*. As is the case with the mad lawyer, a single way of describing reality dominates the thought and expression of all the characters and imposes a kind of absolute unity on their world. Middleton's handling of purgation is so extreme that it almost constitutes a reductio ad absurdum, and this is very important. *The Family of Love* contains the earliest example of a technique that is central to many of Middleton's later comedies: the tendency to push comic conventions and forms to their logical conclusions, thereby rendering them absurd or frightening. Middleton may not have been ready to question New Comedy in *The Family of Love*, but the direction of his later development was already charted.

And so *The Family of Love*, like *The Phoenix*, exemplifies the very extremism it condemns. If we learn anything from these two early works, it is that moderation is not a characteristic of Middleton's technique, or of the world of his plays. Indeed, we must be careful not to dismiss much in either of these dramas as evidence of Middleton's immature or incompetent experimentation. The juxtaposition of opposing and irreconcilable elements we find in *The Phoenix* is present throughout Middleton's corpus. *The Old Law*, written in the second decade of Middleton's career, portrays a world which is as polarized as that of his early allegorical drama. The overt moralizing which we encounter in both *The Phoenix* and *The Family of Love* recurs again and again in his later comedies—in the speeches of the Father in *Michaelmas Term* and in Whorehound's confession in *A Chaste Maid in Cheapside*, for example. Likewise, Tangle's transformation is the model for the extraordinary character reversals we see in subsequent plays.

Essentially, Middleton's later comedies are a composite of important characteristics present in these early works: he often imposes a New Comedy form like the one so clearly worked out in *The Family of Love* on an anticomic society similar to that of *The Phoenix*. And the resulting clash between form and content is the source of the disturbing effects of his more mature dramas. Because the later comedies contain elements which are by nature contradictory, they can neither conclude in the manner of allegory—by depicting the absolute triumph of one extreme over another—nor affirm the truth normally expressed by their comic structure. In *The Phoenix*, good mysteriously triumphs over evil through the interference of a deus ex machina, but there is no such magical power in Middleton's mature dramas. Opposing forces simply coexist.

More important, the doubts about comic assumptions present in Dryfat's plea in *The Family of Love* become increasingly dominant as Middleton continues to write plays. The merchant's mock fear is continually realized as Middleton repeatedly links inclusiveness with confusion. In fact, characters who attempt to impose unity on their fragmented existence—Quomodo, Bounteous Progress, Tim—become foolish or evil and sometimes both. The disorderly society depicted in the later dramas can only fitfully resolve itself through the usual comic virtues of moderation and reconciliation. And in this respect the potential explosiveness which results from Tangle's attempt to reduce everything to the categories of law parallels the tensions created by the problematic unities we find at the end of many of Middleton's plays. The harmony which their comic resolutions demand is constantly undermined by the ineradicable presence of a world which will admit no such harmony.

In order to see more clearly how Middleton questions the assumptions and values of comedy, however, it is now necessary to turn from *The Phoenix* and *The Family of Love* to his more mature works. *Michaelmas Term* and *A Trick to Catch the Old One* are basically New Comedies, but in both plays Middleton creates a society which resists the conventional comic movement toward reconciliation and festivity. In *Michaelmas Term* Middleton subverts the drama's New Comedy structure by juxtaposing that structure to a prodigal son pattern which calls for different responses and emphasizes opposing values. And in *A Trick to Catch the Old One* Middleton successfully integrates the prodigal son parable into comedy, only to create new difficulties by including a subplot that makes an audience's acceptance of the play's apparently joyous conclusion almost impossible.

3
New Comedy & the Parable of the Prodigal Son

And because I see before mine eyes that most of
our heirs prove notorious rioters after our deaths
. . . why should not I oppose 'em now, and break
destiny of her custom?
Quomodo, in *Michaelmas Term*

Ah, here's a lesson, rioter, for you.
Lucre, in *A Trick to Catch the Old One*

As Arthur Kirsch has shown, Middleton's debt to the morality play tradition does not end with *The Phoenix*.[1] Although none of the later comedies is dominated by a Christian allegorical perspective, morality play elements are present in most of Middleton's major plays. Frequently the elements consist of incidents and characters adapted from the parable of the prodigal son and from sixteenth-century plays based upon the parable. In fact, Middleton's interest in this biblical story is apparent in his earliest works, both nondramatic and dramatic, and continues throughout his career.

The second of *Micro-cynicon's* "six snarling satyres," for example, depicts Prodigal Zodon, the "true born child of insatiety" and "son to greedy Gain." This rather unsavory character flies about in a golden chariot and dresses in gold satin. "A

53

base-born issue of a baser sire," Zodon comes to the city to
make his fortune, but in the process he is utterly undone and
soon comes to an appropriate end in the stews. *Father Hubbard's
Tales* contains an even more extended, although less tragic,
description of a prodigal. There we learn of a young gallant
who left his country estate shortly after his father's death and
subsequently became so concerned with dressing in the latest
fashion that he was "metamorphosed into the shape of a
French puppet." Having sold his land in order to pay for his
excesses, the gallant—like so many of Middleton's comic
protagonists—was forced to live by his wits and quickly "out-
stripped all Greene's books *Of the Art of Cony-catching*." In *The
Black Book* Lucifer numbers foolish youths among his most
devoted followers, and Middleton's plays contain numerous
prodigals.[2] Witgood in *A Trick to Catch the Old One*, Follywit in *A
Mad World, My Masters*, Philip Twilight in *No Wit, No Help Like a
Woman's*, Simonides in *The Old Law*, and Leontio in *Women
Beware Women* all owe aspects of their characterization to the
parable and to the tradition of sixteenth century prodigal son
plays.

Middleton was attracted to this particular biblical story, I
believe, because it provided him with a means of expressing his
doubts about New Comedy. In the discussion of *The Phoenix* in
Chapter 2, it was argued that a Christian frame of reference is
often at odds with a comic one. (We might recall that the
triumph of the Christlike prince in that play is accompanied by
the rejection of such positive comic values as youth, festivity,
and reconciliation.) It is not surprising, then, that the respective patterns of judgment and response called for by New
Comedy and the prodigal son parable are incompatible. By
including characters and events drawn from the biblical story
in his comedies, Middleton was thus able to question and, in
some instances, reject the assumptions and values those plays
conventionally should embody. Nowhere is this process more
evident than in *Michaelmas Term*, a drama which contains Middleton's most extensive treatment of the parable. Indeed, the
failure to recognize the comedy's close relationship to the
prodigal son parable and Renaissance prodigal son plays un-

derlies the numerous criticisms of the drama's ambiguity and, more particularly, of its plot.

As the fourth act of *Michaelmas Term* begins, Quomodo, a crafty woolen draper, is putting the finishing touches on his successful attempt to cozen a young prodigal named Richard Easy out of his inheritance. But like so many of Middleton's tricksters, Quomodo is never satisfied; he initiates one last scheme which ironically brings about his own downfall and Easy's recovery. Worried that his son will prove as foolish as the gallant he has just gulled, Quomodo feigns death in order to "note the condition of all" (4.1.104–5): "Because I see before mine eyes that most of our heirs prove notorious rioters after our deaths . . . why should not I oppose 'em now, and break destiny of her custom?" he asks (ll.81–90). Quomodo, however, is unable to oppose "destiny." His son does become a "notorious rioter," Quomodo loses everything, and Easy regains the lands he had earlier let slip through his fingers.

Readers unanimously condemn this sudden reversal in the fortunes of Middleton's clever draper and his former victim. Richard Barker, for example, complains that Middleton weakens "his most interesting character [Quomodo]," and Barker's point is reinforced by Ruby Chatterji: "Thematic unity has not found its dramatic correlative in consistent characterization." Richard Levin perhaps best sums up the problems which seem to be inherent in Middleton's conclusion: "We are evidently expected to side with Easy and enjoy his triumph; and that is the usual response in plays belonging to this comic tradition. . . . Yet the lengthy complication has given us such a vivid impression of Quomodo's and Shortyard's brilliant mastery of the situation, and of Easy's passive gullibility, that our sympathies tend to be reversed."[3]

By focusing attention on the dramatic conventions behind *Michaelmas Term*, Levin indicates the direction that any explanation of the play's puzzling conclusion must take, but he does not develop his insight. The "comic tradition" which Levin mentions is clearly that of New Comedy—a tradition which sanctions the triumph of young lovers (like Easy) over old and usually sterile adversaries (like Quomodo). But Roman com-

edy is not the only dramatic antecedent of *Michaelmas Term*. As
noted above, the play's "lengthy complication" follows the pattern of prodigal son dramas: it traces the fall of a foolish young
heir into misery and his gradual reformation. Because neither
the comic nor the Christian pattern finally dominates the
drama, its conclusion is ambiguous. *Michaelmas Term*'s troublesome ending does not result from faulty plotting or flawed
workmanship. By juxtaposing two contradictory structures,
Middleton has created a play which is deliberately unsettling, a
play which insistently pulls its audience's sympathies in two
opposite directions. But before examining how Middleton
complicates our responses to the drama and subverts its apparent comic form, I wish briefly to consider some sixteenth-
century dramatic versions of the prodigal son parable. These
early Renaissance plays clearly demonstrate why the biblical
tale is usually out of place in New Comedy and thereby provide
a solid background against which to measure Middleton's in-
termingling of the two forms.

Although Renaissance dramatists learned how to write
comedy by imitating Plautus and Terence, the virtues of
Roman comedy were not always self-evident to authors of the
period.[4] The plays, after all, depicted some rather amoral
characters and did not always lend themselves to demonstrating Christian truths. As Gnomaticus, the wise pedagogue in
Gascoigne's *The Glasse of Government*, notes: "[While] out of
Terence may also be gathered many morall enstructions
amongst the rest of his wanton discourses, yet the true christian
must direct his steppes by the infallible rule of Gods woord."[5]
Gnomaticus's view was not unusual, and in general he and his
fellows were right: Roman comedy has little to do with the
moral judgments and spiritual truths which form "the infallible rule of Gods woord." Indeed, the intent of New Comedy is
moral only insofar as what is natural is moral. Comic festivity
reflects an awareness of nature's bounty and of the need to
break away from artifical laws and restrictions in order to act in
accordance with more "natural" laws. Youth triumphs not
because the young lovers are morally or spiritually superior to

those who oppose them (although this is often the case), but
because nature dictates that only the young are fertile and thus
have power to revitalize the community. From a strict Christian
viewpoint, however, such ideas are folly, because nature (like
man) is irrevocably fallen; and as a result, all standards based
upon nature alone are inadequate. To the comic search for
festivity and rebirth in *this* world, the Christian can only answer
that the pagans are looking in the wrong place:

> It is good to be merry
> But who can be merry?
> He that hath a pure conscience,
> He may well be merry.
> . . . .
> What shall he have that can and will do this?
> After this life everlasting bliss,
> Yet not by desert, but by gift, i-wis:
> There God make us all merry![6]

Plautus and Terence would hardly have agreed.

Because many early humanists found classical drama
spiritually lacking, they created the Christian Terence—a body
of plays in which they attempted to assimilate some of the
techniques of classical comedy into stories consistent with
Christian doctrine. The parable of the prodigal son was by far
the favorite subject of these writers, and by the middle decades
of the sixteenth century such prodigal son plays as *Lusty Juventus* (1550), *Nice Wanton* (1550), *The Disobedient Child* (1560),
Misogonus (1570), and *The Glasse of Government* (1575) were an
integral part of English drama. Together with earlier "youth
moralities," such as *Mundus et Infans* (1508) and *The Interlude of
Youth* (1520), these plays form the tradition that stands behind
a large part of *Michaelmas Term*.

There are several reasons why prodigal son plays became
so popular. First of all, many details in St. Luke's story—the
rebellion of the son, his riotous living, the importance of
reconciliation—parallel typical events in New Comedy, and
thus entire scenes from Plautus and Terence could be readily
adapted into dramatizations of the parable. More important,
however, the biblical story approaches these events from a

perspective much different from that of Roman comedy. The authors of the Christian Terence were educators. They wrote to teach, and what they taught was essentially conservative: the virtue of control, the need to preserve the status quo. The prodigal son pattern provides a perfect vehicle for expressing these attitudes, because it negates the comic association of renewal, rebirth, and the triumph of the young. In New Comedy a conflict of generations is inevitable, but the conflict and the equally inevitable victory of youth secures order and continuity by revitalizing an old and moribund society. In the conflict between generations in the decidedly more conservative prodigal son story, however, our sympathies lie on the side of parents. There youth foments disorder and chaos by ignoring its heritage; there the old are the source of all that is truly valuable, because aged wisdom and learning are crucial in a fallen world. The young, not the old, must be reborn at the end of a typical prodigal son play. They do not reform or change their society; instead, they must be altered in order to conform to a society which already exists.[7]

As a result, the prodigal son plays present an extensive critique of comic values. The assumption that it is natural for youth to rebel and to defeat its elders, for example, is attacked in play after play. The author of *Nice Wanton* argues that children must be restrained "from natural wont[,] evil," and demonstrates that Xantippe, the mother in the play, is negligent simply because she believes that children, being children, should have fun. In *Lusty Juventus* a speech which might serve as a definition of New Comedy is assigned, not surprisingly, to Hypocrisy:

> Why should not youth fulfil his own mind,
> As the course of nature doth him bind?
> Is not everything ordained to do his kind?

Similarly, all of the prodigals in these early dramas swear allegiance to festivity and misrule, treating the voices of gravity and seriousness in the same way that Shakespeare's Toby and Maria treat Malvolio. Typically, they verbally abuse their betters, but the Mankind figure in *Youth* goes even further and threatens to murder poor Charity, exclaiming: "Wilt thou reed me / In my youth to lose my jollity?"[8]

The best example of the anticomic vision of the prodigal son plays is Thomas Ingelend's *The Disobedient Child*. Ingelend takes the most positive values of New Comedy and turns them into sources of evil. In fact, he explicitly equates evil with the comic world. Here the prodigal's major fault is that he wants to get married and views matrimony (in good comic fashion) as a form of salvation in itself. Despite his father's frantic attempts to dissuade him, the prodigal marries and is disinherited for his disobedience. A magnificent wedding feast (another comic archetype) follows, and the son and his beloved walk about singing conventional love songs which imply that they have triumphed over restriction and sterility:

> Methought till now I was too sad,
> Wherefore, sadness, fly hence again!
> Away with those words which my father brought out!
> Away with his sageness and exhortation!

But the New Comedy victory is shortlived. The beloved becomes a shrew and terrorizes the young prodigal, beating him in public and treating him like a slave. Humiliated, he finally asks his father's forgiveness and receives it, but the drama does not end happily. The son must bear the consequences of his actions, and the Perorator enters to point the moral in a way which further emphasizes the play's rejection of comic values: "How short a feast is this worldly joying?" he asks.[9] The outcome of the prodigal's marriage feast makes an answer unnecessary.

Ingelend's negation of New Comedy is striking, but it is not, as I have tried to show, unusual. Other writers developed their attacks on youth to such extremes that the prodigals in their plays come to tragic ends. In *Nice Wanton*, Dalila dies of the pox, and her brother Ishmael is hanged. The two elder brothers in *The Glasse of Government* are also destroyed by their misdeeds, and Prodigality is only partially forgiven in *Liberality and Prodigality*. This rather unmerciful severity, so out of keeping with the parable itself, may simply reflect a time when the ideas of men like Luther and Calvin were widely influential. But the tragic fates of many prodigals may also represent a

final attempt to distinguish the dramas from Roman comedy
by erasing any similarities between the conclusions of the two
forms. The writers of the Christian Terence were, as they often
stated, creating a new kind of play, and their attitude is best
summed up by George Gascoigne in the Prologue to *The Glasse
of Government*. Gascoigne rejects mere jesting and "Italian
toyes," urging instead that his audience "gyve eare unto my
Muse":

> A Comedie, I meane for to present,
> No *Terence* phrase: his tyme and myne are twaine:
> The verse that pleasde a *Romaine* rashe intent,
> Myght well offend the godly Preachers vayne.
> Deformed shewes were then esteemed muche,
> Reformed speech doth now become us best.[10]

The lines perfectly convey the difference between the "pagan"
values of conventional comedy and the "godly" precepts of the
prodigal son parable.

   Prodigal sons did not disappear from the stage with the
moralities. In fact, the legacy of these early prodigal son plays
remained strong well into the seventeenth century.[11] Marston
satirizes contemporary instances of the form in *Histrio-mastix*,
and several other playwrights explicitly refer to the earlier
dramas.[12] Like their forebears in the Christian Terence, prodigal son plays written during the flowering of Elizabethan and
Jacobean drama are usually antifestive. For example, the
young murderer in Yarington's *Two Lamentable Tragedies* is
called "Merry," while at the end of act 4 of Jonson's *The Staple of
News*, the Gossips complain that the prodigal's father is spoiling
what might have been a pleasant comedy. In these later dramas
the spendthrifts are generally satiric targets (*Histrio-mastix,
Eastward Ho! The English Traveller*), and are often manipulated
toward reformation by disguised parents or lovers (*The London
Prodigall, The Wise-Woman of Hogsden, The Staple of News*). As in
the earlier plays, their foolishness can lead to tragedy (*Richard
II, Two Lamentable Tragedies, The Miseries of Enforced Marriage, A
Yorkshire Tragedy*). Prodigals who become heroes generally do
so by reforming prior to the action or in the opening scenes of

their respective plays and thus make their prodigality seem insignificant or even nonexistent (*The Merchant of Venice, 1 Henry IV, A New Way to Pay Old Debts*).

As far as I know, most of the Elizabethan and Jacobean playwrights who extensively employ the biblical story avoid mixing it with New Comedy.[13] Middleton is a notable exception. Although *Michaelmas Term* was written in a decade that produced numerous other dramas containing versions of the parable, it breaks rules of composition set down by the early humanists. Middleton's play contains both "*Terence* phrase" and "the godly Preachers vayne."[14] From one perspective the drama appears to be a conventional New Comedy dealing with two love triangles: the conflict of Rearage and Lethe over the hand of Quomodo's daughter Susan and the conflict of Easy and Quomodo over Quomodo's wife Thomasine. Youth triumphs, and the victories of Rearage and Easy are celebrated at the end of the play. As one critic has affirmed: "Easy is energetic, potent, and shows a capacity for growth" in this "life-oriented comedy . . . [that] drives toward overthrow of the old man."[15] But from another perspective *Michaelmas Term* chronicles the prodigal careers of Easy and, less extensively, of Rearage, Lethe, and the Country Wench. It is this second pattern which dominates the opening three acts of the play.

The character Michaelmas Term first introduces the prodigal son theme in the Induction, when he asks, "Shall I be prodigal when my life cools, / Make those my heirs whom I have beggar'd, fools?" (ll.24–25). He answers the question negatively, but his query anticipates the final outcome of Quomodo's plan to gull Easy. More important, although Michaelmas Term states that he is childless, the other Terms enter and hail him as "father of the Terms" (l.35). They in fact are his sons, because they are lesser versions of himself. The ceremonial greeting which follows establishes the significance of the relation of parents and children in the comedy as a whole. Middleton employs rhyme to emphasize the ritual aspects of the scene, and he compares the relationship of parent and child to that of ruler and subject. The three Terms address Michaelmas Term as if he were a king, and he answers using the royal *we*: "Your duty and regard hath mov'd us; / Never till now we thought you lov'd us" (ll.49–50). As is so often the case in Renaissance versions of the parable, familial relationships implicitly become the basis of hierarchy and order in all society.[16] Prodigality is not simply an individual problem. It is an emblem of social discontinuity and chaos. A break between past, present, and future is the inevitable corollary of the prodigal's lack of "duty" and "regard" toward his parents, as Shortyard mockingly tells Easy late in the play: "I should seek my fortunes far enough, if I were you, and neither return to Essex, to be a shame to my predecessors, nor remain about London, to be a mock to my successors" (4.1.14–17). Various characters expend a great amount of energy endeavoring to prevent just such a rupture in *Michaelmas Term*, but most of their efforts are in vain.

The names of the characters who begin the action of the drama proper, *Rearage* and *Salewood*, further emphasize the prodigal son theme, and they are quickly joined by Easy, who reveals his propensity to fall by vowing to become a gallant. Middleton handles these three characters in a relatively straightforward manner. Salewood, Rearage, and Easy might have appeared in any number of prodigal son plays, and their downfall is conventionally described in long scenes of dicing and knavery. Because they are foolish rather than evil, we readily accept the possibility of their reformation. Their mistakes at first do not seem very important. But this lenient picture of youthful folly is soon complicated. The three gallants are suddenly overshadowed by the appearance of Andrew Lethe, whose actions push comedy to the boundaries of the grotesque and transform prodigality from mere folly to a threat to the core of society. Perplexed because he cannot find a suitable messenger for his love letter to Thomasine, Lethe finds help from an unexpected source: "[O that] some poor widow woman would come as a necessary bawd now; and see where fitly comes—my mother!" (1.1.234–36). Mother Gruel does not recognize her transformed son and enters his employ, although the pay is none too high.

Lethe's attempt to ignore his origins (even to the extent of making his mother his bawd) and his plan to woo Thomasine at the same time that he woos her daughter make the prodigal's opposition to hierarchy and order explicit. And the parallel actions of the Country Wench, who first appears in the following scene, having the same effect. By the time we see the parents of both characters unwittingly serving them in act 2, scene 1, prodigality is no longer a laughing matter. And this is important. The seriousness of the Lethe–Country Wench subplots makes it very difficult to condone the apparently innocuous deeds of the other prodigals (notably Rearage and Easy).

The presence of these prodigal son patterns is the reason for the drama's allegorical framework. As Brian Gibbons has stated, "*Michaelmas Term* has for a main plot a modernised, urbanised version of *Everyman*."[17] Indeed, if we view Easy as a composite Everyman, Quomodo and his cohort then become the devil and his allies, while Thomasine, when she stands above the action (2.3.; 3.4.), apparently personifies a beneficent providence which controls the drama's outcome. Moreover, the plot of the comedy takes place on a symbolic landscape which contrasts country and city. As Quomodo implies (1.1.105–7), this opposition superficially reflects the economic struggle of the landed gentry with the middle class, but it also has other, more significant meanings. The first lines of the Induction associate the country with purity and goodness. Michaelmas Term lays aside his white robe symbolizing conscience—"That weed is for the country" (l.2)—and puts on the more devilish "civil black" (l.4). At the same time that the country represents an innocent world in the drama, it also— because of the very qualities of land itself—symbolizes fertility and stability. Shortyard points to these attributes when he argues that Quomodo's love for land is superior to the gallants' amorous inclinations precisely because Quomodo's love concerns something that is lasting: "To be a cuckold is but for one life; / When land remains to you, your heir, or wife" (1.1.109– 10; cf. 1.1.97–101, 2.3.82–85). The acquisition of land thus becomes the only measure of success in *Michaelmas Term*. Land represents everything of value in the play. It is not surprising, then, that Shortyard adopts the name "Blastfield" when gul-

ling Easy, who becomes "Master Prodigal Had-land" after his
fall (5.1.111) and that the loss of Easy's estate, rather than the
loss of Thomasine, threatens to drive Quomodo to madness at
the end of the play.

In contrast to this idealization of the country and land, the
city is presented as a place of temptation or, as Michaelmas
Term intimates, hell itself:

> We must be civil now, and match our evil;
> Who first made civil black, he pleas'd the devil.
> So, now know I where I am.
>
> [Induction, ll.3–5][18]

London is full of dark shops where "spirits" like Shortyard and
Falselight change shape and appearance in a manner which
suggests their father is also the father of lies. It is a city where
one pander is called "Dick Hellgill" and a prodigal takes the
name of a river in Hades (Lethe). Early in the play Hellgill
himself assures us that the "devil reigning, 'tis an age for cloven
creatures" (1.2.8); and so the action of this comedy does not
take place in springtime, as we would conventionally expect,
but in the fall. The season of *Michaelmas Term* thus recalls that
initial triumph of "cloven creatures" which provided the pattern for the fortunes of all later prodigals.

Chaos, confusion, and instability dominate this fallen and
hellish environment. Everything is sterile: law is a "silver harvest" (Induction: l.10); the powers of procreation and the
ability to gather riches seem to be incompatible; Quomodo
equates bonds with children (3.4.135–44); and the Country
Wench turns sex into a business.[19] Linked with this sterility is
the presence of death. The play begins with a discussion of a
lawyer who died because the vacation between terms was too
long, and within three hundred lines we learn that Easy's and
Lethe's fathers have also passed away. These passages in turn
anticipate Quomodo's feigned death at the end of the play.

All of the prodigals in *Michaelmas Term* make symbolic
journeys from the country to the city. "Woe worth th' infected
cause that makes me visit / This man devouring city," laments
the Country Wench's Father, for the city is a place "where I
spent / My unshapen youth, to be my age's curse" (2.2.20–22).

Rearage, Salewood, Easy, Lethe, and the Country Wench all follow in his footsteps. Because they turn away from their ancestry, all prodigals separate their past and present lives. In doing so they reject the order and stability of the country and land for the disorder of the city. The youths' movement from the country to London symbolizes their acceptance of chaos, an acceptance also indicated by their extraordinary ability to forget. Lethe, for instance, is totally true to the meaning of his newly chosen name and does all he can to deny his ancestry. For him the past is irrevocably sundered from the present, and so there is no continuity in his actions and attitudes. Likewise, the Country Wench does not even recognize the parent she employs as her pander. The actions of these two figures are extreme versions of those of the gallants. Like Lethe and the Country Wench, Easy is cursed with a "short memory" (3.4.152) and forgets about the money that he owes Quomodo. Traditionally, prodigality is a denial of heritage, a denial of the advice and models provided by parents. It is precisely this rejection of origins that Rearage, Easy, and Salewood find so odious in Lethe; but by squandering their patrimony, they too have denied the past, have in a sense "forgotten" their heritage.

The prodigals, moreover, not only ignore past events and acquaintances, they also forget themselves, because identity is based upon constancy and continuity. Prodigals are, as the Father notes, "unshapen" youths (2.2.22), and the city only heightens their confusion. The true denizens of urban chaos are ambiguous creatures like Shortyard and Falselight, or masters of deception like Quomodo (who has also denied his ancestry and thus a single identity). But the prodigals fit into neither category. Both Lethe and the Country Wench lack self-knowledge, while Easy has so little sense of his own individuality that when the fictitious Master Blastfield disappears, he laments, "Methinks I have no being without his company" (3.2.6). Instead of being grounded in lineage or in an orderly pattern of behavior, identity becomes a matter of appearance or, more specifically, of clothes. T. W. Craik has demonstrated the importance of symbolic clothing in early prodigal son plays, and Middleton's comedy extensively develops this convention.[20] It is no accident that *Michaelmas Term* begins with a change of raiment in the Induction, that the central character in the comedy is a draper, and that the plot takes place at a time when the clothing industry is particularly healthy (2.3.185–92). Indeed, it might be said that clothes literally make the man in *Michaelmas Term*.

The first three acts of Middleton's comedy are thus dominated by themes and motifs drawn from the tradition of Renaissance prodigal son plays. Most of the drama deals with prodigality and its relation to the chaotic world of the city. Like some of its antecedents, Middleton's play presents a rather pessimistic version of the parable. We watch the prodigals being engulfed in a hellish London, but we never see any of them make a symbolic journey "home" to the countryside. The plot of the play never escapes from the city; green fields always remain somewhere offstage—an almost prelapsarian world of stability and innocence which constitutes a distant source of dreams and desires, but nothing else. As a result, the redemptive aspects of the parable seem to have little significance. Lethe and Mother Gruel are only imperfectly reconciled, and the Father does not even confront his daughter, the Country Wench, at the end of the play. Moreover, the ambiguities and confusion of the drama's urban setting seem to infect even the most upright characters in the comedy. Unlike other disguised fathers in Renaissance prodigal son plays (Old Flowerdale in *The London Prodigall* and Peni-boy Canter in *The Staple of News*, for instance), the Father in *Michaelmas Term* does not recognize his child, and so is unable to manipulate her toward redemption. The noblest character in the play becomes so blinded by appearances that at first he completely misjudges the Country Wench's character, thinking her a lady of good repute rather than the whore she truly is. Mother Gruel's status as moral spokesman is undercut by her desire for young courtiers, and Thomasine's actions similarly become morally questionable as the drama progresses.[21]

Perhaps this pessimism does not matter, however, because

beginning in act 4 the play moves more and more insistently in the direction of New Comedy, tracing the victories of two young lovers (Easy and Rearage) over an old man and his favorite (Quomodo and Lethe). But implicit in the themes and conventions described above is a critique of festivity similar to that of the early prodigal son plays and Middleton's own *The Phoenix*—a critique which unquestionably lessens audience participation in *Michaelmas Term*'s apparently joyous conclusion.

Middleton seems to undermine two central comic assumptions in particular. First, the play denies that procreation is a means of creating order and continuity. None of the children in the drama reproduces his parents' virtues or carries on a heritage. The youths' families are not reborn through them; instead, the prodigals destroy their patrimony, literally beggaring their parents and establishing the incompatibility between riches and children which characterizes the society of the play.[22] Second, as is the case with so many prodigal son plays, *Michaelmas Term* questions the virtues of freedom. In the Induction freedom means the ability to swindle suitors at law, and three of the prodigals discover a new liberty only to be undone by it (1.1.47–48; 1.2.43–44; 4.4.43–45). As his name suggests, Easy's fault is that he is "a fair, free-breasted gentleman, somewhat too open" (1.1.52–53), and after being fleeced by Quomodo, he is ironically told that he has gained complete freedom: "Why, then, Master Easy, y'are a free man, sir; you may deal in what you please, and go whither you will" (4.1.49–50). In *Michaelmas Term* to be free is to be stripped of everything—home, money, heritage. Freedom signifies lack of responsibility and tradition rather than a healthy release from arbitrary restrictions. As such it contributes to the disorderly world of London and is completely opposed to the salutary values of the country.

But *Michaelmas Term* does more than undermine two comic truths. A closer look at the drama's love triangles will show that Middleton complicates the play's New Comedy conclusion in other, more specific ways. From a New Comedy perspective, for example, Rearage is one of the play's heroes. He is a character whom the audience should identify with and admire. Rearage's name and his actions early in the drama, however, immediately label him as a prodigal, and he shows no signs of reforming. We would like to believe the distinctions which Rearage and the other gallants draw between themselves and the more depraved prodigals, Lethe and the Country Wench; but Middleton makes this very difficult. When Cockstone asks Rearage about the latter's plan to marry Susan, "the rich draper's daughter" (1.1.58), his words imply that Rearage has chosen her, at least in part, for her inheritance. Yet Rearage finds Lethe's monetary motives despicable. Hearing of Lethe's desire to marry Susan for her dowry, he exclaims: "And not for love?—This makes for me, his rival" (3.1.205). Rearage probably does not recognize the ironic implications of his statement: he is truly Lethe's rival in seeking Susan's wealth together with her love. Likewise, this apparently conventional New Comedy conflict is thrown into confusion by the fact that Susan initially likes Lethe better than the gallant, instead of the other way way around. As a result, her sudden acceptance of Rearage at the end of the play—"Pardon my wilful blindness, and enjoy me" (5.2.8)—not only casts further doubts on her intelligence, but also undercuts their love. We too would like to assume that she has finally learned the difference "betwixt a base slave and a true gentlemen" (l.10), but her distinction between prodigals is neater than the play will really allow. And Rearage, although outwardly calm and reassured, ironically sounds as surprised as we are: "How soon affections fail, how soon they prove!" (l.12) he exclaims—perhaps a little too soon to be believed.

At first glance Easy seems a less problematic New Comedy hero than Rearage. Although he is the central prodigal of the play and at times shows signs of becoming a truly amoral courtier (3.1.163–64), Middleton ostensibly attempts to raise our estimation of this gull at various places in the drama. Thus Easy turns out to be sufficiently stubborn to elicit a grudging compliment from Shortyard: "I perceive the trout will be a little troublesome ere he be catch'd" (2.3.139–41). Later in the plot Shortyard charitably credits Easy's fall to "good confi-

dence" (4.3.15) and favorably compares the gallant to
Quomodo's son Sim. But even if we are able to ignore Easy's
former folly and his association with prodigality, Middleton
prevents a wholehearted acceptance of his success by complicating this New Comedy triangle, just as he complicated the
relationship of Rearage and Susan. Thomasine, after all, is
Quomodo's wife, and she is a more ambiguous figure than she
first appears. In fact, the symbolic import of the scenes in
which she stands above the main stage and watches the action
below is undercut by her actions in the rest of the play. She does
not reject Lethe out of pious outrage but because " 'tis for his
betters to have opportunity of me" (2.3.7–8). And though
understandable, Thomasine's decision to marry Easy, like her
daughter's acceptance of Rearage, is a little too rapid. Because
it occurs immediately after the coffin of her apparently dead
husband has been carried across the stage, the decision is
disturbingly reminiscent of the prodigals' ability to forget their
families and strike off for the city. Thomasine feels liberated by
the death of another, as did Easy and Lethe, and she eagerly
grasps a chance to break with the past, just as all the prodigals
denied any relation between past and present by rejecting their
heritage. In fact, the sudden marriages of Thomasine and
Susan become additional examples of disorder in the play,
rather than symbols of comic rebirth and the formation of a
new society.

Middleton adds one final twist to prevent an easy identification with these two lovers, for the similarity of Thomasine's
actions to those of the prodigals points to the ambiguous role
that Quomodo fills in *Michaelmas Term*. If we view the play as a
New Comedy, Quomodo is a conventional blocking figure. He
is greedy, old, and apparently impotent. But if we take the
prodigal son material into account, Quomodo no longer seems
so villainous. Two of Quomodo's most cherished values are, in
fact, two of the key positive values in the play—continuity and
family. Sim first appears at the moment Easy is losing his
patrimony, and Shortyard taunts the unfortunate gallant by
noting that Sim is Quomodo's "towardly son and heir" (4.1.28).
All of Quomodo's plots aim at establishing his heirs as landed

ladies and gentlemen, and his attempt to gain land significantly reverses the prodigals' movement from country to city. Even Quomodo's pretended death represents an endeavor to control the future: "For, having gotten the lands, I thirsted still / To know what fate would follow 'em" (5.3.39–40). At the end of the comedy, moreover, Quomodo is clearly associated with the Country Wench's Father. When he announces that he will feign death and "in disguise note the condition of all" (4.1.104–5), he echoes the Father's earlier vow to seek his daughter incognito. Middleton emphasizes the parallel by having the Father appear in the two scenes following Quomodo's decision. He then disappears from the drama, and Quomodo takes his place as disguised commentator on the plot. The Father's lack of an individual name implies that he represents a dramatic type, that he symbolizes all forlorn fathers. Quomodo, when he replaces the Father, acquires some of the same generic qualities.[23] Quomodo the crafty draper is transformed into Quomodo the maligned parent as he is rejected by members of his family (in this case a son and a wife). Likewise, his son proves to be just another prodigal. Sim (like Easy) is gulled out of his inheritance and (like Lethe and the Country Wench) turns away from his heritage. Although he tells the truth about Quomodo, the previous events in the play and Quomodo's conventionally sympathetic role (from the viewpoint of the drama's prodigal son motifs) make Sim's treatment of his father as much a break in hierarchy and order as a moral victory that can be enjoyed.

Quomodo, of course, is not an estimable figure. His attempts to secure stability for his family and himself ironically create untold disorder, disrupting countless families in the process. But Quomodo's association both with the devil and with the drama's highest values is a measure of the careful ambiguity of *Michaelmas Term* and of the moral "doubleness" of almost all its characters. Furthermore, Quomodo does not fail simply because he is evil or foolish. His son's irresponsibility is partially to blame and makes the prodigal son pattern universal in the comedy. *Michaelmas Term* does not contain a single youth who is not prodigal in one way or another. Quomodo's attempt to prevent his heir from becoming a notorious rioter is thus an impossible dream. The same might be said of his desire to gather both money and progeny. Chaos inevitably conquers the attempts (albeit ironic ones) of the cleverest character in the drama to create order and continuity. Quomodo loses both family and riches and, finally, the last vestiges of his identity. When he pleads in court that he has done everything in "jest, my lord; I did I knew not what," the Judge replies: "It should seem so; deceit is her own foe, / Craftily gets, and childishly lets go" (5.3.72–74). *Gets* is a pun on *begets*, and so Quomodo ("deceit" personified) takes on the characteristics of both generations in the prodigal son story: he has "childishly" squandered a patrimony which he himself gathered as a wise and crafty parent. Like all of the other major figures in the play, Quomodo has become a prodigal.

Ambiguity is the salient attribute of the city in *Michaelmas Term*, and in many ways it is also the essential characteristic of the play itself. At the beginning of this drama, as at the beginning of all dramas, the audience asks one basic question: where should its sympathies lie during the unfolding of the plot? Unlike most playwrights, Middleton provides no answer. From the moment Michaelmas Term states that, contrary to the implications of its title, the comedy will not deal with finagling lawyers and greedy suitors, Middleton continually frustrates audience expectations, promising first one kind of play and then another. Apparent spokesmen for authorial intent become ridiculous or depraved. Knaves become fools and vice versa. The drama pulls our responses in two directions at once.

I have tried to show that the reason for this confusion is the juxtaposition of two contradictory structures. New Comedy always values romantic love over family, but the presence of prodigal son material calls this belief into question. As a result, *Michaelmas Term* is a New Comedy in which we tend to despise most of the young and in which the ostensible heroes, Easy and Rearage, do not seem much superior to those they displace. Middleton initially establishes a pattern of judgments and sympathies (e.g., the bonds of family are sacred, children should obey parents), and then forces his audience to violate those patterns if it is to accept the conclusion of the drama. We are asked to admire the Country Wench's Father and Mother Gruel and to condemn their children, while we are paradoxically required to accept Sim, Rearage, and Easy, although they are prodigals, and to be glad at Quomodo's fall, although he, like the Father and Mother Gruel, stands and fights for family. If we "forget" much of the early action, as the play seems to demand, we ourselves become guilty of prodigality. *Michaelmas Term* thwarts any attempt to make easy distinctions and judgments; the play is genuinely ambiguous.

Like *Michaelmas Term*, *A Trick to Catch the Old One* draws upon the traditions of both sixteenth-century prodigal son plays and Roman comedy. Witgood's opening lament over the loss of his estate (1.1.1–8) immediately reveals his former prodigality, and the play closely resembles *Michaelmas Term* in its association of land with stability and order. As is the case with Easy, Witgood's folly has transformed him into master "bully Hadland" (1.2.4; cf. *Michaelmas Term*, 5.1.111), and even the drama's evil characters recognize land as the central good in their society: Witgood's usurious uncle Lucre quickly discovers a new sense of his nephew's worth upon learning that Witgood is betrothed to a widow with a large estate, and Lucre's equally greedy adversary Hoard is "revived" by thoughts of his young wife's green fields rather than by the allurements of her beauty (4.4.4–9). Likewise, all of Witgood's actions center around regaining his lost land and everything which it signifies. Witgood, moreover, is not the only prodigal in *A Trick to Catch the Old One*. The Courtesan enters at the end of his opening lament and notes that the gallant has undone more than his own inheritance: ". . . your lands thrice racked, was never worth the jewel which I prodigally gave you, my virginity" (ll.33–35).

After only forty lines, then, the audience learns that the two central characters of *A Trick to Catch the Old One* are prodigals and that the action of the play will deal with their attempts to regain (symbolically in the Courtesan's case) what has been lost. These attempts essentially follow a New Comedy pattern.[24] At their initial meeting the two young protagonists develop a plan which is intended to trick Lucre into returning the estate he has taken from his nephew, and so enable Witgood to marry the niece of his uncle's archenemy, Hoard. The Courtesan poses as a rich widow who has fallen in love with Witgood and who is perplexed by rumors that the young man is penniless. Viewing the potential match as another chance to enrich himself at his nephew's expense, Lucre agrees to return Witgood's lands, although only temporarily. Meanwhile, news of the rich widow's arrival spreads through London, and Hoard enters the fray, hoping both to frustrate Lucre by preventing Witgood's marriage and to gain the widow for himself. Recognizing that Hoard's interest will enable the Courtesan to escape her less than enviable social position, Witgood urges his former companion to marry the usurer, and she does. With the deed to his estate once more safely in his hands, Witgood then reveals the trick, and the Courtesan unmasks. Defeated, both of the old adversaries accept their fate, and the play ends when both young prodigals ask forgiveness and vow to live virtuous lives. Their victory seems complete.

Middleton thus juxtaposes motifs drawn from both the prodigal son play tradition and Roman comedy in *A Trick to Catch the Old One*, but his use of the two forms is very different from his handling of them in *Michaelmas Term*. In fact, he carefully avoids all of the problems caused by the conjunction of the parable and New Comedy in the earlier play. There are several reasons for this difference. As Richard Levin has stated, Witgood's fall, unlike Easy's, occurs before the main action of the drama, and Witgood's later success is therefore more acceptable.[25] The same is true of the Courtesan. (In this respect we might compare both characters with Shakespeare's Prince Hal and Bassanio.) Moreover, just as Witgood's and the Courtesan's prodigality is deemphasized by never being portrayed on stage, so the prodigals' opponents are more clearly evil than any character in *Michaelmas Term*. There are no sympathetic parents in *A Trick*; no one fulfills the function of the Father in Middleton's earlier play. The characters who attack the prodigality of youth (Lucre, Hoard, the Creditors) are themselves undercut by their own depravity, and the sins of Witgood and the Courtesan seem insignificant in comparison with those of their adversaries. The society which they inhabit is so rapacious that prodigality becomes almost a virtue.[26]

Similarly, whereas *Michaelmas Term* emphasizes the negative aspects of the prodigal son parable—the fall into sin and the accompanying disruption of social order—*A Trick to Catch the Old One* deals with the positive ones: knowledge, forgiveness and mercy, redemption. Lucre ironically points to the first concern when he asks, "Does not he return wisest, that comes home whipped with his own follies?" (2.1.80–81). And at the end of the play the Courtesan argues that her earlier mistakes make her better able to cope with a fallen world, explaining to Hoard: "She that knows sin, knows best how to hate sin" (5.2.140). The prodigals themselves establish the emphasis on forgiveness in the drama's first scene. When Witgood initially encounters the Courtesan, he cruelly calls her "my loathing" (l.28). His speech is reminiscent of Lethe's greeting to Mother Gruel in *Michaelmas Term* and anticipates Allwit's comments on his apparent children in *A Chaste Maid in Cheapside*. Witgood, however, quickly reverses himself and asks her forgiveness (ll.38–39). It is granted, and throughout the remainder of the comedy Witgood strives to be worthy of her trust, an attempt which is best demonstrated by his advice that she marry Hoard: " 'Twould be a great comfort to me to see thee do well, i'faith; marry him, 'twould ease my conscience well to see thee well bestowed; I have a care of thee, i'faith" (3.1.112–14).

As important as these treatments of knowledge and forgiveness are, however, Middleton stresses the theme of redemption most of all. The Courtesan, after she first enters, laments that "lands mortgaged may return, and more esteemed / But honesty, once pawned, is ne'er redeemed" (1.1.36–37), and later in the play Lucre is equally pessimistic about the chances of his nephew's reformation (2.1.8–11). But both are wrong. The prodigals redeem themselves by turning away from their former lives. The Courtesan has not sinned with any man beside Witgood, and at the conclusion of the drama she vows to remain forever chaste. By continually associating success in regaining his land with his own moral reformation, Witgood also helps to dispel any problems we might have reconciling his former prodigality with his status as comic hero. Furthermore, both youths take an important step toward social respectability by marrying. When the Host tells Lucre, "But marriage, by my faith, begins to call him [Witgood] home" (2.1.46–47), Witgood's return "home" implies not only the regaining of Linacre, but also the acquisition of the stability and order which land and home symbolize. The Courtesan also finds marriage a means of redemption and a source of constancy, as she notes after becoming Hoard's wife: "Though I have sinned, yet could I become new, / For where I once vow, I am ever true" (4.4.142–43). The long and, admittedly, somewhat mocking confessional speeches with which the drama ends are the final indication that both of the young protagonists have rejected their former folly and become reputable members of society.[27]

There is one additional way in which Middleton minimizes the potential conflict between prodigal son and New Comedy patterns in *A Trick to Catch the Old One*. As noted above, both forms view misrule in a radically different manner, and thus any play which strongly emphasizes the two structures inevitably becomes ambiguous. Middleton avoids this ambiguity in *A Trick* by making his central character's attitude toward festivity rather conservative and moralistic. After the Host recalls his and the gallant's former merriment, for example, Witgood comments in an aside: "Our merry nights—which never shall be more seen" (1.2.57; cf. 3.1.86–89). Witgood does not view misrule as inherently valuable, but as a means toward a more important goal. (Here, again, we might be reminded of Hal in *1 Henry IV*.) In seeking the Host's aid, the young gallant seeks the help of a man of festivity, a man who is associated with the youth's former folly. And, of course, it is precisely that folly which the gallant is attempting to overcome. Witgood therefore fools the Host into thinking that the success of the plot to gull Lucre will lead to the resumption of Witgood's former debauchery, while assuring the audience that such will not be the case. When the Host agrees to help his friend by saying "If I stand you not in stead, why then let an host come off *hic et haec hostis*, a deadly enemy to dice, drink, and venery" (1.2.48–51), he ironically anticipates the stance toward saturnalia which Witgood will take once his plot is completed. The youth's "trick" is significantly a single one, and because it is not viewed as an end in itself, it is carefully distinguished from the prodigal excesses which led to Witgood's downfall. Similarly, Witgood's actions sharply contrast with those of compulsive tricksters like Follywit in *A Mad World, My Masters*. His involvement in misrule is limited and calculated from the start, and as a result can be reconciled easily with the conservative Christian perspective of the play's prodigal son elements.

Middleton thus carefully integrates aspects of the prodigal son parable into the New Comedy structure of *A Trick to Catch the Old One*. On one hand, he lessens the effect of the biblical material by relegating the folly of his central characters to a time before the opening of the play and by making both Witgood and the Courtesan morally superior to all of the other characters. On the other hand, he also moderates the aspects of the play which are drawn from Roman comedy by making festivity a means to an end rather than an end in itself and by linking the protagonists' success with a rejection of saturnalia and an acceptance of sober Christian values. The drama is free of the conflicting attitudes which run throughout *Michaelmas Term,* and its Christian elements are relatively at home within its comic framework. Indeed, along with *The Family of Love, A Trick to Catch the Old One* appears to be one of the least problematic comedies in the Middleton canon; and the play has remained among his most popular, I think, because it seems so straightforward. But just as *The Family of Love's* apparently typical structure is complicated by Dryfat's warning against comic inclusiveness and the numerous references to purgation in the play, so *A Trick* is not without ambiguities which undermine its ostensibly traditional plot. Having fully examined the contradictory relationship of the prodigal son parable and Roman comedy in *Michaelmas Term*, Middleton carefully integrates the two forms in this later play only to introduce problems of a different nature.

Perhaps the first indication that *A Trick to Catch the Old One* is not entirely conventional is the paucity of love interest in the play.[28] The action begins typically enough. Onesiphorus Hoard discourses on the ability of the young to solve the problems of parents, in this case the feud between his brother Hoard and Witgood's uncle Lucre: "What though there be a dissension between the two old men, I see no reason it should put a difference between the two younger; 'tis as natural for old folks to fall out, as for young to fall in!" (1.1.122–25). But, ironically, Onesiphorus Hoard is talking about the wrong young people—his brother's niece Joyce and Lucre's stepson Sam Freedom—rather than Joyce and Witgood. The audience, however, is not aware of this, because Witgood's amorous intentions are scarcely mentioned until act 3, scene 2, and then only haphazardly (the scene is twenty-one lines long). Joyce later appears in an extraordinarily short balcony scene (five lines). She greets Witgood, and gives him a note arranging their next meeting (which we never see). Witgood speaks five words to his beloved, the last of which ironically are "A word's enough" (4.4.283). And in fact, a word is about all that we hear of their love. As Wilbur Dunkel once complained, "In *A Trick to Catch the Old One* it would seem . . . as if Middleton were avoiding love scenes."[29]

This rather spotty handling of Witgood's feelings for Joyce may seem insignificant at first glance, but it has important effects on the play as a whole. In the world of comedy, love is closely associated with fertility, harmony, and the comic tendency toward inclusiveness which is so fully demonstrated in *The Family of Love.* The success of young lovers at once promises that society will be renewed and symbolizes the harmonious and unified human community toward which comedy moves. The relative absence of this emotion in *A Trick* is symptomatic of a fundamentally uncomic discord at the very center of the society which the drama depicts. For if the flames of love and desire burn only fitfully in this comedy, the flames of anger rise to a fever pitch. In the first scene, for example, we learn that for Hoard and Lucre "anger be the very fire / That keeps their age alive" (ll.111–12). Later their friend Lamprey warns them that "anger is the wind you're both too much troubled withal" (1.3.1–2), and urges: "When the fire grows too unreasonable hot, there's no better way than to take off the wood" (ll.55–56). But neither of the old men follows his advice. Lucre does good only to spite his adversary, and his fondness for vexing others extends even to the members of his own family. Lucre not only swindles his nephew Witgood out of his estate, he also continually provokes his wife, mocking her son's prospects for marriage (2.2.335–39) and sarcastically suggesting that her former husband rescued her from lower class origins because of her ability to cook (4.2.72–76).

Hoard is no better. He spends all of his energy attempting to undo Lucre's plans and at one point vows to pursue his enemy with a "flame of hate" that knows no bounds and to "without mercy fret thee" (1.3.38, 44). The unrelieved malice which characterizes almost all of Lucre's and Hoard's actions dominates the play and overwhelms any positive impression of harmony created in the brief scenes where Witgood and Joyce appear together. The power of love seems insignificant in comparison with the strength of the old usurers' hatred. At the same time, the old men's inability to forgive or be merciful toward one another vividly contrasts with the forgiving natures of both Witgood and the Courtesan. And in fact, the attitudes of Hoard and Lucre are part of a large cluster of motifs and values in the drama which oppose the more beneficent qualities associated with the young prodigals. The import of this contrast in relation to the play's New Comedy structure will become clearer, if we turn back to a concern which was central to *Michaelmas Term*—the ability to forget the past.

To be redeemed or to be forgiven requires both sinner and sinned against to turn away from the past. Almost all comic conclusions demand a degree of forgetfulness on the part of some of their characters and on the part of their audience. Acceptance of the ending of *A Midsummer Night's Dream*, for instance, requires that the audience overlook Demetrius's cruelty toward Helena early in the play and that it, like all of the characters, forget and forgive the foolish actions that take place in the forest. Similarly, the festive conclusion of *The Family of Love* is made possible by Gerardine's and Glister's ability to forgive one another. We, in turn, must not judge Glister and Mistress Purge too harshly if we are to participate in that festivity. Comedies which do not allow us to put aside the implications of much of what happens as their characters are maneuvered toward a happy ending often seem distinctly uncomic. Bert O. States has pointed out that "laughter is essentially a reaction to limited perception, and comedies become progressively less funny and laughter more 'tragic' as awareness increases."[30] Once we realize that the problems which the characters encounter are not simply absurd and that their sufferings are something more than part of a game, once we recognize, in short, that the man slipping on a banana peel might possibly break a leg, it becomes increasingly difficult for us to enter fully into a comic spirit. We encounter a serious side of existence which is usually excluded from the comic world; and because most of us are unable to dismiss the implications of this recognition, our participation in the concluding merriment is inevitably lessened. We cannot, in other words, forget and forgive.

Among the extant Roman comedies, Plautus's *Truculentus* and Terence's *Hecyra* come closest to complicating audience response in this manner—the former because of its unusually harsh tone, the latter because of Pamphilus's hypocritical and callous treatment of his wife. But Plautus and Terence clearly were not interested in examining the relationship of laughter and audience perception in their plays. Shakespeare's *The Merchant of Venice*, on the other hand, perfectly demonstrates the situation States describes. Were Shylock simply a stock figure, his plight would be easy to dismiss at the conclusion of the drama. But as soon as Shakespeare makes the usurer more than a comic automaton, the harmony which the play's last scene attempts to create is rendered impossible. We are too aware of Shylock's humanity to overlook his suffering.

The same problem lies at the heart of *Michaelmas Term*'s

ambiguous conclusion. In Middleton's play the presence of Lethe and the Country Wench makes it hard to dismiss the prodigality of Rearage and Easy and thus undermines an acceptance of the two gallants' triumph. Moreover, because Middleton establishes "forgetting" as both the major sin of the prodigals and a cause of the chaotic world they inhabit, the audience of *Michaelmas Term* cannot easily overlook the past actions of Easy and Rearage unless it wishes to become prodigal as well. And because viewers and readers of the play naturally do not want to be associated with youthful folly, they almost necessarily remain alienated from the drama's joyous conclusion. *Michaelmas Term* suggests that, pushed to an extreme, the ability to forget (and by extension to forgive) creates disorder. Comic inclusiveness and festivity thus have no place in its world.

If Middleton questions the New Comedy status of *Michaelmas Term* by equating comic inclinations to forget and forgive with prodigality, he undermines the apparently conventional form of *A Trick to Catch the Old One* by depicting a society in which the two tendencies are scarcely present. Whereas too many characters forget too easily in *Michaelmas Term*, no one in *A Trick to Catch the Old One*, with the exception of Witgood and the Courtesan, shows much ability either to overlook or to forgive past actions.[31] Lucre, unlike the traditional merciful father of the prodigal son parable, is ready to cheat his foolish nephew at every opportunity. His opening argument with Hoard demonstrates that he even sees himself as an agent of justice: "Upbraid'st thou me with nephew? Is all imputation laid upon me? What acquaintance have I with his follies? If he riot, 'tis he must want it; if he surfeit, 'tis he must feel it; if he drab it, 'tis he must lie by't; what's this to me?" (1.3.29–32). Of course Witgood is nothing to Lucre (cf. 1.3.33–34), and this is the point. When Lucre notes that the name *aunt* has been translated to mean "bawd" (2.1.8–12), he ironically indicates that his unkind actions toward Witgood have also transformed the meaning and role of *uncle*.[32] Although Lucre does say that "most of our beginnings must be winked at" (4.2.76), his actions throughout the play make it evident that he can never ignore the past. The old usurer's attitude is echoed again and again in the drama. Most of the characters in *A Trick* are blessed with similarly fine memories, and the things they remember best are debts.[33] Indeed, the characters expend an enormous amount of time and energy disposing of and collecting various kinds of debts, for the word has a wide range of meaning in the play, as is indicated by Witgood's argument with Hoard over the latter's wish to marry the Courtesan:

> HOARD: Release you her of her words, and I'll release you of your debts, sir.
> WITGOOD: Would you so? I thank you for that sir; I cannot blame you, i'faith.
> HOARD: Why, are not debts better than words, sir?
> WITGOOD: Are not words promises, and are not promises debts, sir? [4.4.187–92]

Using the terminology of *A Trick to Catch the Old One*, forgiving is essentially a matter of releasing someone from former debts, and one aspect of Witgood's success is his ability to trick both Lucre and Hoard into performing symbolic acts of forgiveness which are abhorrent to their natures. Lucre "forgives" his nephew when he unwittingly returns lands taken as punishment for Witgood's prodigality; Hoard absolves Witgood by paying the latter's monetary obligations (appropriately at a reduced rate) in order to marry the Courtesan.

But these are uncharacteristic acts. The three Creditors best embody the normal attitude toward debts in the play. They first appear at the end of act 2, scurrying furtively about like the vermin that they are and speaking in short staccato phrases. They are grotesques, in their own words "bloodsuckers" and "cut-throats" (3.1.71, 73), and the Creditors' final appearance strikingly confirms these qualities. They enter threatening to hang Witgood because of the money he owes them, and when he is apprehended, one of them is nearly ecstatic: "So, so, so, so! It warms me at the heart; I love a' life to see dogs upon men" (4.3.11–12). The Creditor apparently equates the sergeants who arrest Witgood with cruel dogs, but by the end of the episode it is clear that he is really talking about himself and his companions. They are "beasts" (1.45) who "must have either money or carcass" (1.46), and they obviously prefer the latter. As with Lucre and Hoard, suffering, not love, "warms" the hearts of the Creditors.

The Creditors' bloodthirsty nature links the passages in the comedy dealing with debts to those dealing with anger, and the presence of these characters is another important indication of the pervasiveness of hatred and discord in the drama. Furthermore, the Creditors' actions turn debt collecting into revenge. This explains why the usurers Hoard and Lucre are the two individuals most vocally concerned with vengeance in the play. Not only do the old men not forget and forgive, they also unmercifully and joyfully punish those who are in any way obligated to them (see 2.2.40–52; 4.1.96–98). To be told that "you're excellent at vengeance" (4.1.34) is for Hoard and Lucre the ultimate compliment. Moreover, the two old enemies and the Creditors are not the only characters who choose revenge over mercy and forgiveness. After Hoard and Lucre exit from the stage in act 1, scene 3, Lucre's stepson Sam Freedom and a gallant named Moneylove argue over the hand of Hoard's niece Joyce. Moneylove strikes Freedom, and the latter vows to take vengeance through the law (ll.69–72). Similarly, when Lucre taunts his wife over Witgood's new prospects for marriage, she concocts a plan to "cross" him in return (2.1.346–47). And Hoard is ironically forced to become a peacemaker to prevent his allies from absurdly fighting among themselves over their respective contributions to his plot to win the Courtesan. In fact, the spirit of discord is so strong within the play that even the good-natured Host, himself a man of festivity and merriment, succumbs. Noting the Courtesan's plan to gull Hoard, he speculates, "This will be some revenge yet" (4.4.135). One need only recall Gerardine's adopted role as reconciler at the end of *The Family of Love* and his pledge that "all shall end in merriment" (4.2.59) to recognize how far this emphasis on anger and vengeance strays from the usual affairs of comedy.

In essence, the mentality of Hoard, Lucre, and most of the characters in the drama is the mentality of the Old Law. The Old Testament God is a God of strict justice and vengeance, and these attitudes permeate the world of the play. The characters' unspoken allegiance to this pre-Christian frame of mind lies behind both Lucre's emphasis on the need to punish prodigals strictly and the many passages concerning anger, debts, and revenge. The values and qualities of Witgood and the Courtesan, on the other hand, are primarily New Testament ones; they are carefully associated with mercy and forgiveness. Witgood indicates the spiritual consequences of the contrast, when he notes of the Creditors, "He that believes in you shall never be saved, I warrant him" (4.4.277–78). We have reason to believe the young gallant. All of the evil characters in *A Trick to Catch the Old One*, as will be shown below, are associated with the devil. And "Theodorus" (gift of God) Witgood explicitly distinguishes the nature of his own actions (which might be construed as a kind of revenge) from the nature of the actions of his adversaries when he comments on the hatred of Lucre and Hoard midway in the play:

> He has no conscience, faith,
> Would laugh at them; they laugh at one another!
> Who then can be so cruel? Troth, not I;
> I rather pity now, than ought envy.
>
> [4.2.81–84]³⁴

At the same time, this spiritual opposition between the old and new dispensation is part of a larger contrast between anticomic and comic values in the play. Perhaps following the lead of Shakespeare, Middleton brings comedy into a world that is also pervasively Christian by focusing on the aspects of comedy—forgiveness and mercy—which are most compatible with Christianity and by minimizing the amoral aspects of saturnalia which are so out of keeping with Christian values. (As previously discussed, Witgood's trick is not an end in itself, and he promises to reject festivity once he regains his estate.) Thus the essentially Old Testament–New Testament opposition of anger and love, or vengeance and mercy, is paralleled on a more physical level by a traditional comic opposition between sterility and fertility. The death of the spirit is accompanied by the death of the flesh. Not surprisingly, Lucre is childless and his wife is "old, past bearing" (2.1.307). The usurer's treatment of Witgood is itself completely unnatural. And Hoard, we are told on several occasions, is impotent (3.1.238–41; 4.4.1–9). In contrast, the merciful, loving natures of Witgood and the Courtesan are linked with fertility. Like Gerardine and Dryfat in *The Family of Love*, they speak of their plot in words which allude to natural generation (1.1.53–58), and their speeches anticipate the renewal promised by Witgood's marriage to Joyce at the end of the play.

These oppositions between the Old Law and the New and between anticomic and comic values are conventional, and Middleton's greatest contemporary provides several instances in which the two are closely related within a single play. Middleton's use of the contrasts, however, is notably unconventional. On both the spiritual Christian level and the more physical comic one, the negative half of the opposition seems stronger. Anger and sterility rather than love and fertility are the norm in *A Trick to Catch the Old One*; its world seems unable to accommodate some of the central tenets of both Christianity and Roman comedy. And although the anticomic elements in the main plot by themselves are perhaps not striking enough to call Witgood's triumph into question, they are reinforced and intensified by a secondary plot which deals with a figure who seems totally alien in a New Comedy world: a usurer named Harry Dampit.

Dampit first enters the play in act 1, scene 4, and he subsequently appears at the ends of acts 3 and 4. Although Witgood encounters the usurer at one point, the Dampit scenes have no actual bearing on the young gallant's fortunes; they simply portray the old man's gradual decline toward a grotesque, drunken death. Dampit's presence has not, for the most part, been viewed as one of the play's strong points. Some critics have ignored the scenes in which he appears.[35] Others find him out of place: "a remarkably realised character, but one which has no connection with the plot of the play."[36] Dampit, however, is not an unfortunate mistake who might best be overlooked. He is the most important means by which Middleton undermines the comic structure of *A Trick to Catch the Old One*. The usurer does not belong in New Comedy: he is too disgusting and too evil. Like Lethe in *Michaelmas Term*, Allwit in *A Chaste Maid in Cheapside*, and Shylock in *The Merchant of Venice*, he elicits emotional responses which are out of keeping with festivity and saturnalia. In doing so, Dampit calls comedy itself into question by forcing us to confront an aspect of human life which comedy cannot portray and at the same time remain comic. His actions cast a cloud over Witgood's victory which is never really dispersed.

Dampit's introduction recalls the preparation in *The Phoenix* for the appearance of a similarly important figure, Tangle. Witgood and the Host arrive at an inn, and Witgood asks his companion to stay and behold "two the most prodigious rascals that ever slipped into the shape of men: Dampit, sirrah, and young Gulf, his fellow caterpillar" (1.4.5–7). Witgood is also telling the audience to take note of these two "creatures," and his statement indicates that Dampit, like Tangle, should be viewed as an emblem rather than as a personality. Later in the play Hoard's friend Lamprey again points to the usurer's symbolic function, similarly employing a hortatory tone as he describes Dampit's drunken stupor: "Note but the misery of this usuring slave. . . . Here may a usurer behold his end. What profits it to be a slave in this world, and a devil i' th' next?" (4.5.54–59).

In part Dampit embodies the materialistic, Old Testament, anticomic attitudes of the play-world, and statements like the above should make us wary of separating him too distinctly from men like Lucre and Hoard. Indeed, Middleton carefully links the three. All of them are usurers, and they first appear in consecutive scenes (1.3. and 1.4.). When Hoard berates Lucre—"What's all to thee? Nothing, nothing; such is the gulf of thy desire, and the wolf of thy conscience" (1.3.33–34)—his words prepare us for the entrance of Dampit, a "blasphemous, atheistical" rascal (1.4.13) and his servant Gulf. The accusations of monstrosity that the two enemies hurl at one another—"toad," "aspic," "serpent," "viper" (1.3.50–53)—

anticipate Witgood's comment that Dampit and Gulf are "two the most prodigious rascals that ever slipt into the shape of men" (1.4.5–6). Similarly, after Hoard tricks Lucre later in the play, he expresses his joy in a manner that brings the "trampler of time" (1.4.10) Harry Dampit to mind: "Never did man so crush his enemy!" (4.1.105) he shouts. Hoard is also present in the usurer's deathbed scene, and in that episode the similarity between Dampit's quarrel with Gulf and the endless fighting of the old men is driven home by Sir Lancelot: "This is excellent, thief rails upon the thief" (4.5.152). The same is true of Lucre and Hoard.[37]

But Dampit is more than a symbol of greed and rapacity. He is the spirit of discord itself. Dampit's infamous career began with stealing and soon progressed to a point where he became a source of endless conflict. With newly stolen money fresh in his hands, Witgood relates, "The next town he came at, he set the dogs together by th' ears" (1.4.19–20). We need only recall Tangle to understand how appropriate Dampit's interest in law is to his association with strife, and the usurer's love of disorder likewise lies behind his association with the devil. Since Gulf in Dampit's own words is "great Lucifer's little vicar" (4.5.159), then Dampit is Lucifer himself.[38] Dampit's arrival in London before the beginning of the play's action signified the triumph of all that he represents. " 'Twas a merry world when thou cam'st to town with ten shillings in thy purse" (1.4.39–40), Witgood notes, and the past tense of the statement reveals more than the young gallant himself may realize. The world *A Trick to Catch the Old One* depicts is no longer a "merry" one in any real sense. This New Comedy is dominated by anger and revenge rather than by love and mercy. Harmony and festivity have given way to discord and vengeance.

Furthermore, the Dampit scenes themselves qualify our merriment and participation in the play's ostensibly comic world. Without them some of the other problems Middleton introduces into the drama might seem insignificant, but their presence makes the uncomic aspects of the play too insistent to ignore. Dampit appears at the conclusions of acts 1, 3, and 4, while the Creditors (whose bestiality parallels and reinforces the usurer's) close act 2. By evenly distributing these disturbing scenes throughout the drama, Middleton prevents his audience from entering readily into a spirit of carnival or saturnalia. Dampit, true to the nature of his character, brings an element of discord into the overall structure of *A Trick to Catch the Old One* itself.

The last scene in which the old lawyer appears is perhaps the best example of his effect on the drama's comic structure. The episode is one of the most powerful in the play, and because it occurs so near to the end of the comedy, it inevitably affects our reaction to that ending. Moreover, the scene immediately follows Witgood's first meeting with Joyce and so abruptly qualifies any joy we felt in the apparent victory of the young lovers. As the episode begins, we hear Dampit's servant Audrey singing a song which again indicates the usurer's hellish nature (4.5.1–2). Lamprey comments that Dampit lies "like the devil in chains" (l.6), and Sir Lancelot and his friends enter shortly afterward. It is soon apparent that we are watching the culminating scene of vengeance in the play. The gallants gather around Dampit's bed and contemptuously mock a man who once terrorized them all. Lancelot turns and urges silence—"We shall have the better sport with him; peace!" (l.30)—but the quiet he requests is not for the sick usurer's benefit. Indeed, Sir Lancelot's use of the word *peace* strikes a note of profound irony in this least peaceful of scenes in a not very peaceful play. The possibility of harmony seems almost nonexistent in the society these characters inhabit. Dampit's reply is even more startling: "Oh, my bosom Sir Lancelot, how cheer I! thy presence is restorative" (ll.32–33). Here, the key word is "restorative," since it ironically points to the process of rebirth which is so central to comedy. But although Witgood and the Courtesan have been "made new" in the course of the drama, there is no redemption for Dampit. When he requests a drink, the Boy's angry reply underlines the hopelessness of the usurer's situation: "A vengeance sack you once" (l.44), he cries.

Suddenly this overriding tone of hatred and anger is broken. Hoard enters and eagerly invites the dying man to his wedding feast: "Fie, Master Dampit! you lie lazing abed here,

and I come to invite you to my wedding dinner; up, up, up!"
(ll.135–36). In essence, Hoard is asking Dampit to take part in a
typical comic conclusion with its promise of harmony and
rebirth. His hopes are ill-founded, however, for as Dampit's
ironic reply to Sir Lancelot intimated earlier in the scene, the
usurer will never be able to rise, either physically or spiritually,
and enter the "restorative" festivity of the conventional feast
Hoard envisions. Dampit simply has no place there. Moreover,
the shift in tone from the gallants' earlier bitter mockery of
Dampit to Hoard's joyous greeting is grotesque. Indeed, it is so
strange that we might dismiss the radical change as uninten-
tional were it not for a parallel shift at the end of the episode.
While Audrey gently rocks the drunken old man as if she were
rocking a child—"Sleep in my bosom, sleep" (ll.176–77)—Gulf
sputters about threatening to bludgeon his former leader: "A
little thing would make me beat him, now he's asleep" (l.181).

These two juxtapositions of contrary feelings and attitudes
embody on a small scale the relationship of the Dampit scenes
to the rest of the play. Like this episode, *A Trick to Catch the Old
One* is composed of rapidly shifting and opposing qualities, and
Middleton maximizes the effect of the shifts by evenly distributing the Dampit material and the scenes with the Creditors throughout the drama. The contradictory qualities contrast Old Testament with New Testament values, and a distinctly uncomic reality with comic festivity. As noted above,
these oppositions are conventional enough, but, as is not the
case in most plays, the contradictions are never resolved. If *A
Trick to Catch the Old One* essentially depicts a conflict between
revenge and mercy, discord and harmony, and sterility and
fertility, the malign qualities are remarkably resilient. Hate
and vengeance are so dominant in the play that it often seems
to be a bitter revenge comedy, and Witgood's love for Joyce,
because we see so little of it, is lost in the process.

Likewise, although Witgood and the Courtesan are reborn
at the end of the drama, the society they inhabit remains
unchanged. The ironic "restorative" presence of Sir Lancelot
in the last Dampit scene is one indication of this, and we might
also recall that Dampit, in vivid contrast to the young prodigals,

cannot ask forgiveness. Significantly, when he last prayed, he did so to destroy "Poovies' new buildings" (3.4.1–5). Moreover, the presence of young Gulf insures that what Dampit represents will survive the old man's death. And while Hoard does show some sign of changing in the final scene, Lucre does not. After the Courtesan's repentance, he turns to Witgood and says: "Ah, here's a lesson, rioter, for you" (5.2.175). Witgood has learned a lesson; this prodigal has returned home wiser. But what, we may ask, is the lesson that Lucre himself has learned? Curiously, only the least depraved characters in *A Trick* ask forgiveness, indeed, are even aware of their sins. Set against their milieu, Witgood and the Courtesan seem truly miraculous. They, not Dampit or Lucre, depart from the norms of their society, and as a result their victory does not bring with it a renewal of the world they inhabit. That world remains resolutely uncomic. As audience we can applaud the youths' cleverness and success, but *A Trick to Catch the Old One* does not move finally toward the kind of harmonious moderate society which we can become part of. The elements in the play are too disparate and unchanging to form the hypothetically unified community which lies at the heart of conventional comedy.[39]

In its own way, then, *A Trick to Catch the Old One* is as ambiguous and perplexing as *Michaelmas Term*. Just as the contradictions between prodigal son motifs and New Comedy are left unresolved in the earlier play, so Middleton never settles the opposition between an anticomic Old Testament world and a hero and heroine who are associated with both comic and New Testament values.[40] Despite the apparent familiarity of the events it traces, *A Trick to Catch the Old One* is not a conventional New Comedy. The play's uniqueness is perhaps best summed up by one of its own characters. After Mistress Lucre vows to cross her husband for insulting her, Sam Freedom becomes curious about the details of his mother's plan and asks: "Is it a tragedy plot, or a comedy plot, good mother?" (2.1.349). The question might also be asked of the plot of Middleton's play. Significantly, Mistress Lucre does not answer her son's question directly: her plot, like Middleton's, does not easily fit into conventional generic categories. It is, as she states, "a plot shall vex him" (l.350), and her words apply equally well to the effect of the play in which she appears.

Comedy inherently emphasizes moderation and inclusiveness, but *Michaelmas Term* and *A Trick to Catch the Old One* subvert their New Comedy structures by containing opposing qualities so extreme that they refuse to be moderated or reconciled. In the former play Middleton juxtaposes New Comedy and the prodigal son story; in the latter he perfectly integrates the parable into the drama's comic form only to introduce new material which contradicts the festive spirit which comedy requires. In each play the most problematic elements are introduced in the subplots. We can safely say that *Michaelmas Term* would be less troubling if the presence of Lethe, the Country Wench, and their parents did not draw our attention to the more pessimistic aspects of prodigality and the revolt of youth against age. Likewise, *A Trick to Catch the Old One* would be an infinitely more conventional comedy without the Dampit scenes. According to Richard Levin, a playwright using multiple plots ultimately aims "to relate the separate plots, intellectually and emotionally, in such a way that our reaction to one conditions and is conditioned by our reaction to the other, in order that both sets of responses can be synthesized . . . into a coherent overall effect which constitutes the real unity of the play."[41] Middleton's multiple plots do not, it seems to me, always work in this manner. In the two plays discussed in this chapter, the multiple plots do not synthesize our responses, but do the opposite. A set of reactions and moral values called for in one plot is rejected in the other. In fact, Middleton's subplots often complicate rather than reinforce our responses and dislocate rather than pattern our judgments. As a result, they are often key contributors to the ambiguity of his most characteristic plays.

Middleton's handling of subplots, furthermore, is indicative of a more basic reason why *Michaelmas Term* and *A Trick to Catch the Old One* are perplexing. Both plays seem to violate one of the most commonly held assumptions about literature: the belief that form and content should be inseparable. The typical pattern of values and responses implicit in the comic structure of each play is contradicted by events and characters contained within that structure. The comedies are grotesques in Montaigne's sense of the word, "patched and hudled up together of divers members, without any certaine or well ordered figure, having neither order, dependencie, or proportion . . . casuall and framed by chance."[42] But like the apparent formlessness of Montaigne's essays, the confusing surface of Middleton's plays is not really the product of chance, and the discrepancy between form and content is more apparent than real. The dramas' discordant nature is a perfect analogue of the disordered world they portray. More important, by emphasizing a literary form (the prodigal son parable) which undermines central comic values or by stressing figures who are too evil and diabolic to be accommodated easily into comedy (Dampit and the Creditors), Middleton questions the validity of comedy itself. In *Michaelmas Term* essential comic values like festivity and freedom become sources of evil, and in *A Trick to Catch the Old One* comic conventions are revealed to be inadequate to deal with the society within the play. The only way we can accept the apparently traditional conclusions of both dramas is to turn our backs on much of what we have seen, but Middleton makes this very hard to do. Like most of the characters in *A Trick* we cannot "forget" and "forgive" what has come before and enter into the concluding festivities. It is a problem which will frequently recur in relation to Middleton's later comedies.

The plays discussed in this chapter thus develop in a manner similar to *The Phoenix*. Because their worlds are composed of extremes, those worlds, like that of Middleton's estates morality, are basically uncomic. There is, however, one important difference: the two dramas discussed above are not allegories and thus cannot reach a satisfactory resolution (as does *The Phoenix*) through the triumph of one extreme over another. Indeed, they do not reach a resolution at all. The three plays which will be examined in Chapter 4 likewise contain irreconcilable contradictions. But like *The Family of Love* they also focus (more extensively than do *Michaelmas Term* and *A Trick*) on specific comic conventions and values. In *A Mad World, My Masters*, Middleton depicts a flawed symbol of festivity and generosity, Sir Bounteous Progress, and demonstrates that these comic virtues have no validity except on the stage. In *No Wit, No Help Like a Woman's*, he suggests that the harmonious conclusion toward which comedy develops is an unnatural and unreal fiction. Finally, in his greatest comedy, *A Chaste Maid in Cheapside*, Middleton denies that there is a meaningful relationship between New Comedy structure and patterns of natural and spiritual rebirth.

4
Meaningless Forms

This is the commodity of keeping open house, my
lord, that makes so many shut their doors about
dinner time.
                 Bounteous Progress, in *A Mad World,*
                                    My Masters

And now to vex 'gainst nature, form, rule, place,
See once four warring elements all embrace.
           Gilbert Lambston, in *No Wit, No Help*
                                Like a Woman's

Life, every year a child, and some years two;
Besides drinkings abroad, that's never reckon'd;
This gear will not hold out.
                 Touchwood Senior, in *A Chaste Maid*
                                    in Cheapside

Although *A Mad World, My Masters* contains neither the extensive and unsettling juxtaposition of prodigal son motifs and New Comedy conventions found in *Michaelmas Term* nor the harshly conflicting tonalities of *A Trick to Catch the Old One*, its world is recognizably the world of Middleton's other works.[1] The play's society is similarly composed of extremes, and all of the drama's central characters vow allegiance to the excessive humors which form the basis of human action in this "mad world."[2] Virtue alone, Penitent Brothel tells us, "knows a mean" (4.4.64), but no one in the comedy seems able to act upon his insight.[3] Thus the youthful protagonist of the drama's main plot, Dick Follywit, spends all of his time and energy compulsively designing new schemes to amuse himself and his fellows. Unlike Witgood in *A Trick to Catch the Old One* or

93

Gerardine in *The Family of Love*, Follywit does not use his cleverness as a means to gain a single, primary goal. Rather, his trickery, like that of Volpone and Face, is an end in itself; one scheme leads to another until the gallant inevitably undoes himself and his devoted followers. Likewise, the usual victim of Follywit's plots, his grandfather Sir Bounteous Progress, pushes the virtues of hospitality and generosity far past their normal limits. When we first encounter the old knight, we hear one of his guests protesting, "You have been too much like your name, Sir Bounteous" (2.1.1); and shortly after, a disguised Follywit tells his grandfather, "You ev'n whelm me with delights" (2.2.19). The characters in the subplot are equally extreme. Harebrain's jealousy of his wife, for example, is so fantastic that he locks her up in their house, while Penitent Brothel's bawd, Frank Gullman, attempts to gain Mistress Harebrain's favors for her employer by advising, "Put by all kisses, till you kiss in common" (1.2.83). Even Penitent Brothel, a character who at times steps into the role of satiric presenter, falls prey to the madness which permeates the comedy and at one point believes himself under attack by a devilish impersonation of the woman he wishes to seduce.[4] Like *The Phoenix*, *A Mad World, My Masters* contains no norm, no voice of careful reason.

One cause of the characters' inability to act temperately lies in the nature of their personalities. Almost without exception the individuals in the play seem to be ruled by conflicting and often irreconcilable impulses. The discord so dominant in the societies of *Michaelmas Term* and *A Trick to Catch the Old One* here is internalized within the characters' psyches, and as a result, the characters' actions are incoherent and at times unpredictable. In some instances this inconsistent behavior is reflected by the contradictory makeup of individual names—*Folly / wit, Penitent / Brothel, Frank / Gullman*—but in any case the personalities of all the characters are remarkably fluid and inconstant. Bounteous Progress is generous to a fault with those who are not related to him, but refuses to extend a fraction of that generosity toward his grandson. Similarly, the chief knave in the play, Follywit, inexplicably forgets his allegiance to cynicism and trickery near the end of the drama and becomes as foolish as the characters he formerly gulled. This master of false appearances ironically falls prey to an illusion—Frank Gullman disguised as a young maiden—and unwittingly marries his grandfather's whore. At the same time, Frank Gullman herself is transformed into a fool by the match, because she unknowingly marries a thief rather than the prosperous young landowner she assumes Follywit to be.

Other alterations of behavior are even more striking. Follywit's reaction to Frank Gullman's disguise (4.5.68–69), for example, parallels Harebrain's earlier misplaced faith in the courtesan's mother (1.2.30–31), and the echo reinforces the resemblance of the two characters' names.[5] Moreover, the parallel also should remind us that the progress of the madly jealous husband through the drama is the reverse of Follywit's. Whereas the young gallant alters from wit to fool in act 4, scene 5, Harebrain does the opposite a scene earlier. At the end of act 4, scene 4, he overhears Penitent Brothel renounce his adulterous intentions and convince Mistress Harebrain to remain forever chaste. Harebrain steps forward and suddenly becomes a sensible and intelligent man as he embraces both parties and renounces his former attempts to confine his wife.

The most important instance of a total and unpredictable change of personality in the play, however, is Penitent Brothel's rapid transformation from lecher to religious fanatic. In general, Penitent's change has not been popular with readers. It has been attacked as "jarring," as "too sternly moralistic to be applied retroactively to either plot," and as a factor which helps to split the play in two.[6] But when viewed from the perspective of similar reversals in other plays by Middleton (Tangle's in *The Phoenix* and Quomodo's in *Michaelmas Term*, for example) and when placed in the context of the parallel transformations noted above, Penitent's fortunes no longer seem out of keeping with the overall movement of this drama or, indeed, with the general nature of Middleton's art. Like his predecessors in the earlier dramas and analogues in this play, Penitent Brothel moves from one extreme to another. His alteration may be partially prepared

for by his opening aside (1.1.83–111), but it is intended essentially to provide the play's most memorable commentary on the
disunity of human personality. Penitent's behavior is not
reasonable, nor does Middleton attempt to make it seem so.
His remarkable reversal is only one of many examples of
discontinuity in *A Mad World, My Masters*. A grotesque discord
is apparent everywhere, and in everyone.[7]

Clearly, the society Middleton depicts in this play is as
disordered as the societies we encountered in *Michaelmas Term*
or *The Phoenix*. And according to Frank Gullman's Mother, it is
a world which is continually getting worse: "Every part of the
world shoots up daily into more subtlety," she states early in the
play, "The very spider weaves her cauls with more art and
cunning to entrap the fly" (1.1.140–42). Likewise, when
Bounteous Progress's servant Gumwater notes that time has
transformed clothing which was once considered evil into the
latest fashion (4.2.18–21), his master is quick to point out the
reason why: "That was a queasy time," Sir Bounteous confides,
"Our age is better harden'd. . . . Tut, the pox is as natural now
as an ague in the springtime" (ll.22–25). A society which views
syphilis as a natural affliction and which associates spring with
disease is hardly a fertile ground for comic values, and in fact
the discords and extremes which characterize *A Mad World, My
Masters* are, as we have seen, basically anticomic. Like the
marked contrasts of *The Phoenix, Michaelmas Term*, and *A Trick
to Catch the Old One*, they work against the kind of harmonious
society which traditional comedy seeks to create; indeed, they
question the possibility of that very society's existence. As a
result, the hopes of some of the characters to return to an
almost prelapsarian, orderly life are inevitably frustrated.
Frank Gullman's Mother, for instance, seeks to regain Eden by
creating an endless number of new alliances for her daughter
(1.1.155–56), and Follywit believes that marriage to the young
woman impersonated by Frank Gullman will provide a link
with a more harmonious past (4.5.55–57). But both desires are
short-lived. The courtesan's final union is with a former thief
(Follywit), and the woman Follywit thinks a representative of
purity and innocence turns out to be more devious and tainted

than the gallant himself. Like the green fields so highly prized in *Michaelmas Term* and *A Trick to Catch the Old One*, these utopias remain somewhere offstage—a world apart from the lives of the characters.

A Mad World, My Masters thus shares many of the basic qualities of the dramas discussed in Chapter 3, and those qualities have a similar effect on the play's comic structure. The fact that this comedy's contrasts are not as marked or as surprising as the contrasts present in the earlier plays, however, suggests that Middleton's interests have shifted somewhat. And they have. The change, as the above description of the play-world implies, is not a fundamental one. But in *A Mad World, My Masters* Middleton does alter his emphasis from the depiction of an anticomic society enclosed within a comic form to an intensive examination of certain comic conventions and values—specifically, to an analysis of comic festivity, generosity, and inclusiveness—by focusing on a figure who represents those values, Sir Bounteous Progress.

Throughout *A Mad World* the discord which is everywhere apparent is contrasted with a harmony symbolized by music. Harebrain, for example, hopes to "teach the married man / A new selected strain" (1.2.56–57), and both Penitent Brothel and Frank Gullman employ musical images. When Penitent is concerned about Mistress Harebrain's feelings for him and asks the Courtesan, "Did not our affections meet, our thoughts keep time?" she answers: "So it should seem by the music. The only jar is in the grumbling bass viol, her husband" (1.1.118–20; cf. 3.2.144–45). The character most closely associated with music is Sir Bounteous Progress. The pleasant harmonious sounds which pour forth from his incomparable organs symbolize everything that the play-world is not. Furthermore, the knight's music is intimately connected with the festivity so essential to comedy. Like Follywit and Frank Gullman's Mother, Bounteous Progress dreams of a more harmonious existence, but for him that harmony almost seems possible. The festivity so distant from the societies of *Michaelmas Term* and *A Trick to Catch the Old One* and beyond the grasp of the other characters in *A Mad World* suddenly comes to life with the first appearance of this extraordinary old man, treating guests to a sumptuous dinner and allowing them to listen to his renowned organs. It is as if the festive spirit itself were suddenly embodied onstage in a single figure. Before tracing the character and fortunes of Bounteous Progress in more detail, however, it is necessary to consider briefly the drama's comic structure and the knight's place within it. Sir Bounteous Progress's relation to the play's New Comedy form is the most important key to a full understanding of Middleton's critique of comic values in the drama.

Most critics have recognized the New Comedy structure of *A Mad World, My Masters*. In Standish Henning's words, Middleton plays "essentially the game of Latin Comedy."[8] If the drama is approached in generic terms, the role of New Comedy protagonist is divided between Follywit and Penitent Brothel, with Bounteous Progress and Harebrain the respective blocking figures. The main plot centers around Follywit's attempts to gain some of his grandfather's wealth, while the subplot depicts Penitent Brothel's endeavor to lure Mistress Harebrain away from her jealous husband with the aid of Frank Gullman. Follywit, however, commands our attention as the central trickster-hero of the play. Indeed, as the comedy opens, Follywit's companions greet him in a manner which emphasizes this role:

> MAWWORM: Oh, captain, regent, principal!
> HOBOY: What shall I call thee? The noble spark of bounty, the
>   lifeblood of society!
> FOLLYWIT: Call me your forecast, you whoresons. [1.1.1–4]

Besides establishing Follywit as principal wit in the play, these opening descriptions of his character tell us several additional things about the young gallant. His cleverness is closely connected with fertility—the "life-blood of society." Follywit's own preferred name points to his extraordinary imagination and repeated attempts to control the future, or, in fact, to make it present. "Spark" looks forward to Penitent Brothel's vindication of Follywit's knavery as "time's comic flashes" (1.1.93), and perhaps again refers to the youth's imaginative powers. The key word, however, is *bounty*. Curiously, this characterization of Follywit calls immediately to mind the very figure he opposes, his grandfather. In this context *spark* denotes relationship—a small remnant, or small trace of something (*OED*). Hoboy therefore unknowingly describes Follywit as a lesser version of his grandfather, a spark emitted from the peculiar humor which dominates Bounteous Progress's life. Moreover, the knights' obsessive generosity, his bounty, is here connected by juxtaposition with fertility and rebirth, with the very "life-blood of society."

Because the opening lines associate Follywit with his grandfather and intimate that Follywit is really a less impressive version of the old knight, they immediately complicate the play's New Comedy status. As comic protagonist, Follywit should embody most of the positive life-giving forces in the play. He should be young, energetic, fertile. His antagonist, on the other hand, conventionally should be old, stingy, an enemy of mirth and festivity, a Chremes (*Heauton Timorumenos*) or a Theopropides (*Mostellaria*). On the surface, at least, Follywit fits his part well enough, but Sir Bounteous is anything but the typical blocking figure we expect. His values lie on the side of misrule rather than law. His is a spirit of mirth rather than of sobriety. Bounteous Progress's affinities are with Toby Belch in *Twelfth Night* and Old Merrythought in *The Knight of the Burning Pestle* instead of Malvolio and Beaumont's foolish grocer and his wife. Instead, Bounteous Progress's opposition to Follywit is not even total. His will states that the gallant is to inherit the family fortune, and the old knight attempts to gain a position for his grandson with the fictitious Lord Owemuch (ironically, Follywit in disguise).

The surprising nature of this "blocking figure" is stressed from the beginning of the drama. Even if we miss the clue to Bounteous Progress's nature in the opening lines, Follywit's reference to his "frolic grandsire" (1.40) some thirty lines later is difficult to ignore. In fact, we soon hear Penitent Brothel assigning the same quality to Follywit himself (ll.83–85). Furthermore, the old knight, Follywit explains, "keeps a house like his name, bounteous, open for all comers" (ll.60–61). The lavishness of Bounteous Progress's entertainments and his overwhelming bounty reflect essential comic values. His house is a house of festivity, and its "open" doors symbolize the principles of inclusiveness and acceptance so central to the comic spirit. We need only glance at the locked doors and restrictive atmosphere of Harebrain's dwelling to see how far the characteristics of the knight depart from those normally associated with his apparent place in the play's New Comedy structure.

Bounteous Progress first appears, as noted above, amidst praise for his lavish hospitality. "You have been too much like your name," a knight assures him (2.1.1). For Bounteous Progress, the end of one feast simply marks the beginning of another, and when he hears that a certain Lord Owemuch is about to arrive, he is overjoyed:

> I knew I should have him i'th' end; there's not a lord will miss me, I thank their good honors; 'tis a fortune laid upon me, they can scent out their best entertainment; I have a kind of complimental gift given me above ordinary country knights, and how soon 'tis smelt out! I warrant ye there's not one knight i'th' shire able to entertain a lord i'th' cue, or a lady i'th' nick like me, like me. There's a kind of grace belongs to't, a kind of art which naturally slips from me, I know not on't, I promise you, 'tis gone before I'm aware on't. [ll.49–58]

The knight's house is thus a focal point about which the play-society revolves. It is a gathering place where individuals unite in festivity and harmony. It represents qualities so alluring that they seem irresistible. Similarly, by noting that his famous hospitality is a "grace" which is a natural and unconscious product of his personality, Sir Bounteous indicates his essentially emblematic function in the play. The old knight is an abstraction rather than a unique individual. He is an attitude—"Nay, and your lordship know my disposition, you know me better than they that know my person" (2.1.98–99)—amply defined by his name: "Is not my name Sir Bounteous? Am I not express'd there?" (4.3.91).

In his role as mad host, Bounteous Progress is a version of what Northrop Frye has called the "comic buffoon," a character whose "function it is to increase the mood of festivity rather than to contribute to the plot," and he has much in common with the cooks and parasites everywhere present in Plautus's plays.[9] The knight's open doors are, as stated, a symbolic indication of his commitment to the comic spirit, and in act 5 he presides over the kind of feast which usually occurs offstage at the end of a typical Renaissance comedy. Significantly, it is spring, and the feast is closely connected with almost all important comic values. In its inclusiveness the celebration rivals the trial that closes *The Family of Love*. As Bounteous Progress himself notes, "Every jack has his friend today, this cousin and that cousin puts in for a dish of meat" (5.1.3–4). One by one all of the play's main characters gather around to take part in the festivities, and the scene is a perfect example of the comic tendency to include as many individuals as possible in the concluding revelry. Bounteous Progress's commitment to harmony is so great that he even welcomes Frank Gullman despite his belief that she has robbed him. He muses:

> She denies me and all, when on her fingers
> I spied the ruby sit that does betray her
> And blushes for her face. Well there's a time for't,
> For all's too little now for entertainment,
> Feast, mirth, ay, harmony, and the play to boot:
> A jovial season.
> [ll.106–11]

Entertainment, feasting, mirth and harmony—we could not find a better statement of the spirit which permeates comedy and Bounteous Progress as well. Likewise, Bounteous Progress's ability to forget and forgive parallels the traditional comic emphasis on reconciliation. His attitude is that of Gerardine at the end of *A Family of Love*, and it might be recalled that the absence of similar values is what makes the society of *A Trick to Catch the Old One* uncomic. Even after he learns that he has been gulled by the players and robbed a second time, the old knight's anger quickly turns into an appreciation of the scheme's cleverness and an acceptance of its outcome: "Ha, ha, it was featly carried! Troth, I commend their wits!" (5.2.163–64). Anger and revenge have no place in Sir Bounteous's approach to life. He simply accepts and enjoys.[10]

Because the old knight symbolizes many of the essential

values of New Comedy, Middleton's portrayal of Follywit's grandfather is also an examination of the comic attitudes which are so large a part of his makeup. As might be expected, this examination is not a completely sympathetic one. Bounteous Progress is a very attractive figure, and his values are equally enticing. And indeed, the play never really questions the obvious attractiveness of the knight and what he represents. What the drama does question, however, is the ability of the old man to function in the society around him. For if Bounteous Progress is associated with festivity and mirth, the world of this particular comedy, as noted, is anything but harmonious. A clash between this world and the comic qualities which the knight embodies is inevitable, and from Middleton's point of view, at least, the defeat of those comic qualities is also inevitable. It occurs midway in the plot, when Follywit robs his grandfather.

Initially, the episode simply appears to be another of Follywit's endless series of pranks. The gallant disguises himself as Lord Owemuch and arrives at Bounteous Progress's house for an overnight visit. During the night Follywit and his allies tie up the old knight and rob him, pretending to do the same to Lord Owemuch. Released the next morning, Sir Bounteous is crushed that one of his guests could be treated so badly and apologizes profusely to the Lord, never realizing that the fictitious nobleman is his grandson and the mastermind behind the robbery.

The incident, however, is more than an entertaining masquerade. It presents the triumph of a restrictive reality over Bounteous Progress's vision of hospitality and liberality or, more generally, over comedy itself. This symbolic meaning is first indicated by the numerous references to freedom and openness in the episode's early lines—references which reinforce the knight's connection with comic festivity. Sir Bounteous, we learn, is incapable of dissembling his true nature (2.1.90), and he tells the newly arrived Lord that Owemuch is "most spaciously welcome" (l.91). The knight's disguised grandson commends the old man's "bounteous disposition" (l.96). Bounteous Progress returns the compliment by citing

Owemuch's "prodigal fame" and "unbounded worthiness" (ll.103–4). He then invites the lord to hear his famous organs. In contrast, the robbery itself is filled with forms of the word *bind* (see 2.4.33, 34, 36, 45, 46, 47, 70, 72, 76–77, 85)—a word whose connotations of restriction and constipation are, as was discussed in relation to *The Family of Love*, intimately linked with the forces comic misrule seeks to overthrow. The "binding" of Sir Bounteous, then, represents the imprisonment of the comic values he embodies. By tying up his grandfather in front of our eyes, Follywit figuratively signals the defeat of freedom and festivity. The spirit of comedy succumbs to the unfestive forces in the society of the play.

The robbery's significance is further emphasized by the knight's reactions to his predicament. At first, he banters with the thieves in a manner which reflects the essential nature of his personality: "So, take enough, my masters; spur a free horse, my name's Sir Bounteous. A merry world, i'faith; what knight but I keep open house at midnight?" (2.4.41–43). In contrast to the symbolic restrictions being imposed upon him, Bounteous Progress initially reaffirms his allegiance to festivity. He urges the robbers to take what they wish, compares himself to a "free horse," mentions his "open" doors. For Sir Bounteous, the world is still a "merry" one. But just as the merry world Witgood recalls in *A Trick to Catch the Old One* gave way before the onslaught of Harry Dampit, so the old knight's belief in the value of mirth and harmony begins to be shaken as the ropes are brought forward. He quizzically mutters about the injustice of it all—"There should be a conscience if one could hit upon't" (ll.43–44)—and finally condemns his own personality as a cause of his misfortune: "But come, come, bind me, I have need on't; I have been too liberal tonight" (ll.47–48). When the knight asks the thieves to return for supper, he reduces the comic virtue of forgiveness to absurdity. Furthermore, his last hope for reconciliation ends in discord. His magnificent organs are put out of tune both literally and metaphorically as the dissonant music Follywit and his companions symbolize drives out the harmony so dear to Bounteous Progress:

B. PROGRESS: Y'ave deserv'd so well, my masters, I bid you all to
      dinner tomorrow; I would I might have your companies,
      i'faith; I desire no more.
FOLLYWIT: Oh ho, sir!
B. PROGRESS: Pray meddle not with my organs, to put 'em out of
      tune.
FOLLYWIT: Oh no, here's better music.   [ll.52–57]

The old knight's final words are a curse. His spirit has been
defeated. Indeed, it is not the loss of his money so much as this
triumph of restriction over the qualities he prizes so highly
which upsets Bounteous Progress. Although he and his guest
at last are released amidst a chorus of *undo*'s which signals that
freedom and festivity are once more possible (2.6.16–18), the
knight has great difficulty regaining his former exuberance.
Commiserating with Lord Owemuch, he calls munificence,
generosity, and the comic spirit itself into question: "This is the
commodity of keeping open house, my lord, that makes so
many shut their doors about dinner time" (2.6.51–52). The
perpetual comic feast which normally occurs within Bounteous
Progress's "open house" no longer seems so desirable. In a
society where most individuals close their doors at dinner and
cut themselves off from their fellows, the knight's commitment
to festivity is out of place and perhaps even dangerous. The
road to safety lies with restriction and alienation, not freedom
and revelry. Momentarily, at least, comic values are unable to
cope with reality. Bounteous Progress, of course, will eventually rediscover his wonted generosity and good cheer, but the
robbery demonstrates how fragile and foolish his attitude toward life is. And in fact, the next time Bounteous Progress bids
others to take part in his vision of merriment, the outcome will
be the same. At the end of the play Follywit robs his grandfather a second time. In the society of *A Mad World, My Masters*,
the role of comic buffoon seems to be an unfortunate one.

    The first robbery therefore questions basic comic beliefs by
showing how untenable Sir Bounteous's attitudes are in the
world he inhabits. The old knight is a very attractive but very
foolish figure, and Middleton suggests that the same is true of
the comic qualities he represents. The episode complicates the

play's New Comedy form in one other way as well. It was shown above that in terms of the drama's conventional comic opposi- tions Bounteous Progress's role should be that of a blocking figure and that, typically, this role is closely linked to restriction as in the case of Harebrain. Curiously, one of the scenes which most strongly emphasizes this aspect of Harebrain's character (2.5.) follows the scene in which Follywit binds his grandfather. The parallel once more reinforces the similarity between the two characters' names, but it also further indicates Middleton's paradoxical treatment of the main plot's New Comedy pro- tagonist and his chief opponent. Just as the ostensible blocking figure, Bounteous Progress, is associated with freedom rather than restraint, so the apparent hero, Follywit, is continually "binding" others throughout the play. The gallant not only ties up his grandfather during the robbery, he also "binds" Gum- water verbally (4.3.19–24) and at the end of the drama ties up the constable in order to make him part of the gallant's latest scheme, the play-within-the-play. The conventional comic as- sociations of youth with freedom and age with restriction are reversed, and the audience's attitude toward the two charac- ters is greatly complicated as a result.

In keeping with the general instability of everything within the drama's world, however, the reversal is not consistent throughout the play. Bounteous Progress is, as Arthur Marotti has stated, "a kind of comic paradox."[11] If for the most part the knight is a version of Frye's comic buffoon, at times he does act like a typical blocking figure. Bounteous Progress is an imper- fect host; his house is open to all except, strangely enough, his nearest of kin. Follywit's actions are therefore partially jus- tified by his grandfather's less than generous treatment of him. For while the old knight does symbolize the spirit of comic generosity and harmony, he is a remarkably flawed symbol. Like everything else in the play, Bounteous Progress is a lesser, fallen reflection of what had been. In fact, when Penitent Brothel urges Mistress Harebrain to renounce her adulterous intentions, his comments on the growing depravity which he sees around them seem to describe Sir Bounteous himself:

He that kept open house now keeps a quean.
He will keep open still that he commends,
And there he keeps a table for his friends;
And she consumes more than his sire could hoard,
Being more common than his house or board.
                                        [4.4.65–69]

Penitent's references to an "open house" and "quean" should
immediately remind us of Bounteous Progress and his whore
Frank Gullman and lead us to substitute the knight's name for
the impersonal *he* throughout the passage. Thus the decline of
English society becomes characterized by Bounteous Progress's perversion of comic munificence—by a movement from
a past and seemingly praiseworthy generosity to a present
inclination toward panderism (that which is now open to his
friends is his quean) and prodigality which threatens to destroy
all that the knight has. Too often in the drama, Bounteous
Progress seems simply a foolish old man, and somehow his
appearance—"a little short old spiny gentleman" (3.2.5–6)—is
out of keeping with his function as host and promoter of
festivity. Finally, this symbol of bounty, a quality associated
with the lifeblood of society in the play's opening lines, is, we
learn from Frank Gullman, sexually impotent.

    And so Bounteous Progress, like most of the individuals in
the comedy, behaves inconsistently. But Bounteous Progress's
contradictory attitudes and actions reflect more than the
knight's unstable personality. They are also symptomatic of the
radically different parts he must play in the course of the
drama's plot. The knight is both a buffoon and a blocking
figure, and the two roles oppose one another. As Bounteous
Progress moves from one to the other, he continually frustrates our expectations and subverts our patterns of response.
We await actions and attitudes which correspond to one role,
only to be confronted with actions and attitudes which belong
to its opposite. Middleton's handling of the old man is thus very
similar to his ambiguous portrayal of Quomodo in *Michaelmas
Term*, and it has precisely the same result. Our relationship to
Bounteous Progress, and by extension to Follywit, never becomes fixed. The discord which permeates the society de-

scribed in the drama finds an analogue in Middleton's use of the play's comic form. Like everything else, conventions "jar" in *A Mad World, My Masters*.

The comic vision of festivity, mirth, and harmony which Sir Bounteous desires and represents is undermined, then, because it is unable to come to terms with the disunity of the play-world and because in his divided and ambiguous role Bounteous Progress himself is part of that fallen world and reflects its discordant elements. The robbery exposes the fragility of the knight's vision, and his flawed nature likewise suggests that the qualities he values can no longer exist untainted. As in *Michaelmas Term* and *A Trick to Catch the Old One*, Middleton portrays a society which is hostile to most comic values, and at the same time he complicates our relationship with the drama's New Comedy structure to such an extent that we find it hard to affirm the attitudes implicit in that structure. Such a construal, however, constitutes only part of the judgment which Middleton makes on comedy in *A Mad World, My Masters*. The play tests the genre in one other equally important way. Middleton is not content to imply that it is only Bounteous Progress's dream of festivity that is spurious. By making us aware of the artificiality of his own play, he subverts its comic vision as well.

Because his desire for revelry and feasting is forever foundering on the rocks of an antagonistic reality, Bounteous Progress inhabits a fantastic and illusory realm of his own invention, a place where thieves are good-natured fellows and hospitality is the highest good. Sir Bounteous is a dreamer, and the significance of this is demonstrated by a discussion he has with his disguised grandson early in the play:

> B. PROGRESS: Silken rest, harmonious slumbers, and venereal
>   dreams to your lordship.
> FOLLYWIT: The like to kind, Sir Bounteous.
> B. PROGRESS: Fie, not to me, my lord. I'm old, past dreaming of
>   such vanities.
> FOLLYWIT: Old men should dream best.
> B. PROGRESS: They're dreams indeed, my lord, y'ave gi'n't
>   us.   [2.2.9–15]

And he certainly has. The "silken rest" and "harmonious slumbers" which the knight mentions have little place in this drama, as Bounteous Progress himself will find out later that day when Follywit robs him. They are "vanities" not so much in the sense that they are worthless, but because they do not really exist. The same is true of the "venereal dreams" which the knight refers to. Such dreams may be an appropriate extension of reality for a young lord like Owemuch, but they are nothing more than mirages for a man of Bounteous Progress's age. "Old men should dream best" because for them sexuality often is present only in dreams, a state of affairs which Bounteous Progress never acknowledges. Encountering his beloved whore in her sick bed, he quickly finds the cause in his own imaginary physical powers and believes he has made her pregnant. Frank Gullman, however, knows better: "He only fears he has done that deed which I ne'er fear'd to come from him in my life" (3.2.86–88), she confides. As with his hopes for revelry, for "silken rest" and "harmonious slumbers," Bounteous Progress's faith in his potency is based upon his ability to ignore as best he can the pressure of reality and to make the world over in the image of his desires. Bounteous Progress is unable to distinguish what he dreams from what is.

Although the madcap knight is the most important dreamer in the play, he is not the only one. Frank Gullman, for instance, concocts her plans while sleeping (2.5.8–14), and Penitent Brothel is encouraged to repent by a dreamlike vision of a succubus whom he believes to be Mistress Harebrain. *A Mad World* is also full of references to magic and witchcraft (2.4.39; 3.3.64–65; 4.5.17), passages which point to the association of wit and imagination with the supernatural (dreams and magic) in the play. All of these images, moreover, are subsumed into the larger category of madness. References to madness are too numerous to examine in detail, but one passage stands out above all the others: Follywit's announcement that he will marry. After seeing the disguised Frank Gullman, he falls in love and attempts boldly to court her. Rejected, the gallant decides that marriage is the only way to gain what he desires, and asks: "Shall I be madder now then ever I have been? I'm in the way i'faith. / Man's never at high height of madness full / Until he love and prove a woman's gull" (4.5.11–14). In a sense, Follywit's decision seems to arise from a compulsion to attain the greatest possible madness. He marries even though he realizes that he may be undone by his wife (a belief which will prove all too prophetic). His vow is therefore "mad," because the woman he loves may be a figment of his imagination (which she is) and because Follywit is inviting his own downfall. By wishing to marry despite these objections, Follywit demonstrates that the human tendency to accept the mind's illusions and fantasies (two terms synonymous with madness in the play) is almost inescapable. The gallant falls in love with a woman he himself impersonated, and this may symbolically suggest an attachment to his own creations. But Follywit knows nothing of this; to him Frank Gullman is an ideal, and this ideal is as much a creation of his fantasy (madness) as any of his brilliant plots.

We can now see a general pattern emerging from the action of *A Mad World, My Masters*. The various characters' endless plotting and dissembling, Bounteous Progress's vision of hospitality, Harebrain's jealousy, Penitent Brothel's encounter with the succubus, and Follywit's love for Frank Gullman are all alike in bearing witness to the human propensity to create illusory worlds. Their imaginations have gone mad. Furthermore, the characters' tendency to live in worlds of their own making lends added significance to the play's title. According to Standish Henning, the title is "the verbal counterpart of throwing up the hands. But in the strong word 'mad' the phrase recognizes the danger of the world's becoming too intensely or too enduringly unkempt, and so appeals to the hierarchy of values implicit in 'masters.' "[12] Henning correctly focuses on a central concern of *A Mad World*, the relation of madness and control, but he does not see its total importance. The pedagogical overtones of *masters*, for example, are repeatedly emphasized early in the drama, from the Mother's advice to Frank Gullman in the first scene, to the courtesan's and Harebrain's contradictory maxims concerning marriage in the second. Likewise, the "mad world" which the characters must control is, as noted above, the realm of fantasy and imagination. The ability to avoid falling prey to illusion, whether self-created or otherwise, is the measure of this mastery and what separates a knave from a fool in the drama. Significantly, no one avoids falling into the latter category.[13]

The characters' efforts to master appearances also parallel in many ways the artist's. Middleton stresses the parallel by connecting dissembling with art at several points in the play (3.3.1–2; 1.2.75) and by having his characters employ metaphors which describe their plots and disguises as kinds of molding (1.1.115–16; 3.3.111–12). Middleton, however, is not essentially concerned with investigating the general relationship of art and deception. His interests are, I think, more specific than that. The numerous references to imagination in the drama serve to call our attention to a fantasy world we ourselves are taking part in: the comic illusion called *A Mad World, My Masters*. In fact, Middleton makes explicit a close connection between comedy and madness. Midway in the final scene of the play, Bounteous Progress and Harebrain discuss the outcome of the drama that they themselves are watching. The knight is totally enthralled by the work. "By my troth, the maddest piece of justice, gentlemen, that was ever committed," he exclaims (ll.113–14), and Harebrain concurs: "I'll be sworn for the madness on't, sir" (l.115). The reason for the work's madness is generic. It is, as Bounteous Progress recognizes, "a merry comedy and a witty" (l.116). And while this conversation ostensibly deals with Follywit's play, "The Slip," it also clearly refers to Middleton's play. It too is a merry comedy, it too—like all comedies, Middleton would say—is a mad and fantastic piece of justice.

And just as the measure of mastery for the characters in *A Mad World, My Masters* is the ability to recognize illusion for what it is, so Middleton carefully links the madness of their imaginary worlds to that of his own play (and comedy in general) to insure that we, as audience, do not lose control, that is, do not become fools by allowing ourselves to believe that the comic vision we are watching is anything but an empty dream. Middleton thus adds to the critique of comedy present in his portrayal of Bounteous Progress another, more far-reaching examination of the form's madness, an examination which implies that comedy is little more than the product of vain hopes for a more harmonious existence. The focal point of this final aspect of his analysis of comic conventions and assumptions in *A Mad World, My Masters* is the play-within-the-play, which appropriately concludes the action of the drama.

This episode culminates a crescendo of illusions and false appearances which dominates the final scenes of the comedy: Follywit's disguise as a courtesan, Penitent Brothel's vision of the succubus, and Follywit's complementary vision of Frank Gullman impersonating a young virgin. The incident, as previously stated, begins with Bounteous Progress planning to invite all the countryside to a magnificent feast. His preparations are interrupted by an announcement of the chance arrival of players; and, shortly after, Follywit and his friends enter disguised as an acting troupe.[14]

Complications begin here. From this point in *A Mad World*, almost every speech has a double and often a triple significance: (1) for Follywit's play, "The Slip," (2) for the action of *A Mad World, My Masters* as a whole, and (3) for the world of Middleton's audience (or reader). Thus Follywit's new disguise not only reflects his new role as actor in "The Slip," it also recalls his dissembling throughout *A Mad World* and indicates the actual profession of the man who plays the character Follywit. In the latter two senses, Follywit is disguised as what he really is. The audience's awareness of this paradox is strengthened by Bounteous Progress's statement, "I perceive he's your best actor" (5.1.39), a comment which in relation to the play's original London production is probably not far off the mark. Ambiguous passages like this one resonate with increasing power throughout the rest of Middleton's play. Bounteous Progress's happiness at the prospect of "a true feast, a right Miter supper, a play, and all" (ll.72–73) presumably echoed the sentiments and plans of members of the London audience. Earlier in the scene, in fact, he steps into the role of that audience. "Ah, and what play shall we have, my mas-

ters?" he asks (ll.62–63), and Follywit's answer parallels the one
Middleton ostensibly supplies to the viewers of his play who ask
the same question as they are entering the theater. It will be "a
pleasant witty comedy" (l.64), the gallant assures his host.

And in the same way that Follywit's "witty comedy" is a
cause of discomfort for its viewers (Bounteous Progress is
robbed again), so Middleton's play is not, as we have seen, the
frivolous piece of entertainment it at first seems to be. Bounteous Progress, however, is unaware of his imminent gulling and
rejoices at the prospect of the coming revelry (Middleton's
audience presumably does the same): "Ay, ay, ay, a comedy in
any case, that I and my guests may laugh a little" (ll.65–66).
Follywit's play likewise points in various directions. Its subject,
the story of a prodigal nephew and his rich uncle, repeats the
relationship of Follywit and Bounteous Progress with the
added irony that Follywit plays the uncle, not the prodigal.
And the playlet's title has several different meanings. A *slip* is a
counterfeit coin, and we will also soon see Follywit giving the
constable "the slip." Finally, the title recalls the drama's association of spontaneous and rapid motion with the workings of the
imagination, "time's comic flashes," in Penitent Brothel's
words (l.l.93).

In essence, Middleton creates a mirror image onstage of
the actual audience viewing his play. When Penitent Brothel
and Bounteous Progress are troubled that the constable remains tied up for so long, their eagerness that "The Slip"
should end parallels the audience's expectations of the dé-
nouement of *A Mad World, My Masters* and Follywit's conventional unmasking. But their worries are also part of a larger
problem, because the constable is not a character in Follywit's
original play at all and so represents an unwanted intrusion of
"reality" into the world of illusion Follywit has created. The
gallant's attempts to overcome the problems which arise from
this are an important commentary on the power of imagination to transform reality, an ability possessed by almost
everyone in Middleton's comedy. The constable simply becomes part of Follywit's play, and the illusion is so convincing
that Bounteous Progress berates the unfortunate man for talk-

ing to his audience: "To me? Puh! Turn to th' justice, you
whoreson hobbyhorse! This is some new player now; they put
all their fools to the constable's part still" (5.2.76–78). It is not
until much later that the truth is finally revealed. The players
disappear, and the constable at last is able to convince Bounteous Progress that the old man has been fooled once again:

> B. PROGRESS: Give me leave, give me leave. Why, art not thou
> the constable i'th' comedy?
> CONSTABLE: I'th' comedy? Why, I am the constable i'th'
> commonwealth, sir.   [ll.149–52]

From our perspective, of course, he is both.

Thus Middleton shatters the illusion of his own play by
repeatedly making its viewers aware that they, like Bounteous
Progress and his fellows, are watching a totally fictional sequence of events. Just as the audience onstage learns that the
play they have been seeing is a counterfeit, so the audience of
Middleton's play is continually made aware that the drama
they are viewing is also only a hypothetical version of what
might be, not an imitation of what is.[15] Middleton distances us
from the action and makes impossible the suspension of disbelief which often seems so central to the dramatic experience.
The issue is once again control—the ability to recognize illusion and so to avoid falling prey to false appearances and
dreams of unattainable ideals. And the illusion which Middleton wishes to make us aware of is the illusion of festivity and
harmony at the heart of comedy, the illusion of revelry and
concord which his own play represents. Like Bounteous Progress's vision of hospitality and inclusiveness, the drama's New
Comedy form is the product of a fruitless attempt to create
order where none exists. It is the result of the imagination's
desires and hopes, nothing more. And like the old knight,
Middleton's comedy is a strangely flawed embodiment of festivity. Its world is a world of extremes. Its New Comedy protagonist and chief opponent are depicted in an unconventional
and ambiguous manner. It is therefore absolutely appropriate
that Middleton's play ends with an ironic reversal of a traditional New Comedy recognition scene. The apparently com-
promised and penniless girl whom the young hero—in this

case Follywit—loves does not turn out to be a marriageable
young lady of noble birth as, for example, in Plautus's *Curculio*
and *Poenulus* and Terence's *Eunuchus* and *Phormio*. Rather, she
is his grandfather's whore.[16]

One critic has noted that "moral improvement in this play is
the result not of conscience but of coincidence and asserts itself
not through the psychology of the characters but through
contrivances of plot."[17] Surely this is the point Middleton
wishes to emphasize. *A Mad World, My Masters* repeatedly demonstrates that the comic vision is illusory and foolish, attractive
though it may be. Comedy remains as appealing as Bounteous
Progress or, indeed, the play itself, but Middleton never lets us
comfortably ignore the genre's limitations. As Bounteous
Progress himself momentarily recognizes, within the society *A
Mad World, My Masters* describes, festivity can lead only to
misfortune, a misfortune which is the "commodity of keeping
open house" and which "makes so many shut their doors about
dinner time" (2.6.51–52). The old knight's comment spells the
demise of the comic spirit, and although Bounteous Progress
foolishly fails to act on the truth of his words, Middleton
suggests again and again that we would be better off to heed his
warning. Ultimately, the knight and the qualities which he
symbolizes have no place in a world where closed doors are—
necessarily—a way of life.

No Wit, No Help Like a Woman's is an anomaly in the Middleton canon. Until recently, the play was assumed to have been
written well into the second decade of the playwright's career,
but at present most authorities date the time of composition
around the fall of 1611 or spring of 1612.[18] The drama itself
seems to have more in common with the tragicomedies of
Middleton's later career than with the plays considered above.
The main plot is taken from Giambattista Della Porta's *La
Sorella*, and it is much more sentimental and romantic than any
of the plots discussed so far. Indeed, as Lowell Johnson has
pointed out, Middleton seems to be attempting to merge the
elements of his earlier city comedies with Fletcherian romance.[19] The play often sounds more idealistic than most of

Middleton's earlier comedies (with the exception of *The Phoenix*), and some of its characters have aristocratic leanings which are for the most part deemphasized in the earlier plays. *No Wit, No Help Like a Woman's* thus represents an experiment with new materials, an experiment which Middleton turned away from to write his greatest comedy, *A Chaste Maid in Cheapside*, but which later bore fruit in such plays as *A Fair Quarrel, More Dissemblers Besides Women*, and *The Old Law*. But in spite of its apparent affinities with Fletcherian romance, *No Wit* is essentially not very different from the plays examined above. At its core it embodies the same world, the same values, and the same attitude toward comedy. Drawn out of the Italian *commedia erudita*, its main plot, like that of most of the dramas we have dealt with, is basically a New Comedy one.[20] It traces the efforts of a young man named Philip Twilight to gain his beloved Grace, who is disguised as his sister when the play begins. With the aid of a clever servant named Savorwit and his newly returned mother, Philip is able eventually to overcome complications consisting of his father's wishes to marry him to another girl and simultaneously wed Grace to an old fool called Weatherwise, and the mistaken belief that Grace actually is his sister. The young lovers are finally united when it is miraculously discovered that Grace is the daughter of one of Philip's neighbors, and this conventional recognition scene is followed by what seems to be an equally typical reconciliation of all the major characters in the play. The subplot which Middleton adds to his source depicts the wooing of the rich widow Lady Goldenfleece by an assorted group of noblemen and the attempts of an impoverished wife named Mistress Low-water to regain the riches and lands the widow's dead husband had stolen from the Low-water family. The similarity of *No Wit, No Help Like a Woman's* to Middleton's earlier comedies does not end with plot structure, however. The play contains an analysis of comic conventions which is as extensive as any we have seen.

No Wit is dominated by three women: Mistress Low-water, Mistress Twilight, and Lady Goldenfleece. It is Mistress Low-water's wit that the title refers to. Mistress Twilight's help enables her son Philip to escape his father's wrath, and Lady Goldenfleece provides both the major opposition to Mistress Low-water's endeavor to regain her husband's estate and the means of revealing the secret of Grace's identity. The New Comedy hero, in contrast, is ineffectual: his first words are, "I'm at my wit's ends, Savorwit" (1.1.1), and they are certainly fitting. Philip's only response to difficulty is to contemplate suicide (which he does three times), and his intellectual abilities are no match for those of any of Middleton's early trickster heroes.[21] A sense of lost vitality, of things past their time, pervades the play and is reinforced by some of the characters' names: Sandfield, Twilight, Sunset, Low-water. When the foolish old lover of almanacs, Weatherwise, urges Oliver Twilight to betroth Grace quickly—"You will not let your daughter hang past August, will you? She'll drop down under tree, then" (1.1.281–83)—the old man's warning emphasizes the curious overripeness of everything in the drama. Even Savorwit seems a somewhat tired version of a tricky slave.

Philip's lack of wit, however, is balanced by his total concern with love. In contrast to *A Trick to Catch the Old One* and *A Mad World, My Masters*, the society depicted in *No Wit, No Help Like a a Woman's* is permeated by love of all sorts. As in *The Family of Love*, this emotion is a prime motivating force behind the actions of almost everyone in the comedy. But our first view of love's effect is somewhat surprising. The play begins with both Philip and Savorwit on the brink of despair. There are two causes: (1) Philip's father plans to marry his beloved (presently disguised as his sister) to Weatherwise; (2) the old man also has instructed Philip to marry Jane Sunset and as a result has disrupted the youth's friendship with Sandfield, Jane's true love. The situation is nearly too much for Philip to bear. He laments the end of his "old steel friendship" (1.1.16) and be- rates Sandfield (who is not yet onstage) for his lack of constancy and forgetfulness "of the merry hours / The circuits of our youth hath spent and worn" (ll.17–18). Sandfield suddenly enters and, after Philip characteristically offers to kill himself, Savorwit intervenes in order to renew what he calls "the splen- dor / Of a hot constant friendship" (ll.58–59). This rather lofty idealization of friendship, however, only emphasizes the startling nature of the revelation which follows: Philip was recently sent to ransom his captured mother and sister on the continent, but on the way he met a servant girl in Antwerp, fell in love, forgot the purpose of his journey, and spent the ransom money to bring the girl home disguised as his sister—a series of events Savorwit relates with obvious relish. Philip's real sister and mother are presumably still in captivity.

Admittedly, Roman comedy also contains activities which seem at first glance as reprehensible as Philip's. Both *Hecyra* and *Truculentus*, as noted, depict events which do not always seem laughable. Similarly, the youths in Plautus (Calidorus in *Pseudolus* and Philolaches in *Mostellaria*, for instance) sometimes express a bitterness toward their elders which (especially if taken out of context) hardly appears comic. Yet we are seldom, if ever, emotionally involved in the dramas of the Roman playwrights. Even Terence's most decorous plays are dominated by a spirit of holiday and revelry which tells us that nothing tragic can happen, that even the most flagrant violations of morality are not threatening or harmful, and that the topsy-turvy world we are watching will soon give way to the more orderly norms of everyday life. This is not true, I believe, of Middleton's play. Philip's references to the Renaissance ideal of friendship lead us to expect something more than frivolity. They encourage us to place his actions in a moral rather than a festive context. And so, when Sandfield is astounded at Philip's story, he is not astounded, I think, in the same way that we are: "Let me admire thee and withal confess / My injuries to friendship" (l.l.98–99). The ironies are almost too obvious to mention. No one acknowledges the seriousness of what has been done; no one seems to care about "injuries" to family which make Philip's difficulties with Sandfield insignificant in comparison. Indeed, there is a terrifying blind innocence about the entire episode. It is as if we were suddenly thrust back into the world of *Michaelmas Term*, a world where prodigals literally and figuratively destroy their parents and heritage and where romantic love very nearly becomes equated with destruction—an association here given emphasis by Savorwit's punning on Philip's drawn sword (ll.38–40, 48–50). Middleton again pushes the comic commitment to sexual love to an extreme, and again the result is not very attractive.[22]

Such bitter ironies are not confined to the opening scene (see, for example, Philip's initial meeting with his mother in act 2, scene 2), and, as with Easy and Rearage, Philip's actions at the beginning of the drama undermine our sympathy with him and make his role as New Comedy protagonist problematic. When his mother tells him, "You see how hard 'tis now / To redeem good opinion being once gone" (4.1.74–75), she describes the way in which her son's former deeds complicate normal New Comedy patterns of audience identification and response. We might remember that, to be an acceptable comic hero in a Renaissance play, a prodigal usually must reform very early in the plot and his prodigality should be confined generally to a period prior to the time the play depicts. Philip fits neither category very well. Like *Michaelmas Term*, *No Wit, No Help Like a Woman's* contains events which its audience must forget or ignore in order to accept the drama's conclusion, but which are too extraordinary to be easily overlooked.

Philip, furthermore, is not alone in his propensity for unnatural deeds. The Dutch Merchant reports that Mistress Twilight thinks her husband's neglect of her "unkind" (1.3.49–52), and shortly afterward he warns Sir Oliver Twilight about the dangers of being betrayed by friends and loved ones: "Ofttimes, sir, what worse knave to a man / Than he that eats his meat?" he asks (ll.77–78). Many other instances of unnatural behavior concern sex. Philip's sudden fear midway in the plot that Grace is actually his sister and that their love is as a result incestuous is one example, and so too when Weatherwise sees Mistress Low-water disguised as a young gallant and falls in love with the "boy": "If the widow refuse me, I care not if I be suitor to him. I have known those who have been as mad, and given half their living for a male companion" (2.1.180–83). This inclination toward sexual confusion is reemphasized when Lady Goldenfleece unknowingly "thirsts" for a woman (once again Mistress Low-water in disguise) and actively woos her near the end of the play.

Language itself is perverted from its pristine state, because in this drama, as in *The Phoenix*, linguistic corruption accompanies social decay. Thus, during an elaborate banquet Weatherwise stages in her honor, Lady Goldenfleece complains that English has been degraded: "How many honest words have suffered corruption since Chaucer's days? A virgin would speak those words then that a very midwife would blush to hear now, if she have but so much blood left to make up an ounce of grace" (2.1.75–79). The gallants' "saucy courting" (l.40) throughout the scene lends proof to her observation. And late in the drama the gallants corrupt the poetry of Beveril's masque in order to attack the widow, debasing the form's normal honorific function and meaning. As Gilbert Lambston explains: "For the indifferent world, faith, they're apter / To bid a slander welcome than a truth" (3.1.45–46).

Because of the large number of unnatural deeds and attitudes in the drama, forms of the word *strange* appear with great frequency. The word has several meanings in the play, but most commonly it is closely associated with abnormality and "unkind" behavior. For instance, we learn that Oliver Twilight's plan to marry Grace to the aged and foolish Weatherwise is the product of a "strange" wit (1.1.252), while Mistress Twilight, on the other hand, wonders "strangely" at her husband's neglect (1.3.51). When the disguised Mistress Lowwater refuses to go to bed with her after their marriage, Lady Goldenfleece complains that her new husband talks "strangely" (5.1.13; cf. 1.1.229–30; 1.2.74–75; 1.3.131–37; 5.1.371).

In contrast to all of these references to and instances of unnatural behavior, the ways of comedy seem to be linked in the drama with the laws of nature. From a comic perspective, the laws of nature are closely connected with fertility, and thus anything which hinders the sexual union of young lovers which comedy has as its end is by definition unnatural. Savorwit articulates this view in the play's opening scene. Learning that Oliver Twilight plans to wed Grace to Weatherwise, he opposes the match, arguing, "But sir, there's no proportion, height, or evenness / Betwixt that equinoctial and your daughter" (1.1.197–98). The most important words in Savorwit's statement are *proportion* and *evenness*. The marriage of Grace and Weatherwise would be a marriage of extremes, a grotesque and unnatural unity of youth and age. New Comedy rejects this union of opposites by asserting the "natural" rightness of a union between likes, that is, between youth and youth. And later in the same scene Savorwit makes this very point after he has finally convinced Twilight to reject Weatherwise's suit:

> Why, now the clocks
> Go right again. It must be a strange wit
> That makes the wheels of youth and age so hit;
> The one are dry, worn, rusty, fur'd, and soil'd;
> Love's wheels are glib, ever kept clean, and oil'd.
>
> [ll.251–55]

Savorwit's statement is perfectly conventional, if a bit obscene. Even the spurned Weatherwise recognizes the wisdom of returning to "the beaten path again" (ll.294–95) and wooing a more appropriate partner, Lady Goldenfleece.

The first scene of *No Wit, No Help Like a Woman's* thus concludes by twice asserting the New Comedy belief that the laws of nature and proportion require that young love be consummated and that unions between youth and age be rejected. The statements take on added weight by being juxtaposed to the various "unkind" actions in the play. But this conventional contrast between natural actions and comic values, on one hand, and unnatural deeds and anticomic attitudes, on the other, is not as simple as it first appears. For instance, we might recall that Philip's neglect of his mother and sister was an unnatural action which grew "naturally" out of the comic tendency to value romantic love over love for family. More important complications are related to the rejection of a union of extremes discussed above—a union which Savorwit viewed as grotesquely unnatural. The drama itself concludes with just such a combination: the reconciliation of Mistress Low-water and Lady Goldenfleece, characters who until the end of the play have been mortal enemies.

Similar reconciliations occur in most comedies, but, as has

been demonstrated, Middleton's plays seem unable to harmonize the discordant and extreme elements in the society they portray. And while *No Wit, No Help Like a Woman's* does not contain the disturbing excesses of *Michaelmas Term* or *A Trick to Catch the Old One* (with the exception of Philip's commitment to love over family), Savorwit's dismissal of a union of opposites raises questions about the unity with which the drama concludes. Is this unity as perverted as the proposed marriage of Grace and Weatherwise? Is the reconciliation which occurs at the end of traditional comedy in fact fundamentally unnatural? Middleton's answer to these questions lies in the structure of *No Wit, No Help Like a Woman's*. It is, as by now might be expected, affirmative.

The plot of *No Wit, No Help Like a Woman's* is composed of what might be called a series of miniature comedies. The play contains several successive patterns which develop from complication to the apparent resolution of that complication to the sudden introduction of new discord. There are a number of discovery scenes and some indication of a *felix culpa* motif at work (2.2.169–70; 2.3.245–62). Savorwit nicely describes the play's incessant movement from problem to solution to problem to solution and so on when he complains, after being told of the Dutch Merchant's arrival with news of Mistress Twilight, "Pox on't! I thought all had been paid; / I can't abide these after-reckonings" (1.3.118–19). His lament might provide an epigraph for the fortunes of several of the characters.

The first complication in the drama is, of course, Oliver Twilight's plan to wed Grace to Weatherwise and Philip to Jane Sunset. Savorwit solves this problem by convincing Oliver that Sandfield is a better match for Grace. He then proposes a dual marriage—Philip with Jane and Sandfield with Grace—after which, he tells Philip and Sandfield, the gallants can exchange brides and gain their true loves. Savorwit takes on the function of reconciler, reuniting the two former companions after a period of disharmony. "Bless'd be all thy ends / That mak'st arm'd enemies embracing friends," his young master exclaims in admiration (1.1.144–45). Savorwit's solution, however, is quickly destroyed by the arrival of the Dutch Merchant with news that Philip's mother is alive. The new problems which the revelation creates are solved in turn by his mother's almost simultaneous appearance. Philip's reconciliation with Mistress Twilight is rapid and total. When he confesses his guilt, his mother not only quickly forgives his youthful faults, she also agrees to convince her husband that all is well. Her "bounty" will "flow" over the restrictions imposed by his father and establish a period of harmony and festivity (2.2.165). As she states later in the play: "I come in happy time to a feast of marriages" (4.1.152). Mistress Twilight alludes to a comic resolution which she herself has made possible.

But our acceptance of Mistress Twilight's solution to Philip's difficulties is qualified immediately. Just as our knowledge of Philip's disregard for his family complicates our attitude toward Savorwit's plan for a dual marriage and exchange of brides, so it remains to cloud the festivity of this new harmony. Philip's prior deeds are reemphasized by the presence of Beveril throughout the above meeting with his mother. At the same time that Philip is being reconciled with Mistress Twilight, Beveril's laments over his sister's poverty provide examples of the familial loyalty apparently lacking in the other youth, and the passages significantly frame the reconciliation scene (2.2.99–101, 173–81). Similarly, Savorwit's cynical asides (ll.118, 126, 141, 168, 171–72) undermine the incident's idealistic tone by implying that his master has learned nothing from former mistakes, a suggestion which is strengthened when Savorwit later comments that, if given another chance to save a member of the family, Philip "[would] make shift to spend another ransom yet" (4.1.34). It is a poor joke, at best.[23] In the context of Beveril's genuine concern for his sister and Savorwit's running commentary, Mistress Twilight's extraordinarily forgiving response to her son's confession almost becomes absurd. Like the prodigals in *Michaelmas Term*, she extends the comic tendency to forget to extremes and subverts its validity in the process. Philip's position is so indefensible that at times his mother nearly chides him for what he has done (4.1.57–61), but the saintly woman always resists the temptation and then berates herself for having such thoughts—thoughts which from our perspective are much more credible than her usual attitude toward her son. There is, furthermore, one additional complication in Mistress Twilight's attempt to resolve her son's predicament: her apparent discovery that Grace is in fact her daughter and that, as a result, Philip's love for Grace is incestuous. In light of this new information, the comic reconciliation which Mistress Twilight has contrived suddenly becomes one more unnatural event in the play. Philip's love is transformed (if only momentarily) into another example of sexual perversion. Likewise, the disturbing conflict of love and family with which the play began has progressed to a bitterly ironic solution. Philip no longer must choose between romantic involvement and familial ties. By incestuously loving his sister he unites both imperatives. Philip, however, does not find this fact very comforting. He is driven again to despair, and he remains despairing until an even more remarkable and miraculous discovery in the final scene promises to resolve his difficulties, one hopes for the last time.

The same pattern of complication, solution, and new discord is also present in the subplot. For example, in act 2, scene 1, Weatherwise's re-creation of a unified world, his elaborate banquet organized according to the signs of the zodiac, erupts in discord as the gallants argue over the hand of Lady Goldenfleece and Mistress Low-water confronts Lambston with evidence of his libertine nature. In act 3, scene 1, however, the gallants are reconciled in a new pact of friendship, and the episode parallels Philip's meeting with his mother two scenes earlier. But the gallants join together in a spirit of revenge rather than harmony. Their reconciliation results primarily from their wishes to slander Lady Goldenfleece and her new suitor, Mistress Low-water in disguise. The negative quality of the gallants' new harmony reemphasizes a characteristic of all the comic solutions discussed above. Not only are they partial, they are unnatural as well. Philip's initial happiness both at his renewed friendship with Sandfield and at Savorwit's plan for a dual marriage is gained at the cost of overlooking the fact he has left his mother and sister in captivity. Mistress Twilight displays a forgiving nature which is nearly astounding, and she contrives a reconciliation between Philip and his father so that Philip may marry Grace only to discover that Philip's beloved is his sister. The gallants unite in order to destroy.

The masque which Beveril writes in honor of Lady Goldenfleece's wedding is the culmination of all of the motifs present in these "comic" solutions. Technically, the masque is a celebration of the marriage of Lady Goldenfleece and the disguised Mistress Low-water, but it also soon comes to be a celebration of the approaching marriages of Philip and Grace, and Sandfield and Jane Sunset. Indeed, the marriages of the young lovers are linked temporally and causally to the union of their elders, when Oliver Twilight vows that "these young loves shall clap hands together" at the same time that Lady Goldenfleece weds her lover. "The seed of one feast shall bring forth another," he rejoices (4.1.156–57).

The promise of multiple marriages is reminiscent of Shakespearean comedy, where the seemingly endless procession of young lovers to the altar at the end of a given play signifies the formation of a new, harmonious society. The same hope for a new and better world seems to lie behind Oliver's happiness, and Beveril's plan to include a masque in the wedding celebration emphasizes this conventional interpretation of the planned marriages in Middleton's play. As Enid Welsford has shown, "Harmony, particularly social harmony, is the underlying theme of most of the masquing" during the English Renaissance,[24] and Beveril intends that his masque glorify the same values. His hopes, however, never come to fruition. His masque is, after all, written to celebrate two "unkind" unions—one apparently incestuous (Philip and Grace), one homosexual (Lady Goldenfleece and Mistress Low-water)—and the conventional procreative imagery in Oliver Twilight's speech quoted above ironically serves only to heighten our sense of the perversion at the center of the entire episode. Moreover, Beveril's actors do not plan to use the masque to represent harmony at all. Gilbert Lambston and his fellows intend, as already noted, to use the device as a means to slander the widow. Beveril's gratefulness for the "unlook'd for grace" and "voluntary kindness" (3.1.310, 311) of their offer of aid is thus fraught with irony, because grace and kindness are two concepts which have little meaning for these individuals. And when Beveril explains the nature of the entertainment to the gallants, he unintentionally stresses the discord which dominates the wedding. The masque, he tells them, will deal with the four elements, and he then proceeds to recount its theme:

> This the effect: that whereas all those four [elements]
> Maintain a natural opposition
> And untruc'd war, the one against the other,
> To shame their ancient envies, they should see
> How well in two breasts all these do agree.
>
> [3.1.232–36]

Beveril's device is clearly intended to embody a vision of *concordia discors* and to link that vision to Lady Goldenfleece's wedding. But as we have repeatedly seen, opposites do not join to form some greater unity in the world of Middleton's comedies. Rather, they create unnatural tensions which refuse to be resolved. The phrase *natural opposition* recalls the many other unnatural unities in the play and ironically emphasizes the fact that the "two breasts" being celebrated belong to deadly enemies. The passage itself sounds suspiciously like a description of a comic conclusion, a resemblance which is not, I think, accidental.

The traditional function Beveril's masque should have is thus disrupted from its conception. Its occasion is likewise marred by the fact that not everyone in the audience feels that there is something to elaborate. Shortly before the entertainment begins, Mistress Low-water looks across the table and sees Philip sitting in indecorous gloom: "What is yon gentleman with the funeral face there? / Methinks that look does ill become a bride-house" (4.3.14–15). The same might be said of the masque which follows. The gallants enter dressed as the four elements, discard Beveril's prepared text, and gleefully insult the widow until Beveril drives them out. By making explicit the discord which is implicit in the entire wedding feast, they turn masque into antimasque and transform a celebration of harmony and order into an emblem of chaos.[25] Once again unity is replaced by disunity. Once again we see an unnatural reconciliation lead to new discord.

As the masque ends, Gilbert Lambston turns to his audience and announces the device's conclusion: "And now to vex, 'gainst nature, form, rule, place, / See once four warring elements all embrace" (4.3.147–48). In doing so, he indicates that the gallants' reconciliation with one another for the purpose of revenge is as unnatural as any unity in the play and as likely ultimately to dissolve. He also mocks Beveril's initial conception of the piece. More important, however, Lambston parodies the resolution of the play in which he appears. *No Wit, No Help Like a Woman's* progresses to a final reconciliation which is as questionable as are all the reconciliations and solutions which precede it. Mistress Low-water unmasks, gives Beveril her blessing to marry Lady Goldenfleece, and two mortal enemies suddenly become fast friends. "No more my enemy now," Mistress Low-water says of her prospective sister-in-law, "my brother's wife / And my kind sister!" (5.1.354–55). Given all that we have seen, Mistress Low-water's use of the word *kind* to describe this union of opposites is ironic, and Oliver Twilight soon picks up the implications of what she unconsciously states, echoing, I think, our sentiments as well: "Here's unity forever strangely wrought!" he marvels (l.371). Twilight's statement is unmistakably similar to Gilbert Lambston's concluding speech during the masque, and *strangely* is by this point a word with a great many negative connotations. Indeed, the "strange unity" Oliver speaks of is simply one more example of unnatural behavior in *No Wit*, and the entire thrust of Middleton's play is to demonstrate that the principle of comic reconciliation itself vexes " 'gainst nature, form, rule, place" despite the apparent association of comic structure with natural laws.

Several incidents in the concluding scene bear out this analysis. First, Lady Goldenfleece does not seem to be motivated by a genuine change of heart. In fact, her overriding concern throughout much of the scene is revenge (ll.247–51, 309–13, 316–17). Her spiteful tone lends credence to Weatherwise's belief that the present is not a time of harmony but of discord: "For now is Mercury going into the second house near unto Ursa Major, that great hunks, the Bear at the bridge-foot in heaven, which shows horrible bear baitings in wedlock; and the Sun near ent'ring into th' Dog, sets 'em all together by th'ears" (ll.263–67), he explains to anyone who will listen. Likewise, when Oliver Twilight finds this new unity "forever" wrought, and Beveril wishes "perpetual" friendship on all (l.469), their assumption that all problems have reached a final solution contradicts everything we have learned from the structure and events of the play. Until now, no solution has been the ultimate one, and the events of this scene do not indicate that anything has changed. Indeed, if we listen closely, we can hear Oliver Twilight echoing his earlier joy at Philip's proposed marriage to Jane Sunset (cf. ll.391–93 and 4.1.156–57), and there is no assurance that his new happiness will not also prove short-lived. As Twilight himself prophetically stated after being reunited with his wife earlier in the drama, the chances are good that "this weather is too glorious to hold long" (4.1.39).

The old man's metaphoric description of happiness as a beautiful clear day points toward the final and perhaps most significant way in which Middleton shows that his play's concluding unity is false: his portrayal of the foolish astrologer Weatherwise. *No Wit, No Help Like a Woman's* is full of images relating to weather. Mistress Low-water's miseries are like a "foul mist" (1.2.21); Philip's father finds the coming marriages of his son and daughter a "comfortable shine of joy" which "breaks through a cloud of grief!" (1.3.35–36; cf. 1.1.226–27; 1.2.131–32, 133–35, 142–48; 2.1.210–11, etc.). The names of some of the characters—Twilight, Sunset—are also part of this pattern. The goal of the characters is, at the very least, to be able to "endure all weathers" (2.2.27–28), to be, in a sense, "weatherwise." And whereas most of the individuals in the drama advocate stoic resignation as a means of coping with whatever storms life may bring (1.2.142–48; 1.3.111;

2.1.262–63), Weatherwise actively attempts to do just what his name suggests. With the aid of his elaborate table and books, he hopes not simply to withstand the weather but to predict it and to explain all of existence in its terms. He is another Tangle or Bounteous Progress, a character who imposes his own version of absolute unity on a chaotic world. Like all such unifiers in Middleton, he is an important figure, and, like all of them, he is a failure.

Weatherwise's almanac is his method of ordering reality, and the best example of the extraordinary nature of this order is the banquet he constructs in honor of Lady Goldenfleece. Having been rejected in his suit for Grace's hand, Weatherwise decides to woo the widow instead and invites her and her other suitors to his house. There the guests gather around a table which has twelve desserts in the form of the twelve signs, each sign being given to the appropriate guest. Lady Goldenfleece, for example, sits next to Aries because it is the head sign and "a widow is the head / Till she be married" (2.1.100–101); Lambston is seated by Taurus because "they say you're a good town-bull" (l.104), and so on.

The banquet represents Weatherwise's interpretation of the world around him; it is the world made over in the image of his own obsessive beliefs. The fragility of his vision is indicated both by the fact that it is perishable (that is, edible) and by the argument between Mistress Low-water and Gilbert Lambston, which disrupts the harmony of the gathering again and again despite Weatherwise's repeated and finally unsuccessful attempts to keep his order intact (ll.198, 210–12, 279–81). Mistress Low-water's later success in wooing the widow leads Weatherwise to question the validity of his unity for the first time (2.3.194–96), but he soon regains faith in his almanac and is able to withstand Lambston's scornful assertion that the astrologer's unities are "mere delusions" (3.1.129). Lambston, of course, is right, and Weatherwise again questions his calendar in the final scene of the drama. When Lady Goldenfleece pledges her love to Beveril, the old fool complains: "A pox of this! my almanac ne'er gulled me till this hour; the thirteenth day, work for the hangman, and there's nothing toward it"

(5.1.382–84). Suddenly he discovers his mistake, and all is well again: "But now I see the error, 'tis false-figured; it should be, thirteen days and a half, work for the hangman, for he ne'er works under thirteen pence half-penny; beside, Venus being a spot in the sun's garment, shows there should be a woman found in hose and doublet" (ll.385–90). Weatherwise's solution is an absurd rationalization; his unity is, one might say, "strangely wrought."

Indeed, Weatherwise's alternating faith, disappointment, and renewed dependence upon his almanac parallel the recurring pattern of partial comic solutions which forms the overall structure of *No Wit, No Help Like a Woman's*. And just as the main plot of the play ends with the fortuitous discovery of an error of identity and with faith that all will end happily, so Weatherwise finds a mistake sufficient reason for believing that his almanac does in fact explain and order reality. The obvious falseness of his unity helps us to see the play's final harmony for what it truly is: at best a partial and momentary triumph, at worst a fiction which, like Beveril's masque, vexes "'gainst nature, form, rule, place." We can never forget Philip's former actions. Nor can we easily accept the sudden friendship of Lady Goldenfleece and Mistress Low-water. Weatherwise himself best describes the impoverished, hollow quality of this New Comedy when, consulting his calendar to explain the gallants' lack of success in seeking Lady Goldenfleece's hand, he finds the correct day—"The twelfth day, gentlemen, that was our day"—and discovers a message which speaks to the entire play: " 'Past all redemption' " (3.1.122–23).

The judgment of comedy we encounter in *No Wit, No Help Like a Woman's* thus parallels and extends themes and ideas present in *A Mad World, My Masters*. The latter play examines comic festivity and generosity and finds them lacking; the former indicates that the comic resolution, with its emphasis on reconciliation and inclusiveness, is an unnatural fiction. Both plays deny New Comedy some of its most important values, and their comic structures lose, as a result, much of the meaning which conventionally should imbue those structures. The outline of Roman comedy can be perceived in the dramas, but it is an outline only of forms and conventions which have been rendered ambiguous and, in some instances, insignificant.

Although *A Chaste Maid in Cheapside* was written approximately a year after *No Wit, No Help Like a Woman's*, the play's style is closer to that of Middleton's early comedies. The drama contains none of the romantic elements present in *No Wit*. The influence of Fletcher is nowhere apparent. The play is, as has often been noted, the culmination of Middleton's development as a writer of city comedies, and Middleton closes the first phase of his career with a drama which is unquestionably his comic masterpiece, a drama which refines and develops to the fullest the materials which compose his earlier plays. Because of its excellence and pivotal position in the Middleton canon, *A Chaste Maid in Cheapside* has received more and better critical attention than any of Middleton's other comedies. Almost all of the important elements in the play have been discussed in detail. A large part of this critical commentary deals with the conclusion; and before looking at the play in depth, I would like to consider two descriptions of the drama's resolution which are of great interest within the context of the ideas developed in this study.

In his analysis of Middleton's comedies, Wilbur Dunkel complains at one point that the joyous conclusion of *A Chaste Maid in Cheapside* "seems forced and does not emanate from the characters." The play's most perceptive critic, R. B. Parker, similarly finds a degree of artificiality in the ending. However, he argues that this contrivance results not from faulty writing but from a conscious attempt at burlesque: "The serious ambiguities of value in the play are resolved theatrically, not morally, by the trick of the resurrection scene; and the purely literary nature of the solution is emphasized by crediting it surprisingly to Susan and following it with the anticlimax of Tim's marriage."[26] Both critics clearly have a different estimation of Middleton's skill, but at the same time both emphasize the obvious artificiality of the play's conclusion. Dunkel's comment is in this sense only a more extreme version of Parker's.

The two views are, I think, correct, but their real interest lies not so much in the statements themselves as in what they imply. *A Chaste Maid in Cheapside* is basically a New Comedy. The primary plot traces an almost perfect comic conflict.[27] A young lover (Touchwood Junior) schemes to save his beloved (Moll) from an undesirable suitor (Whorehound) forced upon her by her cruel and greedy parents (Maudline and Yellowhammer). And although the subplots develop other material and at times seem to obscure the fortunes of these young lovers, the drama concludes with their victory and marriage amidst countless references to resurrection, portending the birth of a better world and reinforcing the play's Lenten–Easter setting. Moll herself points to the drama's conventional comic structure when she sings of her misfortunes early in act 5 as if she were describing the complications of a New Comedy plot: "O, happy is the maid whose life takes end," she laments, "Ere it knows parent's frown or loss of friend" (5.2.40–41).

Like most New Comedies, *A Chaste Maid* illustrates, in Northrop Frye's words, "a victory of arbitrary plot over consistency of character."[28] All comic endings are somewhat "forced." Most comedies resolve "theatrically, not morally." Is the repentance of Duke Frederick in *As You Like It*, for example, explicable in any other terms? Is the happy conclusion of *Every Man in His Humour* or the sudden realignment of emotional ties in *A Midsummer Night's Dream* less contrived than the conclusion of Middleton's play? In fact, the plots of most conventional comedies are at least as wildly improbable as the plot of *A Chaste Maid in Cheapside*. Yet for the most part we take these other plays seriously; that is, we accept them on their own terms. We do not claim that their endings are arbitrary; we do not usually feel it necessary to explain their resolutions as burlesques. Why then is Middleton's play so difficult to accept in the same way? One answer is that the comedy, like all of Middleton's comedies, is full of extremes which resist being reconciled or harmonized with one another. At times, *A Chaste Maid in Cheapside* is one of Middleton's least humorous plays, and the society it depicts is as chaotic as the society it portrayed in the plays discussed above.[29]

But the reason for many readers' difficulties with the ending is more complex than this. When Parker notes that the conclusion of Middleton's play is "purely literary," he implies that, because the conclusion is so artificial, it seems out of touch with reality as we know it. All dramatic resolutions are, of course, "literary," but they are not normally viewed only as such, because they present events and ideas which appear to be related or applicable to our own lives. Thus the typical comic ending escapes being relegated to a totally artificial existence by embodying (among other things) our intimations of community with one another and our hopes of attaining a victory over death through procreation. The conclusion is an image of our desires which, despite the plot's improbability, appears (while we are watching) right and genuinely attainable.

A Chaste Maid in Cheapside lacks this kind of reality and significance because the play denies the most important source of meaning in comedy: the traditional association of comic structure with patterns of natural and spiritual rebirth. As a result, the comedy's resolution does not convey truths which seem to have a valid place in the world we inhabit. The play's form has no significance beyond itself. It is contrived and arbitrary, nothing more. *A Chaste Maid* thus extends and intensifies the process of emptying comic conventions of meaning which we encountered in *A Mad World, My Masters* and *No Wit, No Help Like a Woman's*. It is a comedy whose form is belied by its content even more fundamentally than was the case with *Michaelmas Term* and *A Trick to Catch the Old One*. Indeed, *A Chaste Maid* is a tissue of patterns and roles—social, linguistic, literary—which no longer have significance. Its world is a world of games which have no substance.

All kinds of contradictory relationships between forms and their respective contents pervade the play. One example is the apparent discrepancy between Moll's character and her name. As any member of Middleton's Renaissance audience would have known, that name is cant for "whore," an association hardly in keeping with the girl's actions in the play or her role as comic heroine. Similarly, as has often been noted, although

Moll is the chaste maid of the title, the women usually "chased" in Cheapside were prostitutes. A second and more important confusion concerns roles pertaining to marriage and the family.[30] *A Chaste Maid in Cheapside* begins with a series of familial disorders: the quarrelling among the Yellowhammers over Moll's refusal to marry Whorehound; the Allwits' curious arrangement with Whorehound in which the knight sires the children and pays the bills while Allwit acts the part of father; Touchwood Senior's forced absence from his wife because the children who yearly result from his phenomenal powers of procreation are literally eating them out of house and home; and the Kixes' endless bickering over who is at fault for their issueless marriage. In each instance socially prescribed roles are left unfulfilled: the Yellowhammers act unnaturally by merchandising their daughter; Allwit retains the appearance but not the responsibilities and activities of father and husband; Touchwood Senior must turn away from his function as head of his household; and Kix fails his duties as progenitor because he is impotent.

Words and the rules of logical discourse are similarly divorced from their normal contents. Just as linguistic corruption accompanied social disorder in *The Phoenix* and *No Wit, No Help Like a Woman's*, so the debasement of social roles in *A Chaste Maid* is paralleled by a subversion of language and conventional methods of argumentation. During the first scene, for example, a Porter enters the Yellowhammer household with a letter from their son, Tim. Confronted by the mumbo jumbo of the young scholar's Latin, both Maudline and the Porter impose two different and equally false interpretations on the same set of words—the citizen's wife finding a directive not to pay the letter's deliverer, and the Porter finding just the opposite. The confusion simultaneously reveals the potential ambiguity of language and the ability of individuals to force their unique meanings on words, thereby transforming reality by transforming the language used to describe that reality. Tim himself is an even more energetic manipulator of words than his mother and the Porter. (See, in addition to the letter, 3.2.133–37, and his extraordinary meeting with the

Welshwoman in act 4, scene 1.) Nor is he content to transform reality merely by subverting language. Tim also employs his own peculiar version of logic to create a world which conforms to his needs, an endeavor perhaps best demonstrated by his farcical dispute with his tutor (4.1.). Indeed, according to Tim, his ability to remake the world by manipulating argumentative techniques has no limits: "By logic / I'll prove anything," he explains to a skeptical Maudline, ominously boasting that he can prove a whore an honest woman (4.1.36–38).

Tim and, to a lesser extent, Maudline and the Porter divorce language and logic from external reality, just as many of the other characters separate role from responsibility. Their actions, like those of Whorehound and Allwit, for example, implicitly alienate forms from their usual contents, destroying the significance of those forms in the process. On one hand, all three characters separate words from their communicative and descriptive purposes by denying normal relationships between signs and what they signify. On the other, Tim destroys any claim that logical discourse might have as a vehicle for discovering truth. By assuming that the rules of argumentation can prove anything, he assures in effect that they prove nothing at all.

Middleton is not, however, interested primarily in role confusion and the misuse of language and logical discourse in this play. His description of these problems reflects a more fundamental concern. As I hope to show in the following pages, the meaningless forms examined above are subsumed into a much more important, if equally meaningless one—that of *A Chaste Maid in Cheapside* itself.

As contrived and unrealistic as comedy often appears, its apparently arbitrary whims traditionally are not without basis, nor are they devoid of significance. It has long been recognized by authors and audiences alike that the structure of comedy parallels the rhythms of renewal and rebirth which man sees about him in the seasonal flow of nature and in his own sexuality. The form's fundamental meaning has its source in this resemblance.[31] No matter how much a given comedy may seem to be rooted in a particular time or in particular abuses, the play's basic issues inevitably center about a conflict of fertility and sterility, or life and death. Christian audiences and writers often point to an analogous and (from their perspective) more important pattern which lies behind comic structure and provides the structure with a symbolic potency: the pattern of Christ's death and resurrection.[32] And indeed, physical and spiritual rebirths often go hand in hand in Renaissance comedy. Such is the case in *A Trick to Catch the Old One* and Shakespeare's *As You Like It*. *A Chaste Maid in Cheapside* is remarkable in the extent to which the play reminds its audience of the two great cyclic patterns which give form and (presumably) meaning to the events depicted in the play. A relationship which is usually intimated in Renaissance comedy becomes explicit as Middleton constructs his plot within a period of Lenten–Easter celebrations, and at the same time fills his comedy with countless references to children and fertility, references which often are connected with a figure of enormous procreative power, Touchwood Senior. But the explicit parallels which Middleton's play seems to sanction do not serve to give the drama added significance. The opposite is in fact true. As we have often seen, Middleton alerts us to fundamental comic truths only to deny those truths before our eyes.

The period of the Christian year stretching from the beginning of Lent through Easter Sunday is an especially fitting setting for a comic play because the period itself, as O. B. Hardison has shown, has an essentially comic structure: "Its descending action begins with Lent. The point of crisis is reached on Good Friday, and Holy Saturday and Easter Sunday are devoted to the entombment and Resurrection, respectively. The reversal-recognition occurs early on Easter morning." As in New Comedy, "the mythical event celebrated is rebirth, not death, although it is a rebirth that requires death as its prelude."[33] The mock resurrections at the end of *A Chaste Maid* and the repeated references to fasting within the play are the most obvious indications of the drama's relation to the Easter story, but the play also contains many other features of the season. The numerous water images and the christening of

Whorehound's child midway in the plot reflect, for example, the importance of baptism during this part of the Christian year. Spiritual purification is an essential feature of the Lenten–Easter celebrations and, together with Whitsunday, Easter was originally the only time infants were baptized into the church. Similarly, the drama's pervasive emphasis upon children parallels the Lenten admonition that the followers of God be "as dere chyldren, and walke in loue," for these "children" have escaped the limitations of the Old Testament ethic: "We are not chyldren of the bondwoman, but of the frewoman," is one lesson which a Renaissance Anglican would have learned on the fourth Sunday of Lent. Passages alluding to blindness (the inscription on Moll's wedding ring, for instance) echo the recurring contrast of light and darkness during Lenten services, as well as the reading (during the first Sunday service in the season) of St. Matthew's account of Christ healing the blind (chap.15).[34] Easter, of course, symbolizes the victory of light over darkness, and the processions which end Middleton's play parallel the great church processions of Easter morning.

From the viewpoint of the drama's Lenten–Easter setting, the most important characters are Whorehound and his newly born child. The period of Lent is a period of death and sterility, a time when man, alienated from God and confronted by the devil, undergoes a period of suffering which precedes the coming glory of the Easter resurrection. The model for this spiritual test is Christ's temptation in the wilderness, and Ash Wednesday opens with a plea for divine aid in the struggle: "Turne thee, O Lorde, and delyuer my soule: Oh saue me for thy mercies sake."[35] In the course of Middleton's comedy, Whorehound endures a similar test. He confronts his own depravity and is beset, as a result, by the forces of evil. After Whorehound is wounded by Touchwood Junior, he suddenly steps into the role of Christian penitent, and Middleton's description of the final meeting between Whorehound and the Allwits reproduces the traditional Lenten struggle of Christian sinner and infernal adversary. Attempting to repent for his past deeds, Walter finds himself opposed by a "devil" who, he laments, "knew the dear account my soul stood charg'd with," and yet, "like hell's flattering angel, / Wouldst never tell me on't" (5.1.21, 25–27). The prize for the victor in the struggle is Whorehound's soul. The same is true of his child. Like its father, the infant must be absolved of its sins, and the significance of the baptism is thus very similar to that of Walter's confrontation with Allwit. The two episodes essentially determine whether or not salvation is attainable for the knight and his youngest offspring.

If Middleton's depiction of both Whorehound's conflict with a hellish Allwit and the christening is in keeping with the overall focus of the Easter liturgy, the outcome of each incident is not. In each case the "devil" triumphs, and these victories cast a pall over the play's relation to the Easter season and the meaning we might draw from that relationship. Middleton's penitent, for example, does not defeat his adversary. In one of the cruelest scenes in all of Renaissance drama, Whorehound's imperfect attempt to repent succumbs to a cynicism without bounds. Allwit suddenly accuses the knight of making advances toward the cuckold's wife, an accusation which Mistress Allwit heatedly denies. And after they learn that Touchwood Junior has apparently died from wounds inflicted by Walter and that the knight has been disinherited because Mistress Kix has conceived, they throw him out of the house. Early in the scene, Whorehound's change of heart leads Mistress Allwit ironically to lament, "He is lost forever" (5.1.51), just at the moment Walter seems to have some hope of being spiritually saved. And yet, she is right. There is no salvation for Middleton's penitent. His end is debtor's prison, an earthly counterpart to hell. The Allwits, on the other hand, go off to the Strand, perhaps to establish a flourishing brothel.

A similar defeat of spiritual values is apparent in the christening scene—an episode which undoubtedly does much more to damn Whorehound's child than to save it. The very makeup of the christening party itself contributes to the overturning of the ritual's spiritual function. Whorehound stands as godfather to his own child, a fact which is doubly ironic because it is the godparents' duty to oversee the infant's moral and spiritual upbringing.[36] Because this particular infant is the product of Whorehound's adulterous union with Mistress Allwit, the knight does not seem to be in a position to undertake that responsibility. Similarly, the baptismal waters which should signify the victory of the spirit over the forces of death are associated instead with human waste (3.2.89–98, 155, 173–75, 184–85). Moreover, these passages are ironically juxtaposed to a speech in which one of the Puritan gossips praises "the wellspring of discipline / That waters all the brethren" (ll.163–64), employing traditional Christian images which have by this point exchanged their normal spiritual associations for much less attractive physical ones. The christening is, as one critic argues, "a flagrant violation of all that the traditional ritual stands for."[37] There are other violations of Christian belief as well. While Mistress Underman defines humility as sexual license, the gossips, glutting themselves with sweetmeats and wine, enact their own version of the last supper and blasphemously parody the Eucharist. We can only wonder about the spiritual fate of Whorehound's child trapped in the midst of such a ceremony.

Walter's unsuccessful repentance and the almost anti-Christian characteristics of his child's christening are indicative of the spiritual wasteland which *A Chaste Maid in Cheapside* delineates. Christian values have no place in the play-society. When they appear, they do so in perverted forms which bear little relation to traditional beliefs. Even the *Agnus Dei* is degraded by being transformed into a series of bawdy puns on *mutton* and *meat*—a degradation which reaches its climax in an absurd parody of the Nativity. Early in the play Touchwood Senior meets the Country Wench carrying a child he has sired. He explains his destitute predicament, gives her money, and urges that she dispose of the child. The Country Wench accomplishes this by an elaborate stratagem. She disguises the infant as a piece of mutton, and her package is confiscated by two Promoters charged with enforcing the Lenten regulations forbidding the eating of meat. Searching for lamb, the informants discover to their surprise a child instead, but this child is hardly the result of an immaculate conception.[38] Like the drama's imitations of Lenten practices and the ritual of baptism, the play's mock nativity debases the original.

This total lack of spiritual awareness inevitably leads the characters to mistake the true nature of Lent. For them it is simply a time of abnormal abstinence. When Allwit asks the Promoters to tell him "where one dwells that kills this Lent" (2.2.73), and later rejects the prohibition against eating meat by asking, "Lent? What cares colon here for Lent?" (l.79), he sums up the attitude of all the individuals in the play toward that part of the Christian year. They are irrevocably tied to the flesh, to the lamb apparently so essential to their diets rather than to the Lamb of God.[39] Lent, of course, is a prelude to a time of spiritual salvation and rebirth, but the drama's characters prove themselves quite adept at killing the spirit, whether by cynically overturning attempts at penitence (Allwit) or by confusing humility with the question of precedence in entering a doorway (the gossips). As a result, the spiritual regeneration inherent in the Easter season is lost on them. More important, because Easter has no significance within the play-world, the validation which the Christian myth would normally provide for the drama's comic structure is also lost. From a spiritual perspective, the resurrections of Moll and Touchwood Junior at the end of the play are hollow, because the community which witnesses them is not morally regenerated, is not, indeed, concerned with moral improvement. Everyone remains unchanged except Whorehound, and for him there is apparently no redemption.

The seasonal and, in the case of humans, generational rebirth which occurs within nature is closely linked in *A Chaste Maid* with the great spiritual renewal of Easter by numerous references to children. As noted above, children are an important symbol during the Easter season, because baptism is a central concern of the period and because children are traditionally associated not only with innocence but also with humility, a particularly characteristic Lenten virtue (see 2.4.11–12). And just as Easter celebrates the fact that God sent his only begotten son to redeem man from the horror of death, so comedy reminds us that, on a more mundane level, children provide a way of overcoming the ravages of time and of providing continuity and order in a confusing world. The creation of new members of society is in many ways the major goal of a typical New Comedy plot, and this certainly seems to be true of the events traced in Middleton's play. The drama is so full of references to fertility that one critic identifies Touchwood Senior with Priapus and argues: "In its joyous celebration of man's procreative energies, *A Chaste Maid* is close in spirit to comedy's origin in phallic song."[40] The statement is extreme, but at first glance it does not seem to be far off the mark. For instance, as the play opens, Maudline urges her daughter to marry in a speech full of sexual double entendres and ambiguous allusions to her own youth, which apparently was far from sheltered (1.1.1–11); and in attempting to "quicken" (impregnate—*OED*) her daughter by bringing her into contact with men (Whorehound), she inaugurates the drama's constant focus on childbearing, a focus which indeed does recall the origins of comedy in phallic songs and seasonal rituals.

Maudline's concern with fertility and reproduction in scene 1 is reinforced by Allwit's comments on his pregnant wife in scene 2 and by Touchwood Senior's description of his extraordinary procreative powers in act 2, scene 1. The impression that *A Chaste Maid* celebrates man's ability to renew himself is further strengthened when, during the christening of Whorehound's child, one gossip mistakenly compliments Allwit on his offspring by saying that she wants "nothing but such getting, sir, as thine" (2.3.25), and another confides after her companion contemptuously dismisses the apparent father: "I would not care what clown my husband were too, / So I had such fine children" (3.2.31–32). We could scarcely find better descriptions of the comic tendency to place an extraordinary value on procreation. Likewise, much of the water imagery in the play (Touchwood Senior's magic water, for instance) is linked to fertility, and dryness is associated with sterility (cf. 2.1.153; 3.3.9–14).

The resurrections at the end of the comedy apparently signify the victory of life and fertility over death and sterility, and the victory is announced when the frequent mentions of death in the drama's final scenes (4.4.37–38; 5.1.1–6; 5.2.1–12, 44 ff.) give way to Sir Oliver's joyous exclamation at the prospect of an heir: "Ho, my wife's quicken'd; I'm a man for ever!" (5.3.1). The Kixes' new hopes seem to provide concrete proof of the close connection between comic structure and the generational renewal of human beings. The miracle of rebirth which Kix alludes to by stating that he will be a man "for ever"—will, in other words, live on through his progeny—parallels the drama's equally miraculous upswing in the final scene. The union of young lovers at the conclusion is thus more than the consummation of a single isolated romance; it promises the renewal of the play-world itself. Placed within the context of seasonal and generational cycles of rebirth, the play's structure no longer seems the product of an author's desire to force events to an arbitrary conclusion which is not warranted. It is a reflection of the wonder of new life we see around us every day, the new life which comedy was first created to celebrate.

Middleton, however, was not content to let the above associations stand unquestioned. In fact, every aspect of the play which initially seems to ground Middleton's plot in cycles of rebirth within the natural world is ironically qualified in some way. The most obvious instance concerns Touchwood Senior. For while this character may have the powers of a Priapus, the result is not very beneficial. Touchwood Senior literally is made destitute by his children. When we first see him, he is planning to leave his wife and making a statement which conventionally should not be possible in comedy. He laments that their desires "are both too fruitful" for their barren fortunes (2.1.9), and concludes that the situation cannot be permitted to continue:

> Life, every year a child, and some years two;
> Besides drinkings abroad, that's never reckon'd;
> This gear will not hold out.
>
> [ll.15–17]

As is his habit, Middleton extends a positive comic value to an extreme and renders it absurd. Not only can one be "too fruitful" in this play, Touchwood Senior's excesses also threaten the health of his sexual organs ("gear"). Furthermore, Touchwood Senior confides at one point that the productivity of his "fatal finger" (l.59) paradoxically opposes the gathering of another kind of natural productivity, the crops planted each spring: "For every harvest I shall hinder hay-making: / I had no less than seven [wenches] lay in last progress" (2.1.61–62). And if we look more closely at some of the other statements concerning procreation noted above, we find similar ambiguities. Maudline's sentiments have a monetary basis: she wants her daughter to make a financially advantageous marriage. Allwit's wife is pregnant by another man, and the Kixes, like the Yellowhammers, view fertility primarily in financial terms. Nor are the gossips unassailable proponents of the comic emphasis on fertility. Indeed, all the conventional statements praising procreation in *A Chaste Maid* come from the play's less admirable characters. Like Bounteous Progress, these characters are flawed spokesmen for comic values which are themselves without significance. And when Tim suddenly blunders into the christening of Whorehound's illegitimate child, we see, as if for the first time, that parental joy does not always have the firmest of bases.

The characters' true attitude toward fertility and procreation is best demonstrated by their attitude toward children.[41] Yellowhammer's recognition that "we cannot be too wary in our children" (1.1.166) is in this drama more than the sentiment of a New Comedy blocking figure. It provides a motto for the entire comedy, and it is paraphrased with increasing intensity throughout. Allwit's angry greeting of his apparent children in scene 2 is closely followed by Whorehound's contemplation about getting rid of his bastards in order to prevent them from incestuously mingling with his legal offspring (ll.109–17). Touchwood Senior then appears lamenting his great powers in the next scene, and his lament leads to the entry of the Country Wench. Her later successful attempt to dispose of their illegitimate child is significantly juxtaposed to the christening. Moreover, Touchwood Senior's relief at her decision to keep the child clearly shows the extent to which children (like everything else in the play) are degraded and materialized: "Here's all I have, i'faith, take purse and all; / And would I were rid of all the ware i' the shop so!" (2.1.99– 100). This is hardly the attitude of a fertility god. And ironi- cally, we hear Allwit echoing Touchwood Senior's sentiments in the next scene, when he rejoices over his cleverness in shifting all the responsibilities of fatherhood onto Whorehound's shoulders: "Fie, what a trouble have I rid my hands on; / It makes me sweat to think on't" (2.2.9–10). His point is borne out some 150 lines later when the Promoters commiserate with one another over the economic burden which the Country Wench's abandoned child will inflict upon them (ll. 157–65).

The drama's most chilling commentary on the relation of parents and children occurs in Whorehound's repentance scene. Placed near the conclusion of the play, the scene's func- tion and effect are similar to those of the final Dampit scene. Once again we encounter an aspect of life which is usually excluded from a comic world and which calls into question the ability of the genre to deal with the reality that we know.[42] As the scene opens, Allwit and his wife are apparently grief- stricken over the wound Walter has received in his duel with Touchwood Junior. Walter enters, and instead of gratefully accepting their offers of aid, he angrily rejects them both. Astounded by the knight's sudden change of heart, Allwit frantically rushes Whorehound's illegitimate children before him, extolling the praises of Wat and Nick, while Davy urges Walter to look at his new girl's pretty smile. Whorehound's response to their actions, however, is not what they expect. He turns away from his children and cries:

> O, my vengeance!
> Let me for ever hide my cursed face
> From sight of those that darken all my hopes,
> And stand between me and the sight of heaven!
> [5.1.66–69]

Cursed paradoxically recalls the "kersen" soul at the christening and thus alludes to the true spiritual worth of that entire business. The two scenes are actually parallel. In the one, a blaspheming drunken group of adults gathers and, effectively (if unwittingly), damns a child they are supposed to be blessing; in the other, illegitimate children enter to damn their begetter. *Cursed* also looks forward to the flood of curses Walter looses on the Allwits later in the scene. Curses, not blessings, dominate the Easter setting of this play. Finally, when Whorehound states that his children "darken" all his hopes, he provides the most striking enunciation of how unconventional the characters' attitudes toward their offspring are. Hope, after all, is precisely what children normally represent in the world of comedy.

Clearly, sexuality is not regenerative, and children do not redeem their parents from the ravages of time in *A Chaste Maid in Cheapside*.[43] Despite the many references to fertility and the presence of Touchwood Senior, the play basically describes a moribund society where procreation is either a source of suffering or used purely for materialistic gain. This rejection of the conventional comic view of procreation prevents us from finding significance in the play's structure by comparing it to seasonal and generational cycles of renewal, just as the characters' analogous dismissal of the spiritual meaning of Lent and Easter hinders any attempt to discover the drama's meaning in parallels between its form and that period of the Christian year. Moreover, the pessimistic view of fertility which *A Chaste Maid* conveys also affects our attitude toward the play's young lovers, Touchwood Junior and Moll, and, more specifically, toward their triumph at the drama's conclusion. In fact, a close examination of the fortunes of these two characters shows that their marriage is far different from the "comic miracle" Richard Levin finds in his reading of the play.[44]

The youths' love is qualified ironically almost from the beginning. Touchwood Junior first seeks his brother's aid in the same scene in which Touchwood Senior leaves his wife, and their discussion about the price of a marriage license (2.1.125–29) is juxtaposed to the Kixes' arguments over the money they have spent trying to ensure her pregnancy and the financial cost of their childless union in terms of lost inheritance. It is hardly an auspicious beginning for Touchwood

Junior's endeavor to bring about a marriage which traditionally is associated with harmony and rebirth. Similarly, the
extraordinary power of love does not always seem very appealing in the play. When Touchwood Junior states that Moll has
escaped from her parents by being "led through gutters, /
Strange hidden ways, which none but love could find, / Or ha'
the heart to venture" (3.3.31–33), he speaks in praise but these
"strange hidden ways" at the same time seem more than a little
defiled. And while Moll at long last emerges from journeys
through mud and filth and from dunkings in the Thames at
the hands of her mother to be resurrected in the drama's final
scene, even that scene is not without its ironies.

Superficially, the conclusion seems very conventional, but
it is undercut from the moment that Touchwood Senior
praises Moll as "the true, chaste monument of her living name"
(1.12). That name, as noted above, is nearly synonymous with
"whore," and Middleton makes sure that his audience does not
miss the pun, by having Allwit comment earlier in the play on
the corrupt practices of Promoters who confiscate meat to give
it to their favorite prostitutes, "their Molls and Dolls" (2.2.65).
The presence of the Allwits, fresh from their triumph over
Whorehound in the most callous scene in the play, further
undermines the apparent mood of idealism in the conclusion.
If anything, their cynicism is even more disturbing than before. Hearing that Tim's new Welsh bride was formerly
Whorehound's mistress, the cuckold confides to his wife, "I
think we rid our hands in good time of him," and she replies
without hesitation: "I knew he was past the best when I gave
him over" (5.4.65–66). Moreover, Kix's offer to hire
Touchwood Senior to administer his magic water to Mistress
Kix on a regular basis repeats the relationship of the Allwits
and Whorehound with little alteration.[45] This rather unattractive triangle is the only thing which is reborn in the comedy. No
new and better society rises out of the old, nor is the old
transformed. For all the bustling activity in *A Chaste Maid in
Cheapside*, the world the drama depicts remains essentially unchanged.

There is one other way in which Middleton indicates that

his play's ending is not as typical as it at first might seem. After Touchwood Junior and Moll are united, Tim enters with his new wife. For the first time his faith in the ability of language and logic to control and shape the world has been shaken. Despite his earlier boast to Maudline, Tim cannot prove a whore an honest woman. The Welshwoman, however, recognizes that the situation is not as hopeless as it seems. There is a solution, she tells her despondent husband: "If your logic cannot prove me honest, / There's a thing call'd marriage, and that makes me honest" (5.4.105–6). But her answer only increases the irony of the situation. The Welshwoman's solution is, as Maudline immediately notes, "a trick" (l.107), just as Yellowhammer's subsequent change from bewailing his son's "unfortunate marriage" (l.81) to rejoicing that "fortune seldom deals two marriages / With one hand and both lucky" (ll.113–14) is a trick.

We may want to believe him in the same way we may wish to believe that the Kix–Touchwood Senior arrangement is significantly different from the Allwit–Whorehound one. But the play will not let us. Furthermore, the notion that marriage is a potential cure for all problems is central (like the patterns of redemption and rebirth discussed above) to comedy. When Yellowhammer is told of Whorehound's evil deeds late in the drama and asks in response, "What serves marriage but to call him back?" (4.1.241; cf. 1.1.34–37), he articulates a belief which comedy often requires of its audience. But the picture of marriage *A Chaste Maid* presents is anything but desirable or redemptive.[46] As is true of the setting of the play and its fertility motifs, Middleton carefully calls our attention to an important comic convention only to debunk it. Like the various social roles in this drama and the structure of its plot, marriage becomes an empty shell—a form devoid of the content and functions which should give it meaning. Within the context of this comedy, Yellowhammer's comment on the benefits of matrimony is, after all, only the cynical statement of a corrupt and materialistic old man.

The happy ending of *A Chaste Maid in Cheapside*, therefore, is contrived and arbitrary in the worst senses of the two words. It cannot be otherwise, because Middleton has systematically destroyed any possible connection between the play's structure and the patterns of spiritual and natural renewal which, for a Renaissance audience (and for us), give comic form its significance. Divorced from the nonliterary patterns which should provide it with meaning, the form of the play is no more than an artificial exercise. And because of this obvious falsity, we are encouraged to view the play's festive conclusion with distrust, to remain distanced and vaguely uncomfortable.

Our relationship to the drama is similar to that of a spectator or participant who suddenly becomes aware of the absurdity of the game he is involved in. Indeed, the comparison is one which Middleton himself seems to have contemplated, for references to *game* and *play* are ubiquitous in the comedy from Allwit's first soliloquy (1.2.50–52) to Whorehound's final speech as he is thrown out of the Allwits' house (5.1.148–49). The drama itself has many of the characteristics of play. In *Homo Ludens*, Johan Huizinga has shown that in spite of its apparent frivolity, play is "a *significant* function" which "creates order, *is* order. Into an imperfect world and into the confusion of life it brings a temporary, a limited perfection." Ultimately, play becomes a repository of man's highest aspirations. In it "man's consciousness that he is embedded in a sacred order of things finds its first, highest, and holiest expression."[47] Huizinga's description of play might well be applied to conventional comedy. Like play, comedy presents an unreal world, but a world that is significant, ordered and embodies some of our most fervent hopes. As Northrop Frye states: "The drive to a festive conclusion . . . is the creation of a new reality out of something impossible but desirable." Thus, "in comedy we see a victory of the pleasure principle that Freud warns us not to look for in ordinary life."[48] Moreover, this paradoxical attitude which views a form—game or comedy—as unreal yet of great value also characterizes the attitudes of a great many Renaissance writers and theorists toward literature. Sidney's "golden world," for example, is an almost perfect analogue of the worlds of play and comedy which Huizinga and Frye respectively describe. It is unreal, indeed must necessarily be recognized as such, but it is also a more orderly and a more clearly meaningful world than the fallen one we live in.[49]

Middleton's comedy is a game of sorts, and at first seems very much like the kind of game Renaissance literary theorists like Sidney envision, but it is a game that has gone wrong. *A Chaste Maid in Cheapside* does not finally fit any of the above descriptions very well, and the reason for its atypical nature lies in our attitude toward its plot. To participate fully in a game or a comedy or any work of literature, we must immerse ourselves within that special world and accept its rules. This is not to say we are not aware that we are involved in something fictional, but that realization must remain, for the most part, in the back of our minds if we are to participate fully in the experience and share in its "temporary, limited perfection." We must play intensely and not question the rules while we are playing. But as I have attempted to show, Middleton makes it very difficult for us to accept the rules of his comic game by continually alerting us to its ultimate meaninglessness. The play does not provide a method of ordering our imperfect world, nor does it represent a hypothetical ideal worthy of contemplation. In a sense, the significance of this game is that it doesn't have any significance at all.

Our relationship to the drama thus closely parallels Whorehound's relationship to Allwit's playing. Just as the knight is first taken in by the cuckold's games and subsequently rejects them when he recognizes they are not the pleasant, harmlesss actions he once believed them to be, so we are slowly made aware of the shallowness of the drama's comic game and finally dismiss it as a result. We become what Huizinga calls the spoilsport, a figure who calls a game in question when he refuses to participate in it any longer: "By withdrawing from the game he [the spoilsport] reveals the relativity and fragility of the playworld in which he had temporarily shut himself with others. He robs play of its *illusion*—a pregnant word which means literally 'in-play'."[50] Huizinga's statement perfectly describes the way in which Whorehound's repentance shatters the festive veneer of the Allwit household. Likewise, it precisely characterizes how Middleton undermines any pretense of truthfulness *A Chaste Maid in Cheapside* might have by forcing its audience into a position similar to that of the spoilsport. As enjoyable as his play may appear, Middleton ensures that we cannot accept the game of comedy it portrays.

In many ways *A Chaste Maid in Cheapside* thus represents the most extensive critique of New Comedy we have examined. The play marks the end of the first phase of Middleton's career, and it is fitting that it brings together and extends several of the techniques discussed in this and the previous chapter. Both *Michaelmas Term* and *A Trick to Catch the Old One*, it was argued, subvert their New Comedy structure by filling it with characters and events which contradict normal comic assumptions and values. The same disjunction of form and content is present in *A Mad World, My Masters*, *No Wit, No Help Like a Woman's*, and *A Chaste Maid in Cheapside*, but Middleton's development of this technique in these plays is, I think, more subtle than in the dramas analyzed in Chapter 3. Instead of simply superimposing New Comedy on a world hostile to its values, Middleton examines in detail certain basic elements of comic form in order to demonstrate their inability to deal with the world as we know it. The comic conventions still are present in the plays, and at times they may seem to work in typical ways, but Middleton repeatedly demonstrates that they are empty and meaningless forms.

A Chaste Maid in Cheapside also deals with one additional theme which is central to most of the city comedies: the relationship of wit (imagination) to fertility and the power of both to create order. In Roman comedy, wit is usually closely connected with love and fertility, since the former (in the person of the *servus*) is normally used to help the young man gain his beloved and triumph over forces associated with sterility.[51] The same union of mind and body is also present in Middleton's *The Family of Love*. There Gerardine takes on the role of both trickster and lover, but he primarily employs wit as a means to win his beloved rather than material possessions. He uses wit, in other words, in the service of fertility. Gerardine's union of intelligence and love, however, is unique among the protagonists in Middleton's early comedies.

   After *The Family of Love*, wit and fertility become more and more distant from one another and at the same time seem incapable of creating the kind of order represented by Gerardine's triumph. In *Michaelmas Term* the central lover (Richard Easy) is a fool, and the play's prodigal son motifs severely qualify the comic assumption that procreation is a means of establishing continuity. The primary wit in the play, Quomodo, is an ambiguous figure, to say the least, and his endeavors to gain the stability of green fields and to oppose his son's destined fall by feigning death are unsuccessful. Witgood seems to unite intelligence and love in *A Trick to Catch the Old One*, but even his cleverness is unable to transform the world he inhabits. And whereas wit and fertility are linked verbally at several points in *A Mad World, My Masters* (3.2.244–46; 3.3.1–2, 68–70), they are not connected with one another in actuality. Neither Follywit's nor Penitent Brothel's plot has a procreative goal, and for Follywit wit is an end in itself. His attempts to "forecast" the future by means of the imagination are therefore essentially sterile. They are also failures. In *No Wit, No Help Like a Woman's*, the New Comedy hero is a prodigal and a complete fool as well, and his servant's mind is not greatly superior to his own. Likewise, Weatherwise's attempt to find order through the use of his almanac is an absurd and futile endeavor. Only Mistress Low-water seems to have some success in shaping her fortunes by the use of her intelligence, but her goal is only incidentally related to procreation.

   A Chaste Maid also considers the ability of both wit and fertility to establish order, and with similar results. The failure of the conventional functions of procreation and fertility has already been recounted, and the drama also demonstrates a parallel failure of the imagination. As in *A Mad World*, imagination and fertility are closely linked verbally—a relationship which is conveyed by the characters' association of words and sexuality. For instance, Whorehound assures his Welsh mistress that their sleeping with one another has naturally been the means of her attaining some proficiency in the English language (1.1.98–99), and at the end of the play Touchwood Senior urges his happy brother to "utter" all his joy at night (5.4.46). Part of the Kixes' problem, on the other hand, is that for them language and sexuality are opposed, an unfortunate state of affairs Touchwood Senior makes explicit when he relates their childlessness to their endless bickering and tells Kix: "Give you joy of your tongue, / There's nothing else good in you" (3.3.42–43).

The plot of *A Chaste Maid*, however, like the plot of *A Mad World, My Masters*, does not really support this verbal connection of wit and fertility for several reasons. First, no one in the comedy shows the same union of intelligence and love present in Gerardine. Touchwood Junior might be a logical choice, but his intrigues are lost in the complexity of the play, and Middleton significantly deflects credit for much of the plotting away from any of the comedy's central characters and onto a minor one, the Yellowhammers' servant Susan. Touchwood Senior is treated too ambiguously to fulfill this ideal role, and the most successful wit in *A Chaste Maid*, Allwit, will have nothing to do with love or procreation. Furthermore, the inversion of his name—"wittol"—implies that this apparent mastermind is actually only a fool. Finally, the character who most strenuously attempts to control existence imaginatively, Tim, is the most laughable figure in the drama. The play-society in *A Chaste Maid in Cheapside*, as in almost all of Middleton's comedies, is too disordered to admit any kind of order, whether it be an order embodied in children or in the constructs of the mind.

Although its critique of New Comedy is thorough and unrelenting, *A Chaste Maid in Cheapside* does not constitute Middleton's final word on the subject. In spite of the fact that he generally turned away from writing plays closely modeled on Roman comedy after this drama, Middleton's interest in exposing the fallacies of comic assumptions did not disappear. Indeed, as we shall see in Chapter 5, the heightened contrasts and conflicts of tragicomedy afforded him a particularly suitable vehicle for exploring the potentially terrifying and diabolic aspects of comedy only touched on in *Michaelmas Term* and *No Wit, No Help Like a Woman's*, among the plays discussed so far. For if from the perspective of *A Mad World, My Masters* or *A Chaste Maid in Cheapside*, comedy is a meaningless structure, from the viewpoint of *The Old Law*, it is a horrifying nightmare.

)

5
The Terror Beneath the Surface

> Open thy knees, wider, wider, wider, wider: did
> you ever see a boy dance clenched up? he needs a
> pick-lock: out upon thee for an arrant ass!
> Sinquapace, in *More Dissemblers Besides Women*
>
> Take hence that pile of years,
> Before [he] surfeit with unprofitable age,
> And with the rest, from the high promontory,
> Cast him into the sea.
> Duke Evander, in *The Old Law*

In general, Middleton's tragicomedies have not fared well with critics. Richard Barker, for example, finds them an inferior lot, and Samuel Schoenbaum warns us that in the later comedies and tragicomedies a reader must "always distinguish between those scenes that Middleton wrote without conviction, in accordance with the prevalent taste for artificial drama, and those to which he seriously applied himself." In a similar vein, Arthur Kirsch argues that Middleton's tragicomedies are often unsuccessful because he "had neither Shakespeare's interest in the resolving epiphanies of *felix culpa* nor his capacity to explore the confrontation of comic and tragic extremes."[1] All three statements imply that in turning to tragicomedy Middleton undermined his natural talents by becoming involved with a dramatic form antithetical to those talents, a form he could not become sufficiently interested in to use effectively. And this attitude does seem partially justified by the plays themselves. On the whole, Middleton's tragicomedies are not as successful as either his city comedies or his tragedies, and they appear to play a transitional role between the early comedies and the late tragic masterpieces.[2]

The tragicomedies differ from the comedies in several ways. Their settings are sometimes more exotic—Milan, Epirus, Ravenna, rather than the streets of London—and the plots give proportionally much more attention to romantic love and idealistic sentiment. Middleton also emphasizes characterization more strongly than in the city comedies (particularly in regard to female figures), and while his interest in the ordering and controlling powers of wit declines, his interest in the influence of sexuality within human society becomes much greater. Thus, as we shall see, *More Dissemblers Besides Women* is truly the fertility play *A Chaste Maid in Cheapside* only appears to be, a fact forcefully symbolized by the pregnant Page's dance near the end of that drama.

Despite these (and other) changes in emphasis, however, the tragicomedies are not—especially from the perspective of Middleton's concern with comic conventions—radically different from his early comedies.[3] Indeed, some of the elements which are usually brought forward to explain the later dramas' inferiority—the rapid reversals of character, the stark contrasts and improbable resolutions—are (as has been shown) present in plays written throughout Middleton's career. *The Witch*, for example, depicts a world of lust, intrigue, and grotesque discords which both is reminiscent of the darker aspects of the city comedies and looks forward to the corrupt society of *Women Beware Women*. Its conclusion is so fantastic that it calls itself into question. (Antonio inexplicably falls to his death through a hidden trap door and so permits the heroine, Isabella, to marry her first love, Sebastian.) *A Fair Quarrel* juxtaposes the noble sentiments of Captain Ager and the Colonel to the nonsensical ranting of Chough and Trimtram and suggests in the process that the idealized code of honor which forms the basis of the former characters' actions is as incapable of dealing with the complexities of existence as the comic ideals examined in Middleton's earlier plays. More important, Middleton's analysis of comic assumptions continues in two of his tragicomedies, *More Dissemblers Besides Women* and *The Old Law*, and this continuation is not accidental. It was inevitable, I think, that Middleton associated the newest of Jacobean dramatic forms with the one he had been immersed in for the first decade of his career and that in doing so he found the values of tragicomedy equally untenable.[4]

While discussing in Chapter 1 the possible relationship of Middleton's use of comic and tragic elements to tragicomic theory, I noted that Guarini envisioned his new dramatic hybrid as a harmonious mixture of two imperfect genres, as a golden mean which avoids the excesses of both tragedy and comedy. I also pointed out that Renaissance tragicomedy is an optimistic form. Closely allied to the *felix culpa* pattern which Renaissance Christians discovered in their individual lives as well as in the history of mankind, the form reflects their confidence that man had truly found the road to salvation. More important, we saw that all of these characteristics—moderation, inclusiveness, harmony, optimism—are essentially comic ones.[5] In spite of the genre's exotic scenes and noble characters, the harmonies which Guarini was so fond of are actually a more dignified variation of the harmonies we find in most comic conclusions. As Guarini himself states (see Chapter 1 above), Renaissance tragicomedy is basically a more serious and aristocratic relative of Renaissance comedy, a fact that Middleton undoubtedly was aware of.

But to Middleton tragicomedy was more than just another expression of harmony which had no basis in reality (although it certainly was that). The new form provided him with an opportunity to develop the darker and more disturbing aspects of comedy only briefly considered in his earlier plays. Cyrus Hoy has shown that Renaissance tragicomedy was inherently an "uneasy fusion" of two normally antithetical elements—"the comic logic of its formal design and the irrational pathos let loose within this symmetrical structure when love—the natural subject of comedy—is raised unnaturally to a tragic power." Middleton found in this mixture of formal design and irrational pathos a means of revealing the potentially demonic energy which lies beneath the surface of Roman comedy but which, in Jackson Cope's words, is "only wanly echoed in society and sentiment and the semblance of order which rationalizes it as New Comedy."[6] For although closely connected at its deepest levels with ritual celebrations of rebirth and renewal, Roman comedy is a remarkably socialized genre. The society it depicts is completely humanized and comfortably recognizable. It is not frightening or mysterious. In *Michaelmas Term* and *No Wit, No Help Like a Woman's*, Middleton begins to peer beneath this palliative veneer to uncover some of the less reassuring impulses behind New Comedy's apparently benign surface, but many of the more unsettling incidents in the city comedies (the Dampit scenes or Whorehound's confession, for example) are, essentially, anticomic elements let loose within a comic framework in order to expose the limitations of that framework.

In the plays analyzed below, however, the more diabolic episodes depict characters and events which are firmly rooted in traditional comedy but which in the context of these plays arouse discomfort instead of mirth. The dark side of these dramas is inextricably intertwined with their comic form and, indeed, is generated by that form. Their terrors are truly comic ones. Middleton initiates this examination of the fearful aspects of New Comedy somewhat tentatively at first, reworking in *More Dissemblers Besides Women* concerns which he had already dealt with from a different vantage point in earlier plays: the movement from restriction to freedom depicted in *The Family of Love* and the emphasis on fertility within *A Chaste Maid in Cheapside*. But in *The Old Law* this tentativeness disappears as Middleton separates comedy from its usual civilized trappings and describes a triumph of comic values which is terrifying.

More Dissemblers Besides Women begins with a song praising the Duchess of Milan's chastity. In it the Duchess is presented as an ideal figure. Her actions are exemplary of true feminine virtue: "To be chaste is woman's glory, / 'Tis her fame and honour's story" (1.1.1–2).[7] The song invites its audience (both in and out of the play) to "come and read her life and praise" (l.5), and two of the characters onstage, a young gallant named Lactantio and his beloved Aurelia, comply. From their discussion we learn that the Duchess has remained constant to a vow of chastity made seven years earlier. Lactantio asks his beloved to make a similar pledge: "What wouldst thou do, faith, now, / If I were dead?" (ll.19–20); and she replies that she would surpass the Duchess by also dying. At the beginning of act 2 the Duchess and her mentor the Cardinal reenact the occasion of her vow. We see that the Duke was himself an ideal figure, a man who passed away to a life of "quiet satisfaction" and "peace" (2.1.86–87) speaking *de contemptu mundi* and warning the Cardinal against guile and his wife against inconstancy. The Duchess, in turn, pledged at her husband's bedside to avoid a prodigal "forgetfulness" (l.72) which would enable her to marry a second time.

But just as the Duke has died, so the ideals he cherished have died with him. The Cardinal will soon become the most artful of manipulators, and the Duchess (as we already know by this point) has newly fallen in love. Like so many of Middleton's plays, *More Dissemblers Besides Women* invokes a distant golden past, a time, according to the Duchess, "when love was simple / And knew no art or guile" (4.2.187–88). The world the play describes, on the other hand, is one of mutability and deception. It is, as the Duchess again points out, "greedy of gain, either by fraud or stealth; / And whilst one toils, another gets the wealth" (3.2.124–25). Thus it is not surprising that the two characters who hear the opening song lack any real understanding of what it is about. Lactantio has already deserted a woman he made pregnant who is now disguised as his page, and later in the play he will turn away Aurelia for the Duchess. Aurelia has likewise rejected her former lover, General Andrugio, and her commitment to chastity is not, to say the least, a wholehearted one. And when the Cardinal later fervidly urges the Duchess to revive her faith in "eternal things" (2.1.104) after he learns that she has fallen in love, he only emphasizes

the irony of his own later change of heart toward her desire to
remarry, once he believes that the object of her desire is his
nephew Lactantio.

In spite of the talk of constancy, vows, and promises in the
opening scenes, change is a way of life for all the characters.
Like the individuals in *A Mad World* and *A Chaste Maid*, they
never seem able to escape the limitations of their fallen existence.[8] When we first see her, the Duchess is a saintly symbol of
all that is good in woman. Indeed, she is so virtuous that she
becomes pompous. When the Cardinal and the nobles urge
her to leave her seclusion and reenter society, she replies by
comparing her virtue to a bright light which shines amidst the
obscurities of an imperfect world:

> I'll come forth
> And show myself to all; the world shall witness,
> That, like the sun, my constancy can look
> On earth's corruptions, and shine clear itself.
>
> [1.3.54–57]

The Duchess's self-assurance, however, is not well-founded.
One short glimpse of "earth's corruptions" in the person of
General Andrugio causes her to fall in love, break her vow, and
ultimately confess with a total lack of irony, "I'm mortal"
(1.107). And she certainly is. Spurred by love, the Duchess
becomes one of the most cunning dissemblers in the play.

The Cardinal undergoes a similar transformation. He too
is more than a little a little enamored of his own worth. He
enters the play apparently praising the Duchess, but in truth
praising himself:

> I shall not be at peace till I make perfect:
> I'll make her victory harder; 'tis my crown
> When I bring grace to great'st perfection.
>
> [1.2.44–46]

The frequency of first person pronouns in this and all of the
Cardinal's speeches is the mark of a great egotist. In fact, when
discussing the Duchess with his noble companions, the Cardinal steps into the role of God boasting to Satan (the lords) about
the virtues of his servant Job (the Duchess). "She's my religious
triumph" (1.64), he says. Like his nephew, the Duchess is one of

his many "good works" (l.131). Moreover, when the Cardinal learns that the Duchess has suddenly fallen in love, his reaction focuses more on his own losses than on the woman's predicament. "If she be lost, / I know not where to seek my hope in woman," he laments, for "I have undone my judgment, lost my praises, / Blemish'd the truth of my opinion" (2.1.95–96, 111–12). But the Duchess's sudden change is more than another chance for the Cardinal to reveal his overly developed sense of self. After she tricks him by saying that she is in love with his nephew Lactantio rather than Andrugio, he begins to move away from his strict religious asceticism and otherworldly concerns. The Cardinal sets "holy anger by awhile" (2.2.2) and become more flexible, more humane. He decides to aid this potential union and, by the end of the play, becomes one of its chief spokesmen for fertility and marriage, although, like Bounteous Progress, he is a somewhat flawed (and certainly self-serving) representative of comic values. And as in the case of his protégée, when the Cardinal turns toward things of the world, he turns toward trickery and deceit.

The changes in the behavior of these two exalted personages are indicative of the way in which everything in *More Dissemblers Besides Women* moves from the ideal to the real, the spiritual to the physical. Because ideals reside outside of time, they have no place in the fallen mutable world the play describes. They belong, like the Duke, to a bygone era. They remain, like Quomodo's green fields or Follywit's simple and innocent virgin bride, totally apart from the lives of the characters. In fact, the value of constancy itself is questioned in the play. After learning of the Duchess's apparent love for his nephew, the Cardinal approaches the nobles and suggests that the woman's vow of chastity is perhaps not completely beneficial. He fears that they may have "sinn'd / In too much strictness" (3.1.297–98) when they urged the Duchess to be faithful to her vow. Indeed, her firm chastity no longer seems admirable: "She cannot truly be call'd constant now, / If she persèver, rather obstinate" (ll.301–2). As usual the Cardinal is arguing in behalf of his own interests (he wants the Duchess to marry Lactantio), but his new evaluation of the Duchess's actions is

accepted without opposition. The metamorphosis of constancy
from a great virtue to a form of stubbornness and obstinancy in
a discussion of some one hundred lines is perhaps the most
emphatic demonstration of the mutability of almost everything
in the play.

Mutability, however, is not necessarily negative—at least
from a comic viewpoint. The movement toward the human,
toward moderation, flexibility, and change is, as was noted in
Chapter 2, essentially a comic movement. *The Family of Love*
also stresses this aspect of comic structure, and the two plays
have much in common. The comic conflict between the forces
of fertility and sterility, or freedom and restriction, so literally
described in the earlier play, is here mingled with a struggle
between chastity and love.[9] This last opposition is introduced
in the opening scene of the drama. After he has listened to the
song which begins the play, Lactantio explains to Aurelia that
the "strange great widow" has "stiffly" vowed to remain chaste
(1.9), an explanation which does not present her actions in a
very positive light, and shortly afterward a lord comments:
"She's too constant, that's her fault" (1.2.40). Cupid's song,
which concludes the masque celebrating Andrugio's return
from battle in act 1, scene 3, again draws our attention to this
central conflict, because it both recalls, by contrast, the song in
praise of the Duchess's chastity and announces that chastity's
defeat as she falls in love with the general. And when the
Cardinal attempts to urge the nephew whom he mistakenly
believes an enemy of all womankind to marry the Duchess, the
opposition of love and chastity is defined in terms even more
typically comic. He reminds Lactantio of the "present barren-
ness" of their house (3.1.153) and the necessity for a "fruitfull
life" (1.156).

Similar kinds of references and images pervade his parallel
discussion with the Duchess shortly after. Fearful that she will
return to her former strictness, the Cardinal assures her that
"fruitfulness / Is part of the salvation of your sex," and urges:
"Unbound a forcèd vow . . . Sinful i' th' fastening" (4.2.31–32,
37–39). As in *The Family of Love*, Middleton conventionally
maps out a conflict of fertility and sterility by associating the

former with words connoting freedom (*unbound, recreation*)
and the latter with words conveying a sense of imprisonment
(*stiffly, forced, fastening*). The mutability that from a moral
Christian standpoint is the product of Adam's curse, from a
comic perspective provides a way toward a natural form of
salvation. Within a comic framework the Duchess's vow of
chastity is evil and unnatural. It is a kind of death. As flawed as
the Cardinal's motives may be, his argument is, from a comic
viewpoint, unassailable. "Fruitfulness" is the only key to im-
mortality in the world these characters inhabit.

The most important way in which Middleton links restriction to sterility is through his use of the commonplace association of chastity with a strong fortress.[10] The Cardinal, for
example, mistakenly believes that Lactantio is one whom "chastity locks up" (3.1.202), and the Duchess laments over her
"vow's breach" after she falls in love with Andrugio (3.2.21; cf.
1.1.11–13). The attempt of Aurelia's father to imprison her in
order to prevent her marriage to Lactantio is a literal version of
the convention. Significantly, the old suitor whom her father
forces upon her is the "Governor of the Fort," and Aurelia
herself makes explicit the connection of the fortress with a
chastity which is itself a form of unnatural restriction. Fer-
vently praying that Lactantio "would seek some means to free
me from this place," she complains: " 'Tis prisonment enough
to be a maid" (2.3.30–31). Aurelia, however, is too wild and
free to be bound by her father's wishes for very long. She
escapes with the aid of her former lover Andrugio. And Aurelia's release represents more than a victory of young love
over parental opposition. It is also carefully linked with fertility, by the allusions to childbirth in her discussion of the escape
plot with the general:

ANDRUGIO: Violence I will not use; I come a friend;
        'Twere madness to force that which wit can end.
AURELIA: Most virtuously deliver'd!
ANDRUGIO: Thou'rt in raptures.
AURELIA: My love, my love!
ANDRUGIO: Most virtuously deliver'd!
        Spoke like the sister of a puritan midwife!
                                [2.3.64–68]

Aurelia's imprisonment and escape is thus analogous to the pervasive emphasis on purgation in *The Family of Love*. In both cases our attention is called to the comic movement from restriction to freedom, and in both that movement is related to a triumph of fertility over sterility. Aurelia's escape from a castle governed by an "old dried neat's tongue" (1.2.190) symbolizes her release from the rigid and life-denying vows of chastity and her acceptance of woman's role as giver of new life. Presumably, the Duchess's rejection of her former constancy has the same significance.

But there is more to Aurelia's escape than this. Aurelia is able to flee because she is disguised as a gipsy, and when she exits from the fortress she suddenly wanders into the midst of a gipsy camp. The gipsies enter the drama at the beginning of act 4 as masters of disguise and deception in a play full of disguises and deceptions. As such, they provide a fitting climax to all of the dissembling and intrigues in the comedy. At the same time, they represent an existence of freedom and ease, the very freedom Aurelia is seeking by breaking her father's decrees. Lactantio's servant Dondolo alludes to this function early in the drama: "As you know," he tells Lactantio, "A merry fellow may pass anywhere" (3.1.31–32), and gipsies "live the merriest lives" of all (l.110). Thus, Dondolo decides not to remain in Lactantio's service because, he states, "I scorn to serve anybody; I am more gipsy-minded than so" (4.1.78–79).

The gipsy camp itself is a world of misrule, a topsy-turvy realm whose nature is best described by the Captain's strange assertion that in his language *arsinio* means nose and *nosario* the hind quarter of a woman (4.1.244–48). The gipsies' nearly incomprehensible language, their purported powers of fortune telling, and blackened faces are all indications of their distance from the normal world and values of the play. Moreover, despite their obvious amorality, the kind of freedom which Middleton associates with the gipsies is markedly different from the freedom of Allwit in *A Chaste Maid* and the various prodigals in *Michaelmas Term*. As in *The Family of Love*, freedom here seems genuinely desirable, genuinely redemptive, for these extraordinary creatures are intimately con-

nected with fertility. As soon as Dondolo proves himself
worthy to be a member of their company, the Captain of the
gipsies offers him a gift which will both be a source of personal
pleasure and ensure the renewal of the community he has just
become part of:

> Thou shalt have all thy heart requires:
> First, here's a girl for thy desires;
> This doxy fresh, this new-come dell,
> Shall lie by thy sweet side and swell.
> Get me gipsies brave and tawny,
> With cheek full plump and hip full brawny.
>
> [4.1.195–200]

Likewise, at the end of the scene the Captain describes their
new booty in terms reminiscent of pregnancy—"Our wealth
swells high, my boys," he sings (l.302)—and the gipsies exit in a
strange dance which anticipates the Page's efforts to please her
dancing master Sinquapace at the moment she is about to give
birth to her child.

The gipsies' behavior is the extreme opposite of the
Duchess's chaste constancy at the beginning of the play. They
are the culminating symbol of the state of mutability toward
which *More Dissemblers Besides Women* steadily develops. Their
trickery is a heightened version of the dissembling of everyone
in the drama. At the same time, this trickery is closely connected with fertility, just as all of the other characters' intrigues
involve love. Thus the play is organized around two opposing
sets of attitudes and actions. On one hand, ideals, constancy,
chastity, restriction, and sterility are associated with one
another. On the other, mutability, deception, love, freedom,
and fertility are intimately related. The contrast which the play
draws between these two groups is conventional. Anticomic
values are confronted by comic values and eventually defeated: the Duchess rejects her vow of chastity; the Cardinal
aids rather than hinders the forces of love; Aurelia outwits her
father's endeavors to marry her to the Governor of the Fort.

But paradoxically, this apparent triumph of freedom and
fertility does not affect us in the same way that it does in *The
Family of Love*. Indeed, there seems to be too much freedom in

More Dissemblers Besides Women, even for comedy. Like the prodigals in *Michaelmas Term*, the characters forget too easily and change too rapidly, moving from partner to partner with a compulsiveness which rivals Follywit's commitment to trickery. The play provides no constant focus for audience identification, and as a result, our sympathies become as mutable as its world. As in *A Chaste Maid in Cheapside* or *A Mad World, My Masters*, characters who at times speak for positive comic values (Aurelia, the Cardinal, the lords) are undercut by the inconsistency of what they do and say. No one in the play seems admirable for very long, and our attempts to find a recipient for our sympathies and to fall into a stable pattern of expectation and response are frustrated again and again.[11]

Lactantio and Aurelia at first appear to be the nominal hero and heroine of the drama, the kind of conventional lovers which might be found in any number of Renaissance comedies. We initially see them pledging their love to one another, and their union is opposed by two typical blocking figures, her father and Lactantio's uncle, the Cardinal. When Lactantio confides that he must dissemble his love by pretending to be a youthful misogynist in order to gull his uncle, his resort to intrigue parallels that of comic protagonists extending back to Plautus and Terence. The Cardinal's actions during his first appearance in act 1, scene 2, are equally typical. He praises the Duchess's chastity and asserts that he is an enemy to love and all things youthful, assuring the lords that he has "ever been in youth an old man / To pleasures and to women" (ll.9–10), and later lauding his nephew's seeming commitment "to old men's goodnesses and gravities" (l.82). Middleton could scarcely have described a conflict between youth and age which appears more conventional than this one.

However, by the end of the second scene we also have our first hint that Aurelia and Lactantio may not be the kind of characters they seem to be. Lactantio's Page states that she is pregnant by him, and Aurelia mentions that she formerly loved General Andrugio, defending her new choice (Lactan-

tio) in words which ironically recall the Cardinal's religious
jargon: "My eye ne'er knew / A perfect choice till I stood bless'd
with you," she tells her new lover (ll.182–83). Finally, like Philip
Twilight in *No Wit, No Help Like a Woman's*, Lactantio gradually
reveals himself to be a rather poor imitation of Middleton's
former trickster-heroes. When Aurelia is taken prisoner by her
father and the Governor of the Fort, he is helpless and laments
in a moment of uncharacteristic insight: " 'Tis a labour / To
keep those little wits I have about me" (ll.227–28). But the
disclosures about the pasts of Lactantio and Aurelia and about
the former's lack of intelligence are not, I think, enough to
alienate us completely from the two characters at this point. As
noted above, Middleton's initial handling of these figures is,
until the middle of the second scene, totally traditional, and the
situation which we are watching is so familiar that we are
encouraged to ignore these early signs that all is not right. The
second scene itself, moreover, ends with a typical New Comedy
vow: "Love bless us with some means to get together / And I'll
pay all the old reckonings" (ll.241–42), Lactantio promises, in
the hope of regaining his beloved.

It is soon evident, however, that these two individuals, like
everything else in the play, are much less ideal that they first
appear. More important, they no longer fit the roles of comic
hero and heroine very well. Lactantio reinforces his foolishness by arriving at the victory parade in honor of Andrugio
garishly dressed in black and yellow (2.1.12), and a lord's aside
concerning Lactantio's hatred for the general reveals another
rather unsavory aspect of the Cardinal's nephew, intimating
for the first time that there will be a shift in protagonist. When
Lactantio learns that the Duchess is ostensibly in love with him,
he rejects Aurelia and with her the conventional opposition of
their love and parental desires which opened the play. And
finally, his cruel treatment of the Page (3.1.) destroys whatever
sympathy we have left for him. Unlike Witgood in *A Trick to
Catch the Old One* and Touchwood Senior in *A Chaste Maid in
Cheapside*, he displays no feelings for a woman he formerly
seduced. Thus, when Andrugio contemptuously dismisses his

antagonist before the Duchess late in the drama, his words merely reemphasize a folly which the play has already made unmistakable:

> But, chaste lady,
> Out of the bounty of your grace, permit not
> This perfum'd parcel of curl'd powder'd hair
> To cast me in the poor relish of his censure.
>
> [4.2.120–24]

Our identification with Aurelia is similarly undermined in the course of the play, primarily because of her treatment of her former lover, Andrugio. For although she no longer loves the general, Aurelia tricks him into helping her escape from the fort by pretending that she will marry him once she is free. In Aurelia's opinion, Andrugio is a "good kind gentleman to serve our turn with," but Lactantio is a "stuff / Will wear out two of him, and one finer two" (2.3.94–96). Her statement reflects both her inability to judge the true qualities of the men in her life and also ironically anticipates Lactantio's dismissal of her in favor of the Duchess. Neither character seems able to comprehend the possibility of a love that is lasting.

More Dissemblers Besides Women thus requires its audience to alter the focus of its sympathy halfway through the play. Middleton repeats a technique he employed earlier in *Michaelmas Term* with a similarly ambiguous and disconcerting effect. The two characters who replace Aurelia and Lactantio as the center of interest are the Duchess and Andrugio, but even here there are problems. Andrugio is a very ineffectual hero, and the Duchess, although far more clever, chooses to remain chaste at the end of the drama instead of marrying the general as we would normally expect. Middleton prevents a typical resolution of this romantic interest by complicating it in much the same way he complicates Rearage's love for Susan in *Michaelmas Term*. Just as in the earlier play Susan at first unconventionally loves Lethe rather than the gallant, so in *More Dissemblers Besides Women* Andrugio loves Aurelia rather than the Duchess, a much worthier partner. The drama's two new protagonists thus cannot join in the type of union which traditionally concludes comedy and which Middleton's play leads us to anticipate. At the same time, Andrugio's true love, Aurelia, similarly spurns him for a lesser figure, Lactantio.

All of these complications in what seems to begin as a standard New Comedy plot lead to a highly ironic conclusion. When the Duchess learns from a servant that Andrugio has been seen wooing a gipsy, she summons the gipsy to her quarters. Aurelia enters soon afterward in disguise and with her face smeared gipsy fashion with dark grease. The Duchess looks at her rival and, with a naiveté which is astonishing after all the dissembling she has seen and been involved in, assumes that Andrugio must be mad to love a creature as "tawny" (5.2.11) as this one. The Duchess inexplicably believes that outer appearances coincide with inner worth, a belief which a few lines later leads her to complain that her servant "decays / In beauty and discretion" (ll. 30–31). And so, when Aurelia reenters without her disguise, the Duchess no longer questions Andrugio's feelings; her rival is more beautiful and thus more worthy: "I confess / I have no wrong at all; she's younger, fairer" (ll. 127–28; cf. ll. 60–66). Andrugio suffers from a similarly deluded faith in the unity of beauty and virtue. When he steps forward to defend his love in the same scene, he bases his defense on outer appearances and argues:

> If here be either baseness of descent,
> Rudeness of manners, or deformity
> In face or fashion, I have lost, I'll yield it.
>
> [ll. 114–16]

But by this point the audience is well aware that Aurelia's exterior charms conceal a much less attractive interior, and as if to reaffirm this judgment, Aurelia displays more than enough "rudeness of manner" in the lines which follow. She suddenly spurns Andrugio for Lactantio, who in turn rejects her because he believes the Duchess is in love with him. Total confusion results. Eventually, however, everything is straightened out; and Aurelia is reunited with the general, Lactantio with the Page, and the Duchess with her vow of chastity. The play has come full circle.[12] Furthermore, despite the apparent movement of the play-society from restriction to freedom, there is an element of restraint in each solution.

Lactantio is "provided for / According to his merits" (ll.211–12) but against his will. Aurelia turns back to Andrugio because of an inner compulsion to bear children. Noting that she was "nineteen yesterday" she recalls a promise "to have a child by twenty, if not twain" (ll.156–57). The Duchess pledges to "bind" herself "more strictly" than before (l.200), and when she calls the thoughts she will have in retirement "fruitfull" (l.204), the word's association with fertility ironically underlines the fact that in her case, at least, the forces of sterility have triumphed. Even the Cardinal's charitable treatment of his nephew is compelled, although much more subtly. The Duchess overcomes his anger with the "meek virtue" (l.247) of a large marriage dowry for Lactantio and the Page.

Surprisingly, *More Dissemblers Besides Women* ends with all of the major characters accepting or acknowledging various forms of restriction. The play's emphasis on the comic movement from bondage to freedom leads first to a dislocation of normal channels of audience sympathy, and then to the unexpected disclosure that almost all of the characters lack real freedom. Only Dondolo, we may remember, stays with the gipsies. Everyone else remains bound. The society which the play depicts is not transformed for the better through misrule, for unlike most comedies the play never establishes a middle ground between misrule and restraint. There are at the end of the plot two extreme states in the drama—total inconstancy and anarchy (represented by the gipsies) and restriction of one kind or another (associated with all of the other characters). And the two are not synthesized within the type of society conventional comedy usually affirms, a society freer than that with which the comedy began but more orderly than the anarchy which brought about the overthrow of the society which existed at the opening of the play. To understand more fully the reasons for the inability of the play's central characters to remain free, however, we must examine some key patterns of imagery in the drama.

The world of the gipsies, as noted above, is one of freedom and contentment. Their song invites its listeners to "come live with us, come live with us, / All you that love your eases"

(4.1.107–8). But for most of the other characters in the drama, life is an eternal contest and struggle. Thus, one lord complains that the Duchess's untried virtue is only partial; because she "has no temptation set before her, / Her virtue has no conquest" (1.2.31–32). The Cardinal replies that he will make the Duchess more perfect by making her "victory harder" (l.45). And although at the beginning of the drama the Duchess feels that her chastity is "arm'd now / 'Gainst all deserts in man" (1.3.19–20), the Cardinal subsequently confronts her with a new test of will, announcing, "I bring war," and telling her, "if now you conquer, / You crown my praises double" (1.3.29–30; cf. 2.2.18–21). The Duchess, of course, is soon "conquered" by the attractions of General Andrugio, a conquest which literally embodies the age-old comparison of human passion with warfare and which indicates another struggle in the drama, one which does not deal with virtue or with chastity, but with love.[13] As the Duchess laments, Andrugio has "won another field since [the battle], and a victory / That credits all the rest" (1.3.115–16). And later in the play when the Duchess decides to call Andrugio's "faith in war now into question" (3.2.67), she is really planning to test his love. Likewise, the Cardinal believes that marriage is a just and honorable battle (4.2.19–22), because, he explains, "the hard war / Of chastity is held a virtuous strife, / As rare in marriage as in single life" (3.1.269–71).

What is most important about these passages is that they portray almost all human behavior as a hard struggle against alien forces. The peace which is often invoked in the drama (1.2.136–37; 1.3.1–5, 122–27) is lost for most of the characters. Moreover, these struggles, whether they have to do with chastity or with love, are inevitably restrictive. Thus, when the Cardinal speaks of freeing the Duchess from her hard vow never to marry again, he surprisingly employs metaphors of restraint: "We'll knit such knots of argument so fast, / All wit shall not undo in haste" (3.1.310–11). Likewise, at the moment Aurelia escapes from the fort, reenacting the comic movement from restriction to freedom and chastity to love, Andrugio is imprisoned by the Duchess because of her love for him. Both Aurelia's freedom and Andrugio's imprisonment therefore reflect the workings of love. And if Aurelia's statements at the end of the comedy about her compulsion to bear children are given the attention they deserve, it is evident that her escape from the fort does not make her free at all. She simply becomes bound in another way. Aurelia's release and Andrugio's imprisonment are, in fact, very nearly the same thing. Both pay tribute to the dominance of human passion in the world of the play.

Instead of conventionally being associated with freedom and the overthrow of unnatural restraints, love is always a restrictive force in *More Dissemblers Besides Women*. Its power is the only constant in the play and controls the actions of all of the major characters either directly or indirectly. During the victory masque in act 1, scene 3, Cupid instructs his female audience that the ability to accept or reject lovers "is not power in you, fair beauties; / If I command love, 'tis your duties" (ll.87–88), and the truth of his words is stressed throughout the drama. Aurelia is the character most susceptible to the power of passion, and Cupid's song significantly echoes her earlier confession to Lactantio that "the power of love commands me" (1.1.66; cf. ll.34–36). The lack of reference to a specific lover in her statement helps explain her otherwise inexplicable rejection of Andrugio for Lactantio and her subsequent reacceptance of the general. Her actions are beyond her rational control. Likewise, when Andrugio questions her faithfulness to him as they plan her escape, her affirmative answer is not the outright lie it at first seems. Aurelia is really swearing allegiance to her hope of "fruitfulness, / Love, and agreement, the three joys of marriage!" (2.3.52–53), rather than to any individual. Aurelia, furthermore, is not the only person in this comedy whose actions are totally dominated by the forces of love. The Duchess loses her "liberty" and "peace" because of love (1.3.126), yet ironically believes that she can "freely" offer a "constant heart" to Andrugio (4.2.181–82). And Lactantio speaks more truth than he knows when, in his feigned role as a young celibate, he attacks this passion before his uncle:

> 'Tis such a madness,
> There is no cure for't; no physician

> Ever spent hour about it, for they guess'd
> 'Twas all in vain when they first lov'd themselves.
>
> . . . .
>
> . . . [to] live a prisoner to a woman's eye:
> Can there be greater thraldom, greater folly?

[1.2.116–30]

Within the context of this play, his final question is a rhetorical one.

The "madness" which Lactantio describes is so pervasive and so dominant in *More Dissemblers Besides Women* that at times it borders on the demonic. Aurelia's frantic drive to bear children before she is twenty, for example, finds an analogue in the fantastic actions of a Tangle or a Dampit. All three characters act as if they are possessed, and the same is true, although to a lesser extent, of many of the individuals in *More Dissemblers Besides Women*. The play contains several allusions to a dark and mysterious world which lies behind its characters' compulsive dissembling in the name of love. The most obvious are the frequent references to physical deformity.[14] Lactantio, for instance, distrusts the ugly appearance of Aurelia's servant; after Aurelia is captured, he believes that the servant has betrayed them and vows: "I'll never trust slave with a parboil'd nose again" (1.2.230). Andrugio's nose is also scarred, although from a wound in battle (2.3.7–11). The servant thus symbolically foreshadows the man who thwarts Lactantio's interests not only in Aurelia but also in the Duchess. And because Andrugio's deformity associates him with mysterious forces which lie outside of normal life, it provides (together with his connection with both love and war) an explanation of why he is the most fitting partner for Aurelia. Similarly, the gipsies' blackened appearance, as well as their skill as shape-changers and their curious language, suggest that they too are linked with the demonic world. Aurelia's disguise as a gipsy is therefore especially appropriate, and when Andrugio finds the Duchess's advances a "strange language" (4.2.194), his description is intended, I believe, to remind us of the gipsies' equally peculiar speech. As a result, her sudden love also takes on mysterious overtones.

The most important symbol of the demonic energies of love and fertility in *More Dissemblers Besides Women* is the dance of the pregnant Page in act 5, scene 1. Like other parallel episodes in Middleton's plays—Dampit's drunken stupor in *A Trick* and Whorehound's confession in *A Chaste Maid*, for example—it occurs near the conclusion of the comedy and thus strongly influences our final judgment of and reaction to the work. It is in every sense the climax of the play, and all of the motifs discussed above are developed to their fullest in this scene. The Page's disguise itself verges on the demonic. As William Willeford states, the "transvestism so common in ceremonial clowning and in saturnalian festivals has deep roots in fertility magic . . . . The reversal of sex roles activated the demonic . . . since these roles are fundamental to the cultural life that holds the demonic at a distance."[15] Dondolo's punning exasperation with the Page points to the sexual anarchy inherent in her disguise (1.4), and her dance is preceded by an almost endless series of sexual allusions. The Page arrives to sing a "prick-song," and almost immediately has a longing to bite off the very long and obviously very phallic nose of one of the musicians (ll.8–14). The frequent references to musical *cliffs* are also bawdy descriptions of female anatomy (*OED*). More in keeping with the outcome of the episode, Crotchet's name signifies both a musical note and a hooklike instrument employed in obstetrical surgery.[16] The presence of the dancing master and fiddler, Sinquapace, similarly may have sexual overtones, since *to fiddle* is to take liberties with a woman (*OED*). And in fact, Sinquapace tells the Page's coquettish companion Celia that "gentlewomen that are good scholars / Will come as near their masters as they can"; indeed, "some lie with 'em for their better understanding" (5.1.126–28). Later in the scene he obscenely urges Nicholao to "enter" the Page, "For the fool's bashful, as they're all at first, / Till they be once well enter'd" (ll.164–66).

But we are hardly prepared for the grotesque dance that follows. The pregnant Page stumbles about clutching her knees in an attempt to delay the inevitable, while Sinquapace circles around her and gestures wildly in an absurd yet frightening parody of a fertility dance, shouting with more truth than he knows:

> Open thy knees; wider, wider, wider, wider: did you ever see a boy dance clenched up? he needs a pick-lock. . . .a pox, his knees are soldered together, they're sewed together: canst not stride? O, I could eat thee up, I could eat thee up, and begin upon thy hinder quarter, thy hinder quarter! I shall never teach this boy without a screw; his knees must be opened with a vice, or there's no good to be done upon him.   [ll. 190–204]

The Page collapses, and Nicholao fears she is dying. But the Page suddenly calls for a midwife, and life miraculously emerges out of death, to the dancing master's utter astonishment:

> A midwife? by this light, the boy's with child!
> A miracle! some woman is the father.
> The world's turn'd upside down.
>
> [ll.224–26]

Sinquapace's wonder is certainly justified, but he has not witnessed, as he believes, an inversion of the natural order. In truth, his wonder arises from a glimpse of the awesome power of renewal inherent in human generation. And the dancing master's reaction to the Page's grotesquely comic and, at the same time, intensely disturbing dance is, I think, intended to direct ours. Middleton places before us a powerful example of the rebirth celebrated by all comedy, but usually from a comfortably symbolic distance. Forces which in conventional comedy are figuratively intimated by conflicts of youth and age and marriages of young lovers are here concretely depicted onstage. And in their unadorned form, these forces are not altogether in keeping with the normally benign, socialized surface we expect of comedy.

The sudden loosening of the Page's locked thighs and the "miraculous" childbirth which results parallel the images of birth which surround Aurelia's escape from the fort. Both episodes seem at first to constitute a movement from bondage to freedom and might remind us of a similar association of this movement with childbirth in *The Family of Love*. But the close resemblance only emphasizes how greatly Middleton's handling of this motif has changed. *The Family of Love* truly celebrates a comic release of energy. There the powers of love and fertility, as strong and as pervasive as they are, still seem attractive. Their effect on the characters' lives may be ludicrous at times, but that is the worst that can be said. In *More Dissemblers Besides Women*, however, love is not a relatively harmless force. It is a form of bondage, and the events of the drama and the play's extensive comparison of love and war illuminate a dark side of human passion which comedy normally overlooks. As the Duchess notes at the moment she first succumbs to this passion, "Love and death / Are brothers in this kingdom" (1.3.111–12). And the Page's deathlike collapse at the end of her dance, followed by a birth of new life which is the first fruit of her love for Lactantio, testifies to the truth of the Duchess's words. Similarly, seen face to face, fertility itself is not the unambiguous blessing comedy would lead us to believe it is. No longer distanced by literary convention, the miracle of rebirth which we as audience witness is still a miracle, but it is also—and this is something comedy usually fails to point out—a brutal fact of nature. The dance, if it is anything, is an embodiment of demonic control. There is no volition, no freedom, no choice. The Page is driven to do what she must by irrational forces she understands, perhaps, but cannot alter.

    In Chapter 2 it was stated that comedy typically attempts to purge excessive and mechanical (and thus overly controlled) forms of behavior in order to make characters freer, more flexible, and better able to adapt to different situations. Nothing like this liberation occurs in *More Dissemblers Besides Women*. By picturing the power of love and fertility as demonic and irresistible, Middleton directly connects his play with energies and impulses which, in order to preserve the vision of festivity so important to the genre, most comedies only vaguely echo. His play is primitive in the most fundamental sense. As a result, the ostensible movement in the drama from restriction to freedom is misleading. Despite the imagery of release and the presence of the gipsies, we take away from the play an impression of struggle and demonic control, inextricably linked with our memory of the Page's dance.

In *More Dissemblers Besides Women*, then, Middleton explores the less attractive and, at times, frightening aspects of the love and renewal celebrated by traditional comedy. Although not immediately appearing to have much in common with Roman comedy, the play continues and extends the examination of comic assumptions I have been tracing throughout this study. That examination comes to a climax in *The Old Law*.

The Old Law is one of the most extraordinary dramas in the Middleton canon, but it is also one of the most neglected.[17] A major reason for this neglect is the general attitude described above toward Middleton's tragicomedies. At the same time, the possibility that *The Old Law* contains the work of two other dramatists—William Rowley and Philip Massinger—has turned attention away from the play itself to problems of authorship. Indeed, although the original text of the drama is corrupt and although its initial publisher was notoriously unreliable, critics have spent a vast amount of time and energy attempting to disentangle the relative contributions of these three playwrights to the drama. It is, however, often very difficult to separate Rowley's hand from Middleton's, and the evidence of Massinger's writing is scanty at best. Thus, if we learn anything by comparing Edgar Morris's questionable assertion that the play was revised at two different times by two different men with David Holmes's belief that Massinger and Rowley wrote little if any of the drama, it is that attempts to divide the comedy line by line or scene by scene inevitably fail.[18] But this does not mean that we cannot establish who is the dominant presence behind the play. All of the critics who have written about *The Old Law* give Middleton the most important share, with the relative contributions of the three playwrights summed up best, perhaps, by Dewar Robb: "Whoever suggested the theme . . . [Middleton provided] the close-knit structure and the artistry which permitted no page to stray from the theme."[19] Middleton's is without doubt the controlling imagination in *The Old Law*, whether or not Middleton himself wrote every scene. The play is the culmination of the investigation of comic values and conventions which runs throughout his work. It is the clearest and, in many ways, the most powerful embodiment of Middleton's comic vision.

In spite of the title page's assurance that *The Old Law* was often presented "with great Applause,"[20] its Renaissance audiences probably experienced as much discomfort as pleasure while watching the play, for much of *The Old Law* strays far beyond the normal boundaries of the tragicomic form Guarini envisioned and Fletcher made so popular. Soon after the action begins, we learn that Evander, Duke of Epire, has recently instituted a law—the "old law" of the title—condemning the aged men and women of the kingdom to death. The fact that almost all of the young people in Epire rejoice over the law's passage only makes this rather distasteful situation worse, and Middleton provides example after example of the youths' disgusting callousness and hypocrisy: Simonides hurries his elderly parents to their death; Eugenia eagerly looks forward to the day her husband Lysander will be executed; Gnotho, the clown, plans a new marriage before his old wife has passed away. Cleanthes and Hippolita are the only young people in Epire who oppose this ruthless edict, but their attempt to save Cleanthes' father Leonides fails, and at the end of the play they are brought to trial as traitors. Without warning Evander suddenly reveals that the law has been a test and that no one has been killed, and he praises Cleanthes and Hippolita for their extraordinary virtue. The play concludes with a traditional but distinctly unsatisfying reconciliation scene.

As the above implies, the society of *The Old Law* is very nearly as polarized as that of *The Phoenix*, a play which the drama closely resembles in many respects. Middleton juxtaposes idealism and cynicism, and virtue and depravity in scene after scene. The play's most important virtuous characters, Cleanthes and Hippolita, are markedly contrasted with its chief villains, Simonides and Eugenia. Thus in the drama's opening scene, Sim's hypocritical treatment of his parents is

balanced by Cleanthes' genuine concern for his. Similarly, both
Hippolita and Eugenia swoon at the end of the comedy, but for
vastly different reasons. Eugenia's lusty, bloodthirsty nature is
the antithesis of Hippolita's innocence and virtue. All four are,
Evander notes, "of sons and wives . . . the worst and best"
(5.1.424), and so it is not surprising that at one point in the play
Cleanthes and Hippolita are associated with heaven, and Sim
and Eugenia with hell. In act 4, scene 2, Cleanthes' father
Leonides momentarily emerges from his forest hideaway to
greet his son. Cleanthes is overjoyed, and his speeches are
filled with religious overtones. He speaks of "heaven" (l.29),
"blessings" (l.38), and "angels" (l.42), and Leonides replies that
Cleanthes is "all obedience, love, and goodness" and "of such
ascending virtue, / That all the powers of hell can't sink [him]"
(ll.50, 54–55). But their mood of idealism is short-lived, for
Leonides' words are truer than he knows: Cleanthes does
indeed contain all that there is of filial obedience, love, and
goodness in Epire. And suddenly a horn sounds, as if symbolizing hell's answer to the old man's boast. Sim, Eugenia, and the
courtiers break into Leonides' Edenic retreat some fifteen lines
later, bringing death and destruction in the person of Cratylus,
the executioner.

Because all of these characters are closely allied either with
total depravity or unswerving virtue, individuals who fall into
these different categories do not interact in any meaningful
way. Cleanthes can rail endlessly in an endeavor to correct
Eugenia's faults, but his attacks are, she states, "nothing to a
mind resolv'd" (3.2.294). Likewise, Sim thinks that Cleanthes is
simply calling him "strange names," and assures his mistress:
"But I ne'er minded him" (ll.311–12). Cleanthes and Hippolita
inhabit a wholly different world from that of Simonides,
Eugenia, and the other youths in the play. There seems to be
no middle ground, no possibility of understanding or even of
dialogue between them. The alienation and lack of communication we earlier saw represented fitfully by the actions of such
characters as Tangle and Tim here become a way of life. The
hypothetical unified human society which comedy proclaims
has been hopelessly and irrevocably fragmented.

As in *The Phoenix*, evil is generally characterized by excess. "For anything too much is vicious" (4.2.106), Cleanthes tells Evander, and the rest of the play bears him out. Sim is, after all, only an extreme example of a character we often find in Elizabethan and Jacobean drama: a young gallant who bridles at his parents' frugality, one whose desires for a mistress (Eugenia) are opposed by an old man (Lysander). Sim's role, in other words, is that of a New Comedy protagonist, and Middleton ensures that we do not miss the similarity. When the play begins, we see the young courtier questioning two lawyers about the power and firmness of a law that condemns aged men and women to death. The reason Sim gives for his interest in the law is simple but important: "I am a young man that has an old father" (1.1.11). By describing both himself and his father only in terms of age, Sim underscores his own typicalness. No other explanation is needed, he seems to say; the fact that he is young and his father old determines all of their respective actions and attitudes. Sim and his father are playing age-old roles in an equally age-old battle of generations.

But what separates Sim from other New Comedy protagonists is the extent of his actions. He does not merely trick his elders in the game of love or swindle them out of their money. Nor does he simply wish his parents dead in a moment of anger (as does Stribax in *Truculentus*, for instance). In fact, Sim's actions go beyond the excesses even of some of Middleton's earlier young gallants—pandering a mother (Lethe), for example, or squandering on a tavern girl money intended to ransom a mother and sister (Philip Twilight). Sim plans to have his parents executed and derives endless pleasure from the prospect of their imminent death, an event he describes, not accidentally I think, with imagery of rebirth: "O lad, here's a spring for young plants to flourish! / The old trees must down [that] kept the sun from us" (1.1.72–73). He is without doubt one of the most depraved characters in all of Renaissance drama, and he never changes during the course of the play.

If Sim's role is disturbingly similar to that of a conventional New Comedy hero, Eugenia's situation—that of a young woman married to a sick old man—is even more obviously typical. Lysander and Eugenia are a Jacobean version of January and May. As such, Eugenia's plight would normally be far from unsympathetic, but in Middleton's play the opposite is true. Just as Evander's law promises to end Sim's financial woes by executing his parents, so it lessens Eugenia's typical marital problems by limiting her life with Lysander. Middleton's handling of a comic convention is again too extreme to evoke anything but a kind of black humor. "I've heard of women, (shall I call 'em so?) / Have welcom'd suitors ere the corpse were cold," Cleanthes laments; "But thou, thy husband living:—thou'rt too bold" (3.2.290–92). The first time Eugenia appears, she is soon besieged by suitors. A familiar and timeworn situation becomes a bit too explicit for comfort as they comment on the desire for young lovers of all women married to old men (2.2.43–45); and she answers, after they call her "widow," " 'Tis a comfort to be call'd so" (l.49). Her final reply to the courtiers' suits is a model of skillful suggestion and hypocrisy:

> Let other women make what haste they will,
> What's that to me? But I profess unfeignedly,
> I'll have my husband dead before I marry.
>
> [ll.107–9]

Eugenia is asking them to kill Lysander. The natural sexual attraction of youth toward youth has been transformed into an impulse to murder. In Epire, even more so than in Milan, "love and death are brothers," and once again we glimpse the potentially terrifying energies which lie behind normal comic values.

The actions of Gnotho are a low-life analogue to Sim's and Eugenia's. Like them, Gnotho is a character who might have appeared in any number of Renaissance comedies. He is a typical clown with an old and presumably shrewish wife. Gnotho solves his problem by bribing the Clerk to alter the record of Agatha's date of birth so that she too will soon be executed by the law. And when confronted by his wife, he displays an audacity at least as remarkable as that of either Simonides or Eugenia. He urges Agatha to kill herself before her time in what is really an attempt at comic assassination. After Agatha swoons at the news she has less than a month to live, Gnotho surmises: "Ay, so! if thou wouldst go away quietly, 'twere sweetly done, and like a kind wife; lie but a little longer, and the bell shall toll for thee" (3.1.326–28). But unfortunately, his wife refuses to succumb to his repeated attempts to frighten her to death. Agatha awakes, and Gnotho is not very pleased by her lack of compliance with his wishes: "What a spite's this, that a man cannot persuade his wife to die in any time with her good will!" (ll.346–47). As Gnotho's complaint demonstrates, moral judgments have gotten completely out of hand in Epire. All traditional values and institutions are sacrificed on the altar of youth.

The portrayal of Sim, Eugenia, and Gnotho is the most obvious example of Middleton's tendency to push comic conventions to an extreme in *The Old Law* and thus make them no longer comic. The actions of all three characters, furthermore, reflect the plot's paradoxical relationship to New Comedy form. *The Old Law* begins with a sense of expectation and change. Sim's repeated questions about the law lend it an almost magical status, and he soon learns that the law is "more grave and necessary" (l.50) than any before devised. Evander has established a new golden age of youth which will end, Sim believes, an insufferable tyranny of aged authority:

> Are there not fellows that lie bedrid in their offices,
> That younger men would walk lustily in?
> Churchmen, that even the second infancy
> Hath silenc'd, yet hath spun out their lives so long,
> That many pregnant and ingenious spirits
> Have languish'd in their hop'd reversions,
> And died upon the thought?
>
> [ll.31–37]

It is indeed a period of rejoicing for "those that have old parents and rich inheritance" (l.29), because Epire has arrived at a time of perpetual spring (l.72). The contrasting images of youth and age, and fertility and sterility which are present in these and other passages in the opening scene are conventional and suggest that the law has brought about the renewal of a moribund society. It has done this by executing aged men and women, because they are "fruitless to the republic" (l.109). Evander's law thus demonstrates man's ability to improve on nature's way; it "shall finish what nature linger'd at" (l.110), the displacement of the old and impotent by the young and fertile. The final result is that end toward which all comedy strives: "Why now, methinks, our court looks like a spring, / Sweet, fresh, and fashionable, now the old weeds are gone" (2.1.34–35).

The Old Law opens with a legislated New Comedy triumph of youth over age and the enforced renewal of an apparently dying society. The play begins where most comedies conclude and paradoxically develops toward something like the normal opening of Roman comedy. As noted in the discussion of *A Chaste Maid in Cheapside*, the meaning of comedy is based upon an analogy between comic structure and both the seasonal renewal of nature and man's ability to recreate himself through procreation. The genre therefore portrays the triumph of the young as a necessary and positive source of continuity in human society. With a horrifying practicality, the citizens of Epire have simply taken these ideas one step further. Not content to await the whims of nature, they plan to hurry "what nature linger'd at." Their law is a logical extension of the central tenets of comedy. Their world has room only for the young and the fertile. But the effect of their actions is anything but festive. Comedy is transformed into nightmare, and, as Cleanthes laments, Epire becomes an earthly hell: "And now, as Epire's situate by this law, / There is 'twixt us and heaven a dark eclipse" (1.1.393–94). The new society which so often awaits somewhere offstage at the end of many comedies is here revealed to be a world of cynicism, murder, and destruction. "Take hence that pile of years, / Before [he] surfeit with unprofitable age," Evander orders when Sim's aged parent is brought before him, continuing, "And, with the rest, from the high promontory, / Cast him into the sea" (2.1.133–36). In Chapter 4, noting Frye's insight that "in comedy we see a victory of the pleasure principle that Freud warns us not to look for in ordinary life,"[21] I argued that the plays discussed there and in the preceding chapter show, more emphatically than is comedy's wont, this triumph to be an illusion not worthy of contemplation. In *The Old Law*, Middleton describes the price a comic victory of the pleasure principle actually would extract. The drive of youth to displace age, the drive for renewal itself, appears as a vision from a dark abyss, and we witness one of the most shocking situations in all of Renaissance drama.

As a result, all conventionally positive comic values become negative ones. The fact that the play's apparent New Comedy hero and heroine, Sim and Eugenia, are despicable is only the most striking example. In *The Old Law*, age, not youth, is innocent (1.1.99–100; 4.2.179), and most of the old men and women in the drama are ideal types. Age is the source of all that is good and beneficial (4.2.196–208), while youth is never a positive attribute; it is something that must be endured and transcended (3.2.280–87). Thus an old man like Lysander, for all his faults, is able to best the youth of the day at their own game: he can dance more gracefully, fence more skillfully, and drink more heartily than any of Eugenia's suitors. Likewise, sexuality is intimately associated with death rather than life. Diocles, we learn, went to his grave "as weeping brides receive their joys at night; / With trembling, yet with patience" (2.1.3–4). And when Cleanthes tells Eugenia that her bloodthirsty nature proclaims her a whore, she calmly replies: " 'Tis dainty, next to procreation fitting; / I'd either be destroying men or getting" (4.2.264–66; cf. 2.1.70). Her sentiments are those of a nature goddess whose powers of renewal are at one with her powers of destruction—a goddess who is a primitive and ambivalent embodiment of the regenerative energies New Comedy celebrates more faintly, and more comfortably, in its entertaining and harmless clashes of young lovers and aged opponents. Ultimately, spring is equated with death, and, as the reactions of Sim and Eugenia to Lysander's youthful costume demonstrate, the play itself might even be called a "killing" joke:

> EUGENIA: O, I shall kill myself with infinite laughter!
>   Will nobody take my part?
> SIM: An't be a laughing business,
>   Put it to me, I'm one of the best in Europe;
>   My father died last too, I have the most cause.
>   [3.2.3–7]

Because the play negates almost all comic values, its true hero and heroine, Cleanthes and Hippolita, appropriately are New Comedy blocking figures. From the courtiers' point of view, Cleanthes is another Malvolio, and early in the first scene Sim complains that his friend is not in a festive mood: "What! 'tis not jubilee with thee yet. . . . How old is thy father?" (ll.78–79). Because Cleanthes does not share the courtiers' careless cynicism and callous disregard for family ties, he is attacked as "a vild example in these days of youth" (5.1.13), a satanic "arch–malefactor" (1.136) and, ironically, a prodigal (ll.195–99). He is brought to trial in the play's final scene for his "grave" opinions and behavior. There, Sim and his allies take on the role of Lords of Misrule about to render comic judgment on a figure who refuses to enter into a spirit of saturnalia.[22]

The episode recalls the mock judgments at the end of innumerable Renaissance comedies (*Every Man in His Humour*, *The Widow's Tears*, and Middleton's own *The Family of Love* are examples). But it is hardly a comic situation, because we do not yet know that all the apparently executed parents are alive.[23] In fact, the scene builds toward a climax of disgust. After Cleanthes prays, "Heaven stand on my side, pity, love, and duty," Sim asks, "Where are they, sir? who sees them but yourself?" (ll.218–19). Suddenly Evander steps forward and music sounds, signifying the end of discord. Cleanthes, enemy of youth and festivity, assumes his rightful position with "grave father[s]" (1.284). He becomes an official *"censor of youth"* (1.304). Misrule is deposed and with it the law which initiated its triumph. We return to the old society, rather than celebrate a new one. The play concludes not by consummating marriages, but by preventing them. Indeed, by the end of the play it has long been apparent that the misrule of Sim and his fellows is not a rebirth at all, but a return to a primitive era of chaos and murderous behavior under the aegis, ironically, of law. And by the close of the play it should also be clear that Evander's law is the law of comedy developed to its logical conclusion. Just as Cleanthes passes judgment on Sim and his companions, so the play as a whole passes judgment—more clearly than any drama we have yet considered—on the assumptions and values of comedy itself.

The chief problem with Evander's law is that it attempts to speed up the natural cycle of generations and so spawns a number of "monsters unnatural" and "wild beasts" (2.2.75, 79). The law attempts to turn the clock forward. Confronted with the prospect of imminent death, Eugenia's aged husband Lysander, on the other hand, tries to turn time backward, "a work ne'er yet attempted" (3.2.229). In the process he too becomes a "monster." When Lysander first sees suitors about his house, he retreats to prayer, but he soon reappears with other plans and consults "the secrets of all art, to make himself / Youthful again" (3.2.15–16). Lysander dons the latest and most youthful fashions, attempts to dye his white beard black, and begins taking dancing and fencing lessons. His outrageous appearance is anticipated by Agatha's overdone makeup (3.1.262–64; cf. 2.1.42–44), and his actions are paralleled by those of the old women in act 4, scene 1. Onstage this "rejuvenated" old man should look as outlandish as possible, because he himself is aware of the absurdity of his actions and worries about the aches and pains they may entail (3.2.60–63, 94–95, 134–37). Lysander defeats youth "at her own virtues" and beats "folly in her own ground" (ll.197–98), but in doing so he equates himself with the courtiers and reveals his own folly. He acts as unnaturally as they do. Lysander becomes a strange hybrid of age and youthful action, and the emblem of this peculiar union is his speckled beard: "Three quarters of his beard is under fifty; / There's but a little tuft of fourscore left" (ll.41–42), Eugenia mockingly confides to the Courtiers. Cleanthes' startled reaction to Lysander implies that it is precisely this juxtaposition of opposites that is so disgusting:

> Methinks, I partly know you, that's my grief.
> Could you not all be lost? that had been handsome;
> But to be known at all, 'tis more than shameful.
>   [ll.211–13]

If Lysander had been more than partly changed, Cleanthes seems to imply, everything would have been all right. As it is,

Lysander is a monster, or more accurately, a grotesque example of "mixt monstrousness" (1.224) and "prodigious folly" (1.246; cf. 5.1.98). There is only one hope. Cleanthes confronts the old man with the foolishness of his actions and is heartened by the results: "I see't has done him good; blessing go with it, / Such as may make him pure again" (ll.256–57). Cleanthes' words do not refer simply to his uncle's state of mind. Lysander must be purified in body as well as soul. He must reject the grotesque dichotomies of his costume and again become "purely," that is, completely, old.

As Cleanthes' speech indicates, purity is very important in *The Old Law*, and this is perhaps the reason that the play contains so many opposites. Most of the characters move toward an extreme state of good or evil. However, this kind of "purity" is itself problematic within a comic world, because it threatens to subvert the typical reconciliation scene with which most comedies and tragicomedies conclude. By finding room for as many characters as possible in the new society, a conventional reconciliation scene (like that of *The Family of Love*, for instance) inevitably lessens distinctions between those characters and so reaffirms the existence of a homogeneous human community—the belief that all men are one, both in wisdom and in folly. But *The Old Law*, like *The Phoenix*, amplifies rather than lessens distinctions between characters and depicts anything but this hypothetically unified human community. How can one reconcile a Cleanthes and a Simonides, or an Hippolita and a Eugenia? The purity which the play seems to value so highly has no place in comedy. In fact, as we have seen, *The Old Law* is so disturbing precisely because Middleton's use of comic conventions is a little too "pure," a little too extreme.

At first glance, Cleanthes appears to provide the key to solving the puzzling relationship between the world of opposing extremes the drama portrays and the reconciliation it ostensibly endorses in its concluding scene. Although he often seems too idealized to serve as a model for a possible union between the warring forces in the comedy, Cleanthes is both young and wise and so represents a potential *concordia discors* of youth (as folly and evil) and age (as wisdom and virtue).

Moreover, his triumph at the end of the drama implies that he performs just this function and symbolizes a new and better Epire. Perhaps he does. Yet as is the case in so many of Middleton's plays, opposites do not join to create some greater harmony and unity in *The Old Law*. Rather, reconciliation is inevitably a form of "mixt monstrousness" or, to paraphrase the words of Oliver Twilight in *No Wit, No Help Like a Woman's*, a union which is "strangely wrought." Middleton demonstrates this by alluding to Lysander's costume early in the final scene, when Sim orders the officers to "attach the grey young man, / The youth of fourscore" (5.1.34–35). The gallant's reference to Lysander's grotesque appearance is reinforced when Hippolita enters shortly afterward and pleads for her husband's pardon:

> Alas! I know not how to style you yet;
> To call you judges doth not suit your years,
> Nor heads and beards show more antiquity;
> Yet sway yourselves with equity and truth,
> And I'll proclaim you reverend, and repeat
> Once in my lifetime I have seen grave heads
> Plac'd upon young men's shoulders.
>
> > [ll.49–55]

Hippolita obviously believes that she is asking for a miracle, for a union of youth and wisdom which she has never seen and does not expect to see. Significantly, her image of "grave heads" placed upon "young men's shoulders" echoes Sim's summons of that "grey young man" Lysander. In effect, Hippolita is asking the courtiers to become grotesques like Lysander by uniting the mind of age with the body of youth. Their reaction to her speech shows that they are all too aware of its meaning: "Hark! she flouts us, / And thinks to make us monstrous" (ll.55–56). The gallants choose the "pure" and characteristic folly of youth, rejecting the "mixt monstrousness" which a taint of wise behavior might bring. In their eyes moderation is not something to be desired.

Hippolita, however, has partially erred in what she says. She has seen one "grave" head placed upon young shoulders. As Sim notes later in the scene, Cleanthes is one who "would have sons grave fathers, ere their fathers / Be sent unto their graves" (ll.138–39). The import of his statement is unmistakable. Sim judges Cleanthes a grotesque just as Cleanthes earlier condemned Lysander's monstrous appearance. And Sim is right. In the world of *The Old Law*, both Cleanthes and Hippolita are unnatural, are grotesques, because they combine the irreconcilable qualities of youth and wisdom. The same is true of the union of young and old with which the play concludes.

This is the reason that the almost otherworldly music which announces the overthrow of Sim and his companions and the wondrous reappearance of the old men and women soon gives way to the peculiar harmony of Gnotho's procession, a harmony which is the antithesis of the pleasant sounds which flow from Bounteous Progress's organs in *A Mad World, My Masters*. In the midst of an effusive tribute to Cleanthes and Hippolita, Evander is interrupted by a series of unusual sounds. "Ha! what strange kind of melody was that?" (l.429) the Duke exclaims, and the clown suddenly enters, followed first by fiddlers and a wedding party and then by a funeral. Like Evander, Cleanthes is astonished by what he sees and hears:

> My Lord,
> I do observe a strange decorum here:
> These that do lead this day of jollity
> Do march with music and most mirthful cheeks;
> Those that do follow, sad and wofully,
> Nearer the haviour of a funeral
> Than a wedding.
>
> [ll.464–70]

Gnotho is off to be remarried and to watch his first wife be executed on the same day—something he does not find at all surprising: "And your grace, in the due consideration, shall find 'em [the two wives] much alike; the one hath the ring upon her finger, the other a halter about her neck" (ll.472–75).

His strange entourage recalls the funeral procession in act 2, scene 1, where Cleanthes and Hippolita gaily follow the hearse of Cleanthes' presumably dead father. The resemblance, however, is a superficial one. In the earlier episode Cleanthes and Hippolita secretly rejoice over their plan to save

Leonides from the law rather than over the old man's death. Their laughing voices and "orient" (l.178) colors expose the hypocrisy of the other youths' "sables" (l.185) by creating a mirror image of the courtiers' true feelings. But Gnotho's procession reverses the import of Cleanthes', just as it reverses the order. Whereas the earlier scene qualifies the triumph of Evander's law, Gnotho's entry undermines the conclusion of the play itself. Gnotho's joy in death is real, not apparent, and like the horn which shatters the peace of Leonides' idyllic hideaway, his "strange melody" disrupts the idealism of the play's last lines.[24]

Gnotho's troupe presents a vision of marriage and revelry reduced to discord by an all too literal juxtaposition of death and rebirth. In keeping with the attempt of all of Epire's youthful inhabitants to improve on nature's way, the clown has gotten things backward. His wedding celebration precedes Agatha's funeral rather than follows it. Gnotho still believes that the law is in effect, but he soon learns that, like his wedding cake, the law, indeed comedy itself, is "out of season" and laments: "Put up your plums, as fiddlers put up pipes, / The wedding dash'd, the bridegroom weeps and wipes" (ll.596, 601–2). Because the procession is a grotesque hybrid of joy and sorrow, it should also remind us of Lysander and Cleanthes, the two other grotesques mentioned in the scene, and reinforce our sense that the conclusion of this comedy is discordant rather than harmonious. At the same time, the procession is a symbol of *The Old Law* itself, for the play is similarly composed of harshly conflicting moods. Joy follows sorrow in the drama's last scene almost as rapidly as Agatha's laments follow her husband's mirthful songs.

As we have seen so often in this study, there is no harmonious resolution at the end of the play. Harmony once more lies somewhere offstage, here specifically in the Edenic retreat where Evander hides the aged men and women of Epire, and which Leonides describes to his awestruck son:

> Oftimes, waking, our unsteady phantasies
> Would question whether we yet liv'd or no,
> Or had possession of that paradise
> Where angels be the guard![25]   [5.1.696–99]

The old people reappear as if in a dream (1.250), but the Epire they return to is no paradise. It is a world which is by now totally familiar, a world of irreconcilable conflicts and grotesque tensions. In essence, *The Old Law* is a New Comedy *reductio ad absurdum*. By delving beneath the surface of comedy to discover the primitive energies which the form embodies and by carrying those energies to their logical conclusion, Middleton creates an unforgettable picture of the destruction which inevitably accompanies renewal, of the death which is prerequisite to new life. In doing so, he gives expression to an aspect of rebirth which, according to conventional comedy, would be better left unsaid.

6
Afterword: The Tragedies

> In time of sports death may steal in securely,
> Then 'tis least thought on.
> Bianca, in *Women Beware Women*

Near the beginning of the second act of *The Changeling*, Beatrice-Joanna is confronted by her father's servant De Flores, an "ominous ill-fac'd fellow" (2.1.53) who seems to plague her every step.[1] De Flores is a true grotesque, a "standing toad-pool" (l.58) whose repulsiveness is unmatched by that of any other character in the Middleton canon. In many ways, however, this strange servant to Beatrice's father, Vermandero, is closely related to several figures we have examined in this study. De Flores's personality, like the personalities of Quomodo, Bounteous Progress, and Whorehound, often seems inconsistent or even contradictory. On one hand, he is helpless and masochistic, a foolish and unworthy suitor who vainly worships at the shrine of a woman who is idealized by everyone and who loathes the sight of him. On the other hand, De Flores is competent, clear-sighted, and practical, and he maintains an unswerving adherence to his love for Beatrice

190

which seems almost admirable, despite the enormity of that love. Like Lethe, Dampit, Allwit, and Simonides, De Flores initially invites our ridicule and then quickly transforms that ridicule into fear and revulsion as we realize that the figure and actions we have been laughing at are not really laughable. To cite only a single example: the scene in which De Flores agrees to murder Alonso de Piracquo, Middleton begins in a predominantly comic mode. From our superior position as audience, we watch first De Flores and then Beatrice each foolishly interpret the other's words according to his own purposes in what is essentially a stock comic situation. And at first the effect, like that of the similarly constructed Porter episode in *A Chaste Maid in Cheapside*, is humorous:

DE FLORES:	You were about to sigh out somewhat, madam.
BEATRICE:	No, was I? I forgot—Oh!
DE FLORES:	There 'tis again,
	The very fellow on't.
BEATRICE:	You are too quick, sir.
DE FLORES:	There's no excuse for't now, I heard it twice, madam;
	That sigh would fain have utterance, take pity on't,
	And lend it a free word; 'las, how it labours
	For liberty! I hear the murmur yet
	Beat at your bosom.
BEATRICE:	Would creation—
DE FLORES:	Ay, well said, that's it.
BEATRICE:	Had form'd me man.
DE FLORES:	Nay, that's not it.

[2.2.100–109]

De Flores is clearly a comic butt at this point. Beatrice-Joanna is cleverly maneuvering her uncomprehending admirer into doing what she wishes, and De Flores's astonishment at her unexpected kindness leads him to respond to her speeches with a blind eagerness which is ridiculous. And indeed, part of us wants to laugh, but only part. The situation is, after all, not finally a comic one, and our laughter is restrained by Beatrice's murderous intention. Moreover, the seriousness of the events we are watching becomes increasingly evident as the scene progresses. De Flores and Beatrice gradually exchange places.

By the end of the episode it is the beautiful beloved rather than the deformed lover who is ignorant of the other's meaning. Yet Beatrice's ignorance (in contrast to De Flores's) is not humorous in the least. Her inability to comprehend either the evils of the murder she urges or the price De Flores asks for the enactment of that murder is appalling. At the same time, we also gradually realize that Vermandero's servant is not a relatively harmless and foolish victim of love, but that he truly is the monster Beatrice envisions. When De Flores exits contemplating the pleasures of holding his beloved in his arms (ll.146–53), his sentiments do not strike us as the vain dreams of a clownish buffoon. The picture he draws is frightening. As in so many of Middleton's plays, what begins in laughter ends in horror.

Middleton's portrayal of De Flores's metamorphosis from a comic to a sinister figure should be familiar: we have encountered similar incidents and characters in several of the plays examined above. Vermandero's servant embodies the "mixt monstrousness" Cleanthes sees in Lysander's attempt to become young again in *The Old Law*. A grotesque both in appearance and action, De Flores personifies the world of Middleton's plays—at once comic and frightening, an unsettling combination of discordant elements. As such, De Flores is one of many links between Middleton's tragedies and the plays discussed in the preceding chapters; and before concluding this study, I would like to investigate briefly a few additional correspondences between the tragedies and Middleton's earlier plays.

Una Ellis-Fermor was the first critic to comment extensively upon the similarities between Middleton's comedies and tragedies, and her ideas have been extended and refined by numerous other writers.[2] The best account of the relationship is Dorothy Farr's. Arguing that Middleton's genius "was essentially comic," Farr finds that "the uniqueness of his tragedies derives a good deal from his ability to develop an inherently comic situation at depth"—a trait we have found to be true of the comedies and tragicomedies as well. She goes on to stress the unheroic nature of Middleton's characters, an unheroic nature which is essentially comic: "It is the character of comic stature brought up against an acute psychological or moral challenge . . . that gives to Middleton's tragedy its characteristic edge." The result of this emphasis on comic situations and unexceptional characters is a version of tragedy which is in its own way as unique as the comic form we have been describing above. In Charles Hallett's words, Middleton violates "almost every major element of tragic form—the hero of stature, the reversal, the suffering, recognition and purification—and has in fact written what we would recognize today as anti-tragedy."[3] Characteristically, Middleton employs an inherited genre in an uncharacteristic manner. Just as his comedies at first glance seem conventional but paradoxically do not develop in traditional ways, so his tragedies follow the surface contours of tragic form while presenting characters and events which are normally excluded from that genre. Thus it is not surprising to find that several interpretations of *The Changeling* parallel those I have advanced for the comedies. We have been told, for instance, that the play is an attack on Petrarchan and romantic love, and that it is a topsy-turvy version of the beauty-and-the-beast fable in which beauty is transformed into a beast rather than the beast into a prince. Likewise, critics have argued that the tragedy depicts a comic rebellion of youth against age which brings only disillusionment, and that the heroine of the subplot violates audience expectations by remaining surprisingly (and unconventionally) faithful to her foolish husband. Even closer to the thesis of this study, it has been suggested that *The Changeling* is "a tonal thrill-show, a roller-coaster ride on hills of many heights and many angles of steepness" which raises expectations it does not fulfill.[4]

But despite these and other analyses of the unusual qualities of Middleton's tragedies, the feeling remains among many critics that the mixture of disparate elements in the plays is not the result of intention but of philosophic or artistic weakness, and that the plays are not organic wholes which fuse comic and tragic in the way *King Lear* and *Hamlet*, for example, do.[5] The persistence of such beliefs suggests (and I think rightly) that the dramas, while they may be coherent intellectually, do not have a coherent effect. And indeed, it is not my intention to argue that these plays exemplify a kind of organic unity in which all parts are perfectly in harmony with one another.[6] The tone of the tragedies, like that of the comedies, is inconsistent; and the tragedies, like most of Middleton's earlier dramas, often pull our responses in two different directions at once, promising first one kind of play and then another.

We need only look at seventeenth-century reactions to *The Changeling* and *Hengist, King of Kent* to find ample proof of the generic confusion inherent in these dramas. In the Renaissance, *The Changeling* was not renowned for the psychologically penetrating scenes which today we prize so highly. Rather, its popularity stemmed from the comic subplot. And when *Hengist, King of Kent* was first published in 1661, it was judged a comedy and given a title, *The Mayor of Queenborough*, based upon the adventures of a clownish tanner who has little to do with the major concerns of the play.[7] Like the strange mixtures of contradictory elements in the dramas discussed in the preceding chapters, the tensions and ambiguous effects of the tragedies mirror the confusions Middleton saw around him. The plays are intentionally disconcerting and intentionally undermine the traditional effect of the form they presumably embody—goals which Middleton makes explicit near the conclusion of *Hengist, King of Kent* when Simon, as noted in Chapter 1, complains about the surprising and unconventional conclusion of the "merry comedy" he had hoped to enjoy.

It is in *Women Beware Women* rather than in *Hengist, King of Kent* or *The Changeling*, however, that Middleton echoes most profoundly several of the concerns discussed in the above chapters. As has often been noted, *Women Beware Women* reproduces Middleton's comic world more closely than do his two other tragedies.[8] Its society, despite the high social rank of many of the characters, is basically bourgeois. The figures in the play never rise to tragic stature, a fact which is reflected by their habit of speaking in asides rather than soliloquies. The frequency of puns and wordplay in the drama is something we usually expect of comedy, not tragedy, and characters such as the Ward and Sordido might have appeared in several of the city comedies.[9]

Likewise, the society of *Women Beware Women*, like that of *A Chaste Maid in Cheapside*, is a society of games which have no substance, a society in which a universal pursuit of pleasure leads to a cynical disregard for all conventional moral codes. More important, in the fortunes of Leantio we see a comic protagonist come full circle: the young factor changes from an apparently typical New Comedy hero to a foolish and jealous cuckold and thence to a would-be revenger on his unfaithful wife and her lover. As in *The Old Law*, Middleton describes what might occur after the traditional comic resolution, after young love has defeated aged obstacles and been consummated in marriage. And as in *The Old Law*, this glimpse of the aftermath of a comic triumph is not reassuring. Leantio passes through a series of comic roles (lover, cuckold) to a tragic one (revenger), and his metamorphosis is symptomatic of the play's bitterly ironic treatment of several potentially comic characters and incidents, a treatment which appropriately concludes when a symbol of harmony and regeneration, a marriage masque, becomes a vehicle of destruction.

The tragedy begins in the manner of conventional comedy—or rather in the manner of a conventional comic conclusion. The young lover (Leantio) enters with his beloved (Bianca) and describes the circumstances of their arrival in words which might have been taken from Plautus or Terence: "From Venice, her consent and I have brought her / From parents great in wealth, more now in rage" (ll.49–50). It is April (1.3.80–84), and Leantio praises the fruitfulness of their love by comparing their feelings with the sterile monetary concerns of the rich (1.1.93–100). The scene also contains several references to birth. Leantio is more dear to his mother than at any any time since his "birth-joy, a mother's chiefest gladness, / After sh' has undergone her curse of sorrows" (1.1.4–5). Bianca speaks of her new home as "the place of my birth now, / And rightly too: for here my love was born, / And that's the birth-day of a woman's joys" (ll.139–41; cf. 80–83, 93–100).

But in spite of these references to the renewal traditionally associated with the victory of young love, it is soon evident that the apparent familiarity of the episode in fact masks attitudes totally out of keeping with the comic victory it initially seems to describe. We might note, for example, that the mother's opening reference to childbirth stresses the pain and suffering of delivery as well as the joy of new life; and, as we saw in *More Dissemblers Besides Women,* the former qualities are usually excluded from the idealized comic view of procreation. And although Leantio states that the fruitful poverty of true love is superior to the sterile riches of aged misers, he worries constantly about his financial status and views his wife in materialistic terms—as a precious jewel to be hoarded from the world. Similarly, the young lovers' escape from Venice does not embody a conventional comic movement from restriction to freedom. Leantio must accept the restraints imposed upon him by the necessity of making a living, and his jealousy in turn imprisons his wife.

The ironies surrounding Leantio and Bianca's New Comedy victory largely result from the fact that Middleton thrusts these characters out of the wish-fulfillment fantasies of their comic dreamworld and into the harsh realities of a world where comic values have no place. By showing us the life of young lovers after they have consummated their love (something we seldom see in conventional comedy), Middleton exposes the fragility of the promise of future happiness with which most comedies conclude. Again and again, problems and attitudes intrude which slowly erode the idealism of Leantio and Bianca's love: the Mother's acknowledgment of the pain connected with childbirth, her comments on the different social status of Leantio and Bianca, Leantio's worries about adultery and money. In *Women Beware Women,* romantic love and comic optimism belong to a distant past, and Middleton invokes that past in the play's first scene only to show that it cannot be recovered. Thus, after Leantio leaves his new wife for the first time in act 1, scene 3, his mother turns to a weeping Bianca and says, "Come, 'tis an old custom / To weep for love" (ll. 71–72). Romantic involvement, she advises, is old-fashioned and of little use, and the Mother's sentiments are echoed by the Duke's later argument that Bianca give in to his desires and so "play the wise wench, and provide for ever" (2.2.382), and by

Livia's comments to Leantio on the foolishness of youthful love:

> Young gentlemen that only love for beauty,
> They love not wisely; such a marriage rather
> Proves the destruction of affection.
>
> [3.3.282–84]

The three statements perfectly characterize the society of *Women Beware Women*, a society which rejects idealistic sentiments and in which romantic love is foolish and perhaps destructive. Within such a setting Leantio has no choice but to concern himself with material possessions and to lock up his wife in order to keep her faithful to him. There is no place in Florence for New Comedy heroes. Leantio's metamorphosis from young lover to jealous husband is the inevitable result of leaving his house—a private, secluded sanctuary for love—and entering the light of everyday reality. Similarly, Bianca's alteration from innocent beloved to lustful intriguer is not simply the product of choice or moral weakness. It also suggests that the role she plays at the beginning of the drama does not and cannot exist in the play-world. As comic types in a comic situation at the opening of *Women Beware Women*, Leantio and Bianca are anachronisms, vestiges of a past which no longer has meaning for those around them. The price for entering the society of the drama, for becoming (in a sense) up to date, is the exchanging of those comic roles for tragic ones.

The world of *Women Beware Women*, like that of most of the plays discussed above, is thus hostile to comic values, and Middleton demonstrates this by beginning his play where many comedies end and then tracing a tragic metamorphosis in the relationship of the young lovers, a metamorphosis which is caused by their unavoidable reentry into reality from a comic-fantasy world. Comic revelry, Middleton shows us, must stop eventually; and when it does, the result is disillusionment and suffering. At the same time, the tragedy, like *A Chaste Maid in Cheapside*, questions the curative powers of matrimony. We might recall that in the earlier play Yellowhammer and the Welshwoman cynically manipulate this belief for their own purposes. In *Women Beware Women*, on the other hand, Leantio

and the Duke accept the premise at face value, and in doing so
both men reveal their own folly and the absurdity of the belief
they so heartily affirm. Leantio, for example, enters the play as
a prodigal who has been reformed by marriage. Bianca's
beauty protects him from the abyss of adultery (1.1.26–34),
and he assures his Mother that his theft has received a pardon
"sealed from heaven by marriage" (l.45). He could not be more
wrong. The Duke's faith in the redeeming power of matrimony is greater and so more deluded. After he has been
confronted by the Cardinal, the Duke suddenly repents for his
sins and vows never again to visit Bianca unlawfully. He is not,
however, ready to give up his mistress, and he plots to murder
Leantio so that he may make her "lawfully" his own (4.1.273).
The ironies are almost too obvious to mention. The Duke
foolishly believes that marriage can absolve all his sinful deeds,
even the murder which must necessarily precede his taking
vows. Thus comforted, he ironically envisions that he will be
reborn on his wedding day, soliloquizing: "Live like a hopeful
bridegroom, chaste from flesh; / And pleasure then [after
marriage to Bianca] will seem new, fair and fresh" (ll.277–78).
The Duke's statement is one which might describe the effect of
marriage in numerous comedies, but in *Women Beware Women*
it simply reinforces his moral blindness. The Duke's traditional
comic solution to his predicament is a prelude to disaster. His
wedding will bring death, not new life.

    This bitterly ironic treatment of the comic emphasis upon
the curative power of matrimony is reinforced by Middleton's
portrayal of the play's central matchmaker, Livia. Hippolito's
sister first enters as an apparent defender of love: she opposes
Fabricio's plan to wed Isabella to the Ward. Livia's honesty and
wit are attractive, and she plays, as Parrott and Ball note, "the
role of the intriguer in a comedy."[10] Livia describes her powers
to Hippolito using images of birth and pregnancy (2.1.26–32),
and according to Leantio she is "a cheerful and a beauteous
benefactor too, / As e'er erected the good works of love"
(4.1.71–72). Moreover, Livia's house, like Bounteous Progress's, is a place of feasting and revelry. We see her presiding
over a sumptuous banquet in act 3, scene 3, and, like Middle-

ton's frolic knight, she prides herself on her generosity toward friends, on the "bounty [which] is the credit and the glory / Of those that have enough" (2.2.240–41). But Livia's association with such comic values as love, generosity, and festivity simply reemphasizes the impossibility of affirming those values in the world of the play. As intriguer, her plots lead to destruction rather than rebirth, in one instance creating an incestuous union of uncle and niece (we might recall the threat of incest in *No Wit, No Help Like a Woman's*), in another helping to consummate an adulterous love which proves the undoing of almost everyone in the play. Livia is a sinister combination of Savorwit and Bounteous Progress and a logical development of misrule's amoral opposition to restriction and restraint, an opposition which here (as is usually the case in Middleton's plays) is not regenerative in any sense.[11] In Livia we see the comic emphasis upon freedom, hospitality, and the necessity of fulfilling youthful sexual desires transformed into cynicism and exploitation. And given the society of the play, the metamorphosis (like the ones of Leantio and Bianca) seems to be inevitable. When she exchanges the role of matchmaker for that of revenger late in the drama, Livia makes explicit what has always been implicit: the promise of consummated love she offers is, in *Woman Beware Women*, a promise of destruction.

Livia's revenge reaches its climax in the play's final scene. Her part in Gratiano's masque, that of the marriage goddess Juno Pronuba, is one she has played throughout the drama, and during the revels she confers (as she always has conferred) death, not life, murdering Hippolito and Isabella, the lovers she had earlier helped to unite. The final scene itself is perhaps the most striking example of the way in which *Women Beware Women* continually transforms potential comic values and situations into tragic ones. The episode begins as if it were a conventional reconciliation scene. Despite his reservations about his brother's marriage to Bianca, the Cardinal professes peace and accepts them both. But this hope of harmony is short-lived. Bianca reveals in an aside her plan to murder the Cardinal, and the masque begins its destructive course. As was noted in the discussion of *No Wit, No Help Like a Woman's*, a marriage masque conventionally symbolizes harmony and fertility. Here, however, as in the earlier play, that purpose is frustrated: Gratiano's masque is a vehicle of death. In a sense we are watching a reconciliation scene which denies the possibility of such scenes, a scene in which harmony—marriage, forgiveness, the masque—gives way before the forces of discord. The drama's conclusion is thus not unlike those of many of the plays we have encountered in this study, although it is certainly the bloodiest.

Once again, we see that harmony has no place in the world of Middleton's plays. Once again, we see that comic values— reconciliation, mercy, acceptance—are irrelevant in the society he depicts. Indeed, when Bianca notes that "in time of sports death may steal in securely, / Then 'tis least thought on" (5.2.22–23), her statement at once describes the plight of all of the characters (including herself) in this final episode and provides an epigraph for most of the plays we have been examining, plays in which antifestive forces suddenly and unexpectedly disrupt what initially seems to be a conventional comic world. Similarly, when the Duke states that the metamorphosis of his nuptial celebration into "great mischiefs" (l.171) is "prodigious" (l.172), his words both link the events he has witnessed to the grotesque ("prodigious") discords which characterize so many of Middleton's dramas and parallel our reaction to those discords. His expectations shattered, his laughter turned into bewilderment and horror as he stands before a spectacle—the masque—which promises mirth but instead brings suffering, the Duke is a tragic mirror of our responses as we encounter the unconventional and disturbing characters and events which constitute the essence of Thomas Middleton's comic vision.

Notes

Chapter 1

1. See, for example, Geoffrey Hartman, "Toward Literary History," *Daedalus* 99 (1970): 355–83; Walter Jackson Bate, *The Burden of the Past and the English Poet* (Cambridge, Mass.: Harvard University Press, Belknap Press, 1970); and Harold Bloom, *The Anxiety of Influence: A Theory of Poetry* (Oxford: Oxford University Press, 1973). Both Bate and Bloom are interested primarily in Romantic and post-Romantic writers.

2. Northrop Frye, *Anatomy of Criticism: Four Essays* (Princeton, N.J.: Princeton University Press, 1957), pp. 163–165. Cf. Frye's descriptions of New Comedy in "The Argument of Comedy," *English Institute Essays, 1948*, ed. D. A. Robertson, Jr. (New York: Columbia University Press, 1949), pp. 58–74; and in *A Natural Perspective: The Development of Shakespearean Comedy and Romance* (New York: Columbia University Press, 1965).

3. But only a few. Of the twenty plays by Plautus which have survived relatively intact sixteen have plot structures which parallel in large part the one Frye outlines (*Asinaria, Aulularia, Bacchides, Casina, Cistellaria, Curculio, Epidicus, Mercator, Miles Gloriosus, Mostellaria, Persa, Poenulus, Pseudolus, Rudens, Stichus, Trinummus*). And although *Captivi* and *Menaechmi* both deal with a sudden discovery of individuals long believed dead rather than (or together with) the consummation of young love, their focus simply represents—as Shakespeare realized in his reworking of the latter in *The Comedy of Errors*—another method of expressing a concern with rebirth more explicitly developed in plots detailing the difficulties of young love. *Amphitruo* is a mythological travesty and so belongs to a different dramatic tradition from Plautus's other plays; and *Truculentus*, despite its somewhat

harsh tone, includes as part of its resolution the promised marriage of a young man (Diniarchus) to a young woman he had formerly seduced and abandoned and his recovery of their newborn child. Five of Terence's plays closely resemble Frye's model (*Andria, Heauton Timorumenos, Eunuchus, Phormio, Adelphoe*), and *Hecyra* is certainly compatible with his ideas, although here the opposition to young love comes from one of the lovers rather than from some external source.

4. Attacks on Frye's theory of comedy usually presuppose a rigidity that is not actually present. See, for example, A. N. Kaul, *The Action of English Comedy: Studies in the Encounter of Abstraction and Experience From Shakespeare to Shaw* (New Haven, Conn.: Yale University Press, 1970), pp. 18–23; and Morton Gurewitch, *Comedy: The Irrational Vision* (Ithaca, N.Y.: Cornell University Press, 1975), pp. 17–19. Likewise, Erich Segal wrongly chastises Frye for stating that a harsh father is always the blocking figure in New Comedy—something Frye does not do—in *Roman Laughter: The Comedy of Plautus* (Cambridge, Mass.: Harvard University Press, 1968), p. 92, a study that, in fact, closely parallels Frye's point of view.

5. Renaissance commentators on comedy were, among other things, more didactic and Aristotelian in approach. But their ideas are not incompatible with Frye's. In fact, Renaissance descriptions of the various character types found in Roman comedy closely resemble those in the *Anatomy of Criticism*. See Marvin T. Herrick, *Comic Theory in the Sixteenth Century* (Urbana: University of Illinois Press, 1950), esp. pp. 147–59.

6. Madeleine Doran, *Endeavors of Art: A Study of Form in Elizabethan Drama* (Madison: University of Wisconsin Press, 1954), p. 153. T. W. Baldwin's analyses of English grammar school curricula during the sixteenth century can be found in *William Shakspere's Small Latine & Lesse Greeke*, 2 vols. (Urbana: University of Illinois Press, 1944); and *Shakspere's Five-Act Structure* (Urbana: University of Illinois Press, 1947). For Renaissance discussions of Terence, see Herrick, *Comic Theory in the Sixteenth Century*. On the relation of classical and Renaissance comedy, see Doran, *Endeavors of Art*, pp. 152–60; George Duckworth, *The Nature of Roman Comedy: A Study in Popular Entertainment* (Princeton, N.J.: Princeton University Press, 1952), pp. 396–431; Leo Salingar, *Shakespeare and the Traditions of Comedy* (Cambridge: Cambridge University Press, 1974), esp. pp. 76–174; Ashley H. Thorndike, *English Comedy* (New York: Macmillan Co., 1929), pp. 30–34; and Richard Hosley, "The Formal Influence of Plautus and Terence," *Elizabethan Theater*, Stratford-upon-Avon Studies, no. 9 (London: Edward Arnold, 1966), pp. 131–45.

7. Salingar, *Traditions of Comedy*, provides the best account of the ways in which these various literary kinds intermingle in Renaissance comedy. See also Doran, *Endeavors of Art*, pp. 167–69, 172–75. Helpful studies of Italian comedy include Douglas Radcliff-Umstead, *The*

Birth of Modern Comedy in Renaissance Italy (Chicago: University of Chicago Press, 1969); Marvin T. Herrick, *Italian Comedy in the Renaissance* (Urbana: University of Illinois Press, 1960); and Kathleen M. Lea, *Italian Popular Comedy*, 2 vols. (1934; reprint ed., New York: Russell and Russell, 1962). Bruce R. Smith examines the modification of New Comedy in court productions in "Sir Amorous Knight and the Indecorous Romans; or, Plautus and Terence Play Court in the Renaissance," *Renaissance Drama* n.s. 6 (1973): 3–27. Brian Gibbons, *Jacobean City Comedy: A Study of Satiric Plays by Jonson, Marston and Middleton* (Cambridge, Mass.: Harvard University Press, 1968); and Alexander Leggatt, *Citizen Comedy in the Age of Shakespeare* (Toronto: University of Toronto Press, 1973) discuss the nature and origins of Jacobean city comedy. Because he limits literary influence to the adaptation of specific plays, Michael Shapiro wrongly argues against a close relationship between Roman comedy and Jacobean plays in *Children of the Revels: The Boy Companies of Shakespeare's Time and Their Plays* (New York: Columbia University Press, 1977), p. 154. But his own statement that the "new" form of comedy invented for the children's companies encouraged "spectators to identify with a roguishly attractive young gallant locked in conflict with one or more caricatured figure of authority" (p. 56) suggests that the opposite is, in fact, true.

8. As will be noted in the following chapters, the plots and characters of most of Middleton's comedies have been related to Roman comedy by a wide variety of critics. Gail Kern Paster has even argued that Middleton is Plautus's chief heir on the English stage in "The City in Plautus and Middleton," *Renaissance Drama* n.s. 6 (1973): 29–44.

9. See, for instance, R. B. Parker, "Middleton's Experiments with Comedy and Judgment," *Jacobean Theater*, Stratford-upon-Avon Studies, no. 1 (New York: St. Martin's Press, 1960), pp. 179–200; Richard Barker, *Thomas Middleton* (New York: Columbia University Press, 1958), p. 46; Anthony Covatta, *Thomas Middleton's City Comedies* (Lewisburg, Pa.: Bucknell University Press, 1973), pp. 38, 57, 102; and Charles A. Hallett, "Middleton's Overreachers and the Ironic Ending," *Tennessee Studies in Literature* 16 (1971): 1–13.

10. Among the most helpful studies of the influence of expectations and generic norms on interpretation are: Kenneth Burke, *Counter-Statement*, 2d ed. (Los Altos, California: Hermes Press, 1953), pp. 123–83; E. D. Hirsch, Jr., *Validity in Interpretation* (New Haven, Conn.: Yale University Press, 1967), pp. 68–126; Barbara Herrnstein Smith, *Poetic Closure: A Study of How Poems End* (Chicago: University of Chicago Press, 1968); Martin Steinmann, Jr., "Convention," in *Encyclopedia of Poetry and Poetics*, ed. Alex Preminger, Frank J. Warnke, and O. B. Hardison, Jr. (Princeton, N.J.: Princeton University Press, 1965), pp. 152–53; Stanley E. Fish, *Self-Consuming Artifacts: The Experi-*

ence of Seventeenth-Century Literature (Berkeley: University of California Press, 1972); E. H. Gombrich, *Art and Illusion: A Study in the Psychology of Pictorial Representation* (London: Phaidon Press, 1959); and Leonard B. Meyer, *Music, the Arts and Ideas: Patterns and Productions in Twentieth-Century Culture* (Chicago: University of Chicago Press, 1967), pp. 5–21. Both J. L. Styan, *Drama, Stage and Audience* (Cambridge: Cambridge University Press, 1975), and Bernard Beckerman, *Dynamics of Drama: Theory and Method of Analysis* (New York: Alfred A. Knopf, 1970), pp. 129–67, stress the importance of audience reactions in the theater, but neither critic discusses the expectations which are built into specific dramatic forms.

11. The frustration of audience expectations in Middleton's tragedies has been examined by Robert Jordan, "Myth and Psychology in *The Changeling*," *Renaissance Drama* n.s. 3 (1970): 157–65; J. B. Batchelor, "The Pattern of *Women Beware Women*," *Yearbook of English Studies* 2 (1972): 78–88; and Raymond J. Pentzell, "*The Changeling*: Notes on Mannerism in Dramatic Form," *Comparative Drama* 9 (1975): 3–28. Paradoxically, however, there has been little interest in this aspect of his comedies. Dorothy M. Farr does note that when the "fun [of Middleton's comedies] sometimes takes a sinister turn it owes much of its effect to the familiarity of the associations it suggests," but she does not develop the point further in *Thomas Middleton and the Drama of Realism: A Study of Some Representative Plays* (Edinburgh: Oliver and Boyd, 1973), p. 15.

12. Here, as elsewhere, my ideas about comedy are heavily indebted to Northrop Frye. I have also benefited from the following studies of comedy and related forms: E. K. Chambers, *The Medieval Stage*, 2 vols. (London: Oxford University Press, 1903); Francis Macdonald Cornford, *The Origin of Attic Comedy*, ed. Theodor H. Gaster (1914; reprint ed., Gloucester, Mass.: Peter Smith, 1968); C. L. Barber, *Shakespeare's Festive Comedy: A Study of Dramatic Form and its Relation to Social Custom* (Princeton, N. J.: Princeton University Press, 1959); Suzanne Langer, *Feeling and Form: A Theory of Art Developed From Philosophy in a New Key* (New York: Charles Scribner's Sons, 1953); Henri Bergson, *Laughter: An Essay on the Meaning of the Comic*, trans. Cloudesley Brereton and Fred Rothwell (New York: Macmillan Co., 1911); and Leo Salingar's work cited above. All of my generalizations about comic values and assumptions apply only to New Comedy and may not be relevant to other types of comedy. Unless otherwise noted, comedy, Roman comedy, and New Comedy are used interchangeably throughout.

13. See, for example, Una Ellis-Fermor, *The Jacobean Stage: An Introduction* (1935; reprint ed., New York: Random House, 1961), pp. 128–53; Samuel Schoenbaum, "*A Chaste Maid in Cheapside* and Middleton's City Comedy," in *Studies in the English Renaissance Drama*: *In*

Memory of Karl Julius Holzknecht, ed. Josephine Waters Bennett, Oscar Cargill, and Vernon Hall, Jr. (New York: New York University Press, 1959), pp. 287–309; Gibbons, *Jacobean City Comedy*, p. 205; Farr, *Drama of Realism*; and the studies of Middleton's tragedies cited in note 2 of Chapter 6.

14. The quotations are taken from *A Trick to Catch the Old One*, ed. G. J. Watson, The New Mermaids (London: Ernest Benn, Ltd., 1968).

15. R. C. Bald follows the manuscript version of the play and prints Hengist's outburst as "Vnreasonable folly" in his edition of *Hengist, King of Kent; or, The Mayor of Queensborough* (New York: Charles Scribner's Sons, 1938), p. 90. The reading I have chosen has its source in the 1661 edition of the play and is, I believe, more in keeping with the tenor of the scene. The quotations are taken from *The Works of Thomas Middleton*, ed. Arthur Henry Bullen, 8 vols. (1885–86; reprint ed., New York: AMS Press, 1964), 2:102, 105.

16. Claudio Guillèn, "Poetics as System," *Comparative Literature* 22 (1970): 202. Robert Ornstein points out that "Middleton is a realist who studies literary illusions as part of human experience" in *The Moral Vision of Jacobean Tragedy* (Madison: University of Wisconsin Press, 1960), p. 182.

17. R. B. Parker, ed., *A Chaste Maid in Cheapside*, The Revels Plays (London: Methuen, 1969), p. lix.

18. Frye, *A Natural Perspective*, pp. 46, 92.

19. Frye, *Anatomy of Criticism*, p. 184.

20. Ben Jonson, *Timber; or, Discoveries*, in *Ben Jonson*, ed. Charles H. Herford, Percy Simpson, and Evelyn Simpson, 11 vols. (Oxford: Oxford University Press, Clarendon Press, 1925–53), 8:567. On Renaissance attitudes toward inherited forms see Rosalie L. Colie, *The Resources of Kind: Genre Theory in the Renaissance*, ed. Barbara Lewalski (Berkeley: University of California Press, 1973), and *Shakespeare's Living Art* (Princeton, N.J.: Princeton University Press, 1974); Bernard Weinberg, *A History of Literary Criticism in the Italian Renaissance*, 2 vols., (Chicago: University of Chicago Press, 1961), esp. chapters 13, 16–21; Baxter Hathaway, *The Age of Criticism: The Late Renaissance in Italy* (Ithaca, N.Y.: Cornell University Press, 1962), p. 438; and Claudio Guillèn, *Literature as System: Essays Toward the Theory of Literary History* (Princeton, N.J.: Princeton University Press, 1971), p. 109.

21. This is an oversimplification, but it is, I think, true to the basic tendencies of English Renaissance literature. Extended analyses of Renaissance uses of literary tradition have usually focused on the methods of revising tradition which are here associated with Christian Humanism. Middleton's attitude toward inherited forms is the product of beliefs which basically oppose those of the early humanists.

22. Douglas Bush, *English Literature in the Earlier Seventeenth Century*, 2d. ed., The Oxford History of English Literature (Oxford:

Oxford University Press, Clarendon Press, 1962), p. 2; Herschel Baker, *The Wars of Truth: Studies in the Decay of Christian Humanism in the Seventeenth Century* (New York: Staples Press, 1952), p. 303.

23. For general discussions of this aspect of seventeenth-century literature see Frank J. Warnke, *Versions of Baroque: European Literature in the Seventeenth Century* (New Haven, Conn.: Yale University Press, 1972), p. 158; Anthony Caputi, *John Marston, Satirist* (Ithaca, N.Y.: Cornell Univ. Press, 1961), pp. 7–15; and Jackson I. Cope, *The Theater and the Dream: From Metaphor to Form in Renaissance Drama* (Baltimore: Johns Hopkins University Press, 1973), pp. 1–13. The studies dealing with individual authors who remake older forms according to their own purposes are too numerous to be mentioned here, and the comments which follow are simply intended to indicate the directions those studies have taken.

24. Stanley Fish in *Self-Consuming Artifacts*.

25. Stephen Booth, "On the Value of Hamlet," in *Reinterpretations of Elizabethan Drama*, Selected Papers from the English Institute, ed. Norman Rabkin (New York: Columbia University Press, 1969), p. 152.

26. On the questioning of misrule in *2 Henry IV* see Barber, *Shakespeare's Festive Comedy*, pp. 213–16. Gabriele Bernhard Jackson discusses Jonson's parodic uses of traditional "interactive comedy" in the introduction to her edition of *Everyman in His Humour*, The Yale Ben Jonson (New Haven, Conn.: Yale University Press, 1969), pp. 1–34. And John Finkelpearl has described Marston's attack on holiday in *What You Will* in *John Marston of the Middle Temple: An Elizabethan Dramatist in His Social Setting* (Cambridge, Mass.: Harvard University Press, 1969), pp. 164–77.

27. I am here speaking only of Renaissance tragicomedy and not modern plays associated with the term. Likewise, I am only concerned with Renaissance definitions of the genre. Guarini's ideas have been discussed by Doran, *Endeavors of Art*, pp. 203–9; Weinberg, *Literary Criticism*, 2:656–62, 679–85, 1074–1105; Marvin T. Herrick, *Tragicomedy: Its Origin and Development in Italy, France, and England* (Urbana: University of Illinois Press, 1962), pp. 130–42; Walter F. Staton, Jr. and William E. Simeone, eds., *A Critical Edition of Sir Richard Fanshawe's 1647 Translation of Giovanni Battista Guarini's "Il Pastor Fido"* (Oxford: Oxford University Press, Clarendon Press, 1964), pp. ix–xvi; and Arthur C. Kirsch, *Jacobean Dramatic Perspectives* (Charlottesville: University Press of Virginia, 1972), pp. 7–15. G. K. Hunter argues that Guarini's treatises, although not published in translation during the seventeenth century, were known generally to English dramatists in "Italian Tragicomedy on the English Stage," *Renaissance Drama* n.s. 6 (1973): 123–48.

28. See Kirsch, *Jacobean Dramatic Perspectives*, p. 10.

29. Giambattista Guarini, *Compendium of Tragicomic Poetry* (trans. of *Compendia Della Poesia Tragicomica*), trans. Allan H. Gilbert, in Allan H. Gilbert, *Literary Criticism: Plato to Dryden* (1940; reprint ed., Detroit: Wayne State University Press, 1962), pp. 507, 509, 512, 523–24. All quotations from Guarini are taken from this partial translation.

30. Ibid., p. 507.

31. Philip Edwards, "The Danger not the Death: The Art of John Fletcher," *Jacobean Theater*, Stratford-upon-Avon Studies, no. 1 (New York: St. Martin's Press, 1960), p. 175. Cf. Kirsch, *Jacobean Dramatic Perspectives*, pp. 38–47; and Eugene M. Waith, *The Pattern of Tragicomedy in Beaumont and Fletcher* (New Haven, Conn.: Yale University Press, 1952), pp. 39–41.

32. Indeed, John F. McElroy has argued that Middleton's tragicomedies present "a deliberate and sustained . . . ironic deflation" of the techniques of Beaumont and Fletcher in *Parody and Burlesque in the Tragicomedies of Thomas Middleton*, Jacobean Drama Studies, no. 19 (Salzburg: Institut für Englische Sprache und Literatur, 1972), p. 24. In many ways McElroy's study parallels my own, and he finds instances of literary parody throughout Middleton's career. But McElroy asserts that the early comedies "do not in general demonstrate the same sense for the satiric possibilities of form itself that the later [tragicomic] works do" (p. 94). I believe that the opposite is true, that the uses Middleton makes of tragicomic form repeat in a slightly different fashion techniques and concerns already fully developed in the comedies. As noted, it is doubtful that Middleton found much difference between the values and assumptions of comedy and those of tragicomedy.

33. Giason Denores, *Discorso intorno a' que' principii, cause, et accrescimenti . . .* , trans. Bernard Weinberg, in Weinberg, *Literary Criticism*, 2:1076 (cf. 2:1084); and Herrick, *Tragicomedy*, p. 136; Sir Philip Sidney, *The Defense of Poesie*, in Gilbert, *Plato to Dryden*, p. 451; Guarini, *Compendium*, p. 512.

34. Michel de Montaigne, "Of Friendship," *The Essayes of Michael, Lord of Montaigne*, trans. John Florio, 3 vols. (London: J. M. Dent and Sons, 1928), 1:195.

35. On the history and qualities of the grotesque, see Wolfgang Kayser, *The Grotesque in Art and Literature*, trans. Ulrich Weisstein (Bloomington: University of Indiana Press, 1963); Arthur Clayborough, *The Grotesque in English Literature* (Oxford: Oxford University Press, Clarendon Press, 1965); Willard Farnham, *The Shakespearean Grotesque* (Oxford: Oxford University Press, Clarendon Press, 1971); Lee Byron Jennings, *The Ludicrous Demon: Aspects of the Grotesque in German Post-Romantic Prose*, University of California Publications in Modern Philology, no. 71 (Berkeley: University of California Press, 1963); and Mikhail Bakhtin, *Rabelais and His World*,

trans. Helene Iswolsky (Cambridge, Mass.: MIT Press, 1968). According to Farnham, *Shakespearean Grotesque*, p. 8, the words *antic* and *grotesque* were synonymous in the Renaissance.

Bakhtin, *Rabelais*, argues that the disturbing and frightening qualities usually associated with the grotesque were not always present. It is only as man becomes alienated from his folk origins (the seventeenth century is a key turning point) that these negative associations begin to dominate, because "seriousness and fear reflect a *part* that is aware of its separation from the whole" (p. 254). Montaigne's essays seem to lie on the borderline between what Bakhtin sees as the true grotesque and the modern grotesque, but Middleton's plays definitely fall into the latter category and at times (the Dampit scenes in *A Trick to Catch the Old One*, the appearance and activities of De Flores in *The Changeling*) create the unsettling atmosphere which now seems central to the term's meaning.

36. Questions concerning the authorship of Middleton's dramas have been extensively analyzed by David J. Lake, *The Canon of Thomas Middleton's Plays: Internal Evidence for the Major Problems of Authorship* (Cambridge: Cambridge University Press, 1975). See also Chapter 2, note 7, and Chapter 5, note 18. Because Bullen's standard collection of Middleton's works is often unsatisfactory, I have employed readily accessible modern editions of the plays whenever possible. The specific texts being used are cited at the beginning of each chapter.

On the dates of Middleton's plays see Alfred B. Harbage *Annals of English Drama, 975–1700*, rev. Samuel Schoenbaum (London: Methuen, 1964); R. C. Bald, "The Chronology of Thomas Middleton's Plays," *MLR* 32 (1937): 33–43; Lake, *Canon*; and the introductions to the editions cited in the following chapters.

Chapter 2

1. On the political aspects of the play see Clifford Davidson, "*The Phoenix*: Middleton's Didactic Comedy," *Papers on Language and Literature* 4 (1968): 121–30; and a series of articles that link Phoenix with James I: N. W. Bawcutt, "Middleton's *The Phoenix* as a Royal Play," *N & Q* 201 (1956): 288; Marilyn L. Williamson, "*The Phoenix*: Middleton's Comedy *de Regimine Principum*," *Renaissance News* 10 (1957): 183–87; Daniel B. Dodson, "King James and *The Phoenix*—Again," *N & Q* 203 (1958): 57–61. For the play's relationship to the estates morality tradition, see Alan C. Dessen, "Middleton's *The Phoenix* and the Allegorical Tradition," *SEL* 6 (1966): 291–308.

2. J. W. Lever has traced the origins of this tradition in his introduction to the Arden Shakespeare *Measure for Measure* (London: Methuen & Co., 1965), pp. xliv–li. In its use of the disguised magistrate, *The Phoenix* closely resembles both *Measure for Measure*, Marston's *Malcontent*, and Middleton's own *Your Five Gallants*.

3. All quotations from *The Phoenix* and *The Family of Love* are taken from *The Works of Thomas Middleton*, ed. Arthur Henry Bullen, 8 vols. (1885–86; reprint ed., New York: AMS Press, 1965).

4. Angus Fletcher, *Allegory: The Theory of a Symbolic Mode* (Ithaca, N.Y.: Cornell University Press, 1964), p. 49, defines demonic agency in allegory in a manner that helps explain Tangle's behavior: "If a man is possessed by an influence that excludes all other influences while it is operating on him, then he clearly has no life outside an exclusive sphere of action."

5. Samuel Schoenbaum, "*A Chaste Maid in Cheapside* and Middleton's City Comedy," in *Studies in the English Renaissance Drama: In Memory of Karl Julius Holzknecht*, ed. Josephine Waters Bennett, Oscar Cargill, and Vernon Hall, Jr. (New York: New York University Press, 1959), p. 287. He is echoed by Anthony Covatta, *Thomas Middleton's City Comedies* (Lewisburg, Pa.: Bucknell University Press, 1973), pp. 66–72. The views are fairly characteristic of Middleton criticism.

Dessen, "Middleton's *The Phoenix*," pp. 291–308, has shown that Middleton "by conscious use of earlier dramatic conventions, has managed to maintain the realistic or 'literal' surface that we expect in Jacobean comedy while, at the same time, achieving the scope and general significance characteristic of the morality tradition" (p. 292). Although he does not explicitly note the sight imagery and the importance of clarity in the play, Dessen implies that the purpose of the conclusion is definition: "The various 'estates' (Lawyer, Magistrate, Courtier, Noble, Citizen's Wife) and the various principles (Honor, Loyalty, Justice, Law, Patience, Private Lust) . . . are thus brought forward . . . and conveniently labeled in Middleton's characteristic pseudo-allegorical fashion" (p. 305). Arthur Kirsch, *Jacobean Dramatic Perspectives* (Charlottesville: University Press of Virginia, 1972), pp. 84–85, reinforces Dessen's argument by stressing the relationship of Middleton's strange mixtures to the morality play tradition.

6. Lever, *Measure for Measure*, pp. xliv–li. Both Phoenix and Duke Vincentio in *Measure for Measure* have been interpreted as complementary portraits of James I (on *The Phoenix* see note 1 above). If this reading is correct, it further supports the points I have been stressing. Davidson, "Middleton's Didactic Comedy," pp. 121–30, has noted the relationship between Phoenix and Christ, although in his view the phoenix is primarily "a symbol of the way the kingship renews itself" (p. 124). He also relates Proditor to "the figure of Satan in the Garden of Eden" (p. 128).

7. Fletcher, *Allegory*, p. 222. He goes on to point out that "the same sharpening of opposition, the same denial of a natural moral continuum, the same withdrawal of moral and ethical and spiritual problems into two polar opposites, affects agency" (p. 223).

8. Although the great majority of critics believe that Middleton is the sole author of *The Family of Love*, some questions regarding collab-

oration have been raised. Gerald J. Eberle, "Dekker's Part in *The Family of Love*," *J. Q. Adams Memorial Studies*, ed. James G. MacManaway, Giles E. Dawson and Edwin Willoughby (Washington: Folger Library, 1948), pp. 723–38, has suggested that Dekker wrote parts of the play, and more recently David J. Lake, *The Canon of Thomas Middleton's Plays: Internal Evidence for the Major Problems of Authorship* (Cambridge: Cambridge University Press, 1975), pp. 91–108, has argued that David, Lord Barry revised nearly all of the work. Eberle's statements have gained little support, however, and Lake himself admits that his theory "is one about which I am not confident in detail" (p. 107). Whatever the contributions of Dekker and Barry (if any), the controlling imagination behind the play is clearly Middleton's.

9. For example, Clifford Davidson, "Middleton and the Family of Love," *English Miscellany* 20 (1969): 92, argues that the play was "written to exploit the contemporary curiosity about a notorious sect."

10. Richard Levin, *The Multiple Plot in English Renaissance Drama* (Chicago: University of Chicago Press, 1971), p. 61.

11. Ibid, p. 65.

12. Davidson, "Middleton and the Family of Love," p. 91, correctly notes that while Gerardine and Maria are superior to the other characters in the play, they are not different in kind; but his judgment that *The Family of Love* "is simply most successful in telling what love is not" (p. 92) seems to miss the real point of the play.

13. The possible parallel to *Romeo and Juliet* was first pointed out by W. J. Olive, "The Imitation of Shakespeare in Middleton's *Family of Love*," *PQ* 29 (1950): pp. 75–78. John F. McElroy extends Olive's insight and argues that the entire play is an example of "antiromantic burlesque" in "Middleton, Entertainer or Moralist? An Interpretation of *The Family of Love* and *Your Five Gallants*," *MLQ* 37 (1976): 37–41.

14. Failure to recognize this gradual modification of all idealistic sentiments in the drama lies behind, I believe, the general critical discomfort with Gerardine's sudden transformation. See, for instance, Alexander Leggatt, *Citizen Comedy in the Age of Shakespeare* (Toronto: University of Toronto Press, 1973), p. 107; and David Frost, *The School of Shakespeare: The Influence of Shakespeare on English Drama 1600–42* (Cambridge: Cambridge University Press, 1968), pp. 31–33.

15. Purge's name is self-explanatory. A *glister* (clyster) is a medicine injected into the rectum to empty or cleanse the bowels, an injection, an enema, and sometimes a suppository. It is also the pipe or syringe used to inject enemas and a contemptuous name for a doctor (*OED*). Arthur F. Marotti, "The Purgations of Middleton's *The Family of Love*," *Papers on Language and Literature* 7 (1971): 80–84, relates the passages on purgation to Renaissance medical theory. His summary of the uses of the term in the play is similar to mine, but Marotti does not relate the concept of purgation to the general comic movement

from restriction to freedom, or to Gerardine's role as playwright. Covatta, *City Comedies*, pp. 61–62, also notes the pervasive references to purgation, and argues that Gerardine "purges the play world of evil, giving metaphorical value to the rather coarse image that dominates the play" (p. 61).

16. For physiological theory, see Mary Claire Randolph, "The Medical Concept in English Renaissance Satiric Theory," *SP* 35 (1938): 125–57. For a general overview of Renaissance analyses of catharsis, see Baxter Hathaway, *The Age of Criticism: The Late Renaissance in Italy* (Ithaca, N.Y.: Cornell University Press, 1962), pp. 205–300. Samuel Henry Butcher argues that the Italian sixteenth-century critic Antonio Minturno rediscovered this medical interpretation of catharsis, in *Aristotle's Theory of Poetry and Fine Art with a Critical Text and Translation of the Poetics* (London: Macmillan and Co., 1902), pp. 244–47. Other contemporary Italian critics also comment upon the medical analogy, Agnolo Segni, Lorenzo Giacomini and Giambattista Guarini, among them. For representative statements by these writers see Bernard Weinberg, *A History of Literary Criticism in the Italian Renaissance* (Chicago: University of Chicago Press, 1961), 1:303, 627; 2:658, 739. Milton's famous preface to *Samson Agonistes* echoes the views of these Italian critics and is further indication of the influence of medical interpretations of catharsis during the Renaissance. See Ingram Bywater, "Milton and the Aristotelian Definition of Tragedy," *Journal of Philology* 27 (1900): 267–75; and Martin Mueller, "Sixteenth-Century Italian Criticism and Milton's Theory of Catharsis," *SEL* 6 (1966): 139–50. The best modern commentary on this aspect of catharsis is that of Franz Susemihl and Robert Drew Hicks in *The Politics of Aristotle: A Revised Text with Introduction, Analysis and Commentary* (London: Macmillan and Co., 1894), pp. 641–56.

Gerald F. Else has questioned the validity of a medical interpretation of catharsis in *Aristotle's Poetics: The Argument* (Cambridge, Mass.: Harvard University Press, 1957), pp. 224–32, 423–47. But for our purposes the issue is not the correctness of the Renaissance's use of catharsis as a medical analogy; what is important is that the use of the analogy was relatively common.

The *OED* cites no record of the word *catharsis* in English before 1803, when its primary meaning was the purgation of the body's excrement. However, the adjective *cathartic* was common in the seventeenth century and referred to various means of aiding defecation.

17. At least one other contemporary work, John Harrington's *A New Discourse of a Stale Subject, Called the Metamorphosis of Ajax*, ed. Elizabeth Story Donno (London: Routledge and Kegan Paul, 1962), similarly associates sex, defecation, and spiritual concerns. Harrington's tract is at once a mock encomium, a utilitarian treatise on sanitation, and a satiric attack upon "malcontents, Epicures, Atheists, hereticks, & careless & dissolute Christians, and especially against

pride & sensualitie"(p. 182). Like Middleton, Harrington associates the pleasures of orgasm and of evacuation: "This surpassing pleasure [lechery] . . . bred no more delectation to him (after the first heate of his youth was past) then to go to a good easie close stoole, when he hath had a lust thereto (for that was his verie phrase)" (p. 84). Moreover, his concern with physical cleanliness leads him to speculate about spiritual purity: "A good stoole might move as great devotion in some man, as a bad sermon" (p. 92), he notes at one point. Harrington links the devil to excrement (p. 94), and concludes the *Metamorphosis* by advising his reader "To keepe your houses sweete, cleanse privie vaults, / To keepe your soules as sweete, mend privie faults" (p. 186).

18. Robert C. Elliott, *The Power of Satire: Magic, Ritual, Art* (Princeton, N.J.: Princeton University Press, 1960), pp. 1–98, examines the relationship between satire, magic, and fertility.

19. Caroline Lockett Cherry, *The Most Unvaluedst Purchase: Women in the Plays of Thomas Middleton*, Jacobean Drama Studies, no. 29 (Salzburg: Institut für Englische Sprache und Literatur, 1973), finds similar oppositions throughout Middleton's work and argues that it "indicates the basically aggressive, sexual nature of commerce; it is in fact misdirected sexuality" (p. 68).

20. Compare Maria's speech at 1.1.18–22.

21. Cf. Fletcher, *Allegory*, p. 30: "There is nothing like the feeling one gets of a common humanity binding together the characters of a mimetic drama." Thus there is "no place for either comedy, which solves problems communally, or tragedy, which resolves by the death or exclusion of the hero from the community" (p. 338). The same is true, although to a lesser extent, of *Your Five Gallants*, a comical satire which approaches allegory in its use of marked oppositions and a masque as part of its conclusion.

22. See Henri Bergson's comments on this aspect of comic characterization in *Laughter: An Essay on the Meaning of the Comic*, trans. Cloudesley Brereton and Fred Rothwell (New York: Macmillan Co., 1911), pp. 140–48.

Chapter 3

1. Arthur Kirsch, *Jacobean Dramatic Perspectives* (Charlottesville: University Press of Virginia, 1972), pp. 75–96.

2. All quotations from Middleton's nondramatic works are taken from *The Works of Thomas Middleton*, ed. Arthur Henry Bullen, 8 vols. (1885–86; reprint ed., AMS Press, 1964): *Micro-cynicon*: 8:120–21; *Father Hubbard's Tales*: 8:65–88; *The Black Book*: 8:22. Quotations from *Michaelmas Term* and *A Trick to Catch the Old One* are taken from *Michaelmas Term*, ed. Richard Levin, Regents Renaissance Drama Series (Lincoln: University of Nebraska Press, 1966); and *A Trick to*

Catch the Old One, ed. G. J. Watson, The New Mermaids (London: Ernest Benn, Ltd., 1968).

3. Richard Barker, *Thomas Middleton* (New York: Columbia University Press, 1958), p. 50; Ruby Chatterji, "Unity and Disparity: *Michaelmas Term*," *SEL* 8 (1968): 359. Levin, *Michaelmas Term*, p. xviii. Anthony Covatta, *Thomas Middleton's City Comedies* (Lewisburg, Pa.: Bucknell University Press, 1973), argues that the drama is a unified example of "life-oriented comedy," but paradoxically goes on to say that Easy is not much of a hero: "It is difficult to summon much sympathy for him in the first two-thirds of the play. . . . At that, he is treated rather gently; the play's other gallants evoke much less sympathy" (pp. 91, 95).

4. For accounts of the humanist reception of Roman comedy and the resulting development of the Christian Terence and prodigal son plays, see E. K. Chambers, *The Elizabethan Stage*, 4 vols. (Oxford: Oxford University Press, Clarendon Press, 1923), 1:236–41; Charles H. Herford, *Studies in the Literary Relations of England and Germany in the Sixteenth Century* (Cambridge: Cambridge University Press, 1886), pp. 84–88; Marvin T. Herrick, *Tragicomedy: Its Origins and Development in Italy, France, and England* (Urbana: University of Illinois Press, 1962), pp. 16–62; R. W. Bond, "Introductory Essay" to *Early Plays from the Italian* (1911; reprint ed., Benjamin Blom, [1967]), pp. xciii–cix; Robert Y. Turner, "Dramatic Conventions in *All's Well that Ends Well*," *PMLA* 75 (1960): 497–502; Richard Helgerson, *The Elizabethan Prodigals* (Berkeley: University of California Press, 1976), pp. 34–43; Alexander Leggatt, *Citizen Comedy in the Age of Shakespeare* (Toronto: University of Toronto Press, 1973), pp. 33–53; and especially Ervin Beck, "Terence Improved: The Paradigm of the Prodigal Son in English Renaissance Comedy," *Renaissance Drama* n.s. 6 (1973): 107–22.

5. George Gascoigne, *The Glasse of Government*, in *The Complete Works of George Gascoigne*, ed. J. W. Cunliffe, 2 vols. (Cambridge: Cambridge University Press, 1907–10), 2:17. Herford, *Literary Relations*, p. 87, quotes a similar passage from Georgius Macropedius's *Asotus* and states that such remarks were "a hackneyed commonplace of every prologue." For additional Renaissance comments of this kind see Herrick, *Tragicomedy*, pp. 26–27. Helgerson, *Prodigals*, p. 35; Leggatt, *Citizen Comedy*, p. 40; and Beck, "Paradigm," pp. 110–15, all note that the parable contrasts many of the values of Roman comedy, but their points of emphasis are different from mine. None of them, moreover, examines in detail how comic values are questioned in specific sixteenth-century prodigal son plays.

6. From a song that concludes *Nice Wanton* (1550), in *A Select Collection of Old English Plays*, ed. Robert Dodsley, rev. W. C. Hazlitt, 14 vols. (1874–76; reprint ed., New York: Benjamin Blom, 1964), 2:183–84. All quotations from sixteenth-century prodigal son plays

except *The Glasse of Government* are taken from this collection. Dates for the prodigal son plays are based upon Alfred B. Harbage, *Annals of English Drama, 975–1700*, rev. Samuel Schoenbaum (London: Methuen, 1964).

7. Cf. Beck, "Paradigm," pp. 112–13. The essential conservatism of the parable is best shown by the radical changes that must be made in its structure to transform it into a vehicle urging change. *Lusty Juventus*, written by a Protestant militant named Richard Wever, represents just such an attempt. Wever's prodigal is misled not by his friends or by other youths but by his elders, who clearly signify the Catholic Church. In fact, there are no virtuous parents in the play, since tradition is evil and rebellion is called for. Likewise, the prodigal does not fall because he revolts against the status quo. He falls because he obeys mature voices which urge that he be subservient to an older generation. In using the biblical story for revolutionary purposes, Wever thus composes a play which resembles New Comedy. But despite the structural similarity between *Lusty Juventus* and classical drama, the moral outlook of Wever's play is still opposed (as later quotations will show) to that of Roman comedy.

8. Dodsley, *Collection*, 2:11, 88, 163.

9. Ibid., 2:288, 320.

10. Gascoigne, *Glasse of Government*, 2:6.

11. A partial list of plays employing prodigal son motifs and written between 1590 and 1626 might include *Two Lamentable Tragedies* (1594), *Richard II* (1595), *The Merchant of Venice* (1596), *1 Henry IV* (1597), *Histrio-mastix* (1599), *The London Prodigall* (1604), *The Wise-Woman of Hogsden* (1604), *Eastward Ho!* (1605), *The Miseries of Enforced Marriage* (1606), *The Knight of the Burning Pestle* (1607), *A New Way to Pay Old Debts* (1621), *The English Traveller* (1625), and *The Staple of News* (1626). For a more extensive list of prodigal son *comedies* see Beck, "Paradigm," pp. 121–22. The import of Beck's fine article is lessened, it seems to me, by the fact that he deals only with comic versions of the parable and thus excludes tragic plays which represent a logical development of the parable's antifestive perspective.

12. At one point during an abortive prodigal son play in *Histrio-mastix*, a roaring devil enters "with the *Vice* on his back, *Iniquity* in one hand; and *Juventus* in the other" (*The Plays of John Marston*, ed. H. Harvey Wood, 3 vols. [Edinburgh: Oliver and Boyd, 1939], 3:265). Similarly, in Heywood's *The Wise-Woman of Hogsden*, the young gallant Chartley is greeted by being called "*Lusty Iuventus*" (*The Dramatic Works of Thomas Heywood*, ed. R. H. Shepherd, 6 vols. [1872; reprint ed., New York: Russell and Russell, 1964], 5:325). In *The Staple of News* (*Ben Jonson*, ed. Charles H. Herford, Percy Simpson, and Evelyn Simpson, 11 vols. [Oxford: Oxford University Press, Clarendon Press, 1925–53], 6:323) Mirth explains that the play is an allegory in which we see

"Prodigality *like a young heyre, and his* Mistress Money . . . *prank't up like a prime* Lady."

13. The key word here is *extensively*. Leggatt, *Citizen Comedy*, pp. 44–53, examines several plays which mingle New Comedy and the prodigal son paradigm, but in all of the plays he discusses, the prodigal son material is given very little emphasis. In fact, some do not appear to be prodigal son plays at all.

14. This does not mean that Middleton did not know how to write a conventional prodigal son play. Both *Micro-cynicon* and *Father Hubbard's Tales* demonstrate that he could deal with the story in a straightforward manner if he wished; and, as will be shown below, Middleton reconciles the parable with New Comedy in *A Trick to Catch the Old One* (1605) by having the prodigals in that play reform in the opening scene. In later plays like *No Wit, No Help Like a Woman's* (1613) and *The Old Law* (1618), however, Middleton exploits the same ambiguities present in *Michaelmas Term*.

15. Covatta, *City Comedies*, p. 91.

16. For a particularly intricate expression of an hierarchical principle linking obedience to parents with social and spiritual order, see *The Glasse of Government*. Gascoigne even compares the relationship of parent and child to that of Christ and his flock (2:21). While commenting on Bartholomew Cokes's similarity to the protagonists of early "moralities of youth," Alan C. Dessen, *Jonson's Moral Comedy* (Evanston, Ill.: Northwestern University Press, 1971), p. 167, notes: "The fate of youth in such plays . . . is important not only in terms of his individual salvation but also in terms of the future health of society."

17. Brian Gibbons, *Jacobean City Comedy: A Study of Satiric Plays by Jonson, Marston and Middleton* (Cambridge, Mass.: Harvard University Press, 1968), p. 129; cf. Chatterji, "Unity and Disparity," p. 350.

18. Gail Kern Paster relates Middleton's urban environment to the setting of Plautus's plays in "The City in Plautus and Middleton," *Renaissance Drama* n.s. 6 (1973): 29–44; and Charles Hallett argues that the play attacks urban excesses in *Middleton's Cynics: A Study of Middleton's Insight into the Moral Psychology of the Mediocre Mind*, Jacobean Drama Studies, no. 47 (Salzburg: Institut für Englische Sprache und Literatur, 1975), pp. 24–44.

19. In *The Multiple Plot in English Renaissance Drama* (Chicago: University of Chicago Press, 1971), pp. 168–83, Richard Levin demonstrates that success in money matters is usually at odds with sexual prowess in Middleton's comedies.

20. T. W. Craik, *The Tudor Interlude: Stage, Costume, and Acting* (London: Leicester University Press, 1958), pp. 49–78. For examples of this symbolic use of clothing see *Mundus et Infans, Youth, Eastward Ho!*, and *The Staple of News*.

21. Mother Gruel states that "there's no woman so old but she may learn, and as an old lady delights in a young page or monkey, so there are young courtiers will be hungry upon an old woman, I warrant you" (1.1.299–301). Thomasine's ambiguity will be explained later in the text. The disappearance of the Father, who is the only completely upright character in the play, suggests that the world of *Michaelmas Term* is hopelessly corrupt.

22. The children in the play thus tend to have symbolic rather than natural parents. Hellgill states that persons like the Country Wench are begotten by "tirewomen and tailors" (3.1.5); Shortyard is Quomodo's true heir (5.1.2); and the Father provides Lethe with an alternative ancestry when he states: "He that can / Be bawd to woman never leapt from man; / Some monster won his mother" (3.1.265–67).

23. The prodigal son tradition is filled with parents who stand aside and comment on their children's misdeeds or go in disguise to seek out their foolish progeny. See, for example, *Misogonus, The Disobedient Child, The Glasse of Government, The London Prodigall*, and *The Staple of News*.

24. Signi Falk suggests that Middleton's plot is based upon a specific Roman play in "Plautus' *Persa* and Middleton's *A Trick to Catch the Old One*," *MLN* 66 (1951): 19–21. But Watson, *A Trick*, p. xiv, argues more convincingly that the drama is generally indebted to New Comedy rather than to a specific play. He adds that Middleton shifts the usual New Comedy emphasis from "the ingenuity and vitality of the deceivers . . . to the greed and folly of the deceived" (pp. xiv–xv). As will be seen, this slight change in focus has an important effect on our response to Middleton's play.

25. Richard Levin, *Michaelmas Term*, p. xix. His point is reinforced by Beck, "Paradigm," p. 118: "The more the [prodigal son] paradigm is abbreviated the more the resultant play imitates Roman comedy, both in idea and in form." This result is precisely the case with *A Trick to Catch the Old One*.

26. Thus Leggatt, *Citizen Comedy*, p. 39, states that in some plays the prodigal's "fate can be seen as a criticism of a society so obsessed with money that anyone who mishandles it is virtually destroyed."

27. Watson, *A Trick*, p. xxii, argues that the concluding speeches are ironic, and burlesque "the traditionally moral exit of the prodigal," but his view is, I believe, too extreme. Witgood and the Courtesan certainly mock the language of conventional reformation speeches, but their words are indicative nevertheless of their desire to turn away from the follies of their past.

28. Love is not, of course, necessarily a major concern in Roman comedy (in Plautus's *Casina* the young lover does not even appear), but Madeleine Doran, *Endeavors of Art: A Study of Form in Elizabethan Drama* (Madison: University of Wisconsin Press, 1954), pp. 171–82, has shown that Renaissance dramatists usually give much greater

emphasis to romance than do their Roman predecessors. Her findings have been corroborated by Leo Salingar, *Shakespeare and the Traditions of Comedy* (Cambridge: Cambridge University Press, 1974), pp. 28–75; and Bruce R. Smith, "Sir Amorous Knight and the Indecorous Romans; or, Plautus and Terence Play Court in the Renaissance," *Renaissance Drama* n.s. 6 (1973): 3–27. Middleton's handling of Witgood and Joyce is therefore more extraordinary than it first appears.

29. Wilbur Dunkel, *The Dramatic Technique of Thomas Middleton in His Comedies of London Life* (Chicago: University of Chicago Libraries, 1925), p. 94; cf. Charles Barber, *A Trick to Catch the Old One*, Fountainwell Drama Texts (Berkeley: University of California Press, 1968), p. 4: "The 'romantic' story of Witt-good's marriage to the Neece is treated with utmost perfunctoriness."

30. Bert O. States, *Irony and Drama: A Poetics* (Ithaca, N.Y.: Cornell University Press, 1971), p. 65. The trouble with Shakespeare's problem plays, States goes on to say, is that some of the characters "come too near to making infinite judgments about their finite problems" (p. 68).

31. Dampit does forget some of his companions while he is in a drunken stupor (4.5.), but this is not thematically very significant. It is a sign of his failing health, rather than an indication of any change in his attitudes.

32. The relationship of Lucre and Witgood is not the only example of perverted familial relationships in *A Trick*. Mistress Lucre, in contrast to her husband, displays a love for her son which is a bit too passionate. When she notes, "If I were a widow, I could find it in my heart to have thee myself, son; ay, from 'em all," he answers: "Thank you for your good will, mother, but indeed I had rather have a stranger" (2.1.363–66).

33. Massinger understood this aspect of Middleton's play very well when he gave his adaptation of *A Trick* the name *A New Way to Pay Old Debts*.

34. The careful contrast that Middleton draws between Witgood and the other characters also distinguishes the gallant's trick from the actions of Harry Dampit. Like Witgood, Dampit first gains riches by use of his wits (1.4.24–26), but this one similarity only serves to emphasize the great differences between the usurer's unending and ultimately evil trickery and Witgood's highly moral single plot.

35. Thus David M. Holmes, *The Art of Thomas Middleton* (Oxford: Oxford University Press, Clarendon Press, 1970), p. 82, because he relegates Dampit to a footnote, can read the play as an example of the success of a character whose "saving grace is a dawning, infant-like ability to respond to wholesome influence."

36. Barber, *A Trick*, p. 7; cf. Covatta, *City Comedies*, pp. 102–3.

37. Richard Levin, on the other hand, argues that Dampit is not

closely associated with Hoard and Lucre in "The Dampit Scenes in *A Trick to Catch the Old One*," *MLQ* 25 (1964): 140–52. According to his reading Dampit is "a sort of emotional lightning rod, someone who can draw off from Lucre and Hoard to himself the audience's normal detestation of the usurer" (p. 147). Levin's treatment of the play in *Multiple Plot*, pp. 127–37, also stresses the contrasting function of the Dampit scenes. Cf. Leggatt, *Citizen Comedy*, p. 58; and Watson, *A Trick*, pp. xxx–xxxi. In my opinion the parallels between the subplot and the main plot are at least as crucial as the differences. The Dampit scenes, as the general discomfort with them suggests, are not an emotional lightning rod; they complicate rather than simplify our responses to the primary action.

38. Levin, "The Dampit Scenes," p. 150, connects all three usurers with the devil, the "old one" of the play's title. The Creditors are also linked to hell (4.3.61–62). As previously noted, Witgood is separated from all of these characters by the meaning of his Christian name, and Middleton emphasizes the separation in the meeting between the youth and the drunken lawyer. Shortly after Witgood states that Gulf walks so low in order to be "nigher hell by a foot and a half than the rest of his fellows" (1.4.36–37), Dampit greets the gallant, saying, "My sweet Theodorus" (l.38).

39. A brief look at Massinger's revision of *A Trick* may shed further light on the ways in which Middleton undermines his New Comedy. In *A New Way to Pay Old Debts*, Massinger combines the roles of Lucre and Hoard into a single character, Giles Overreach, while he divides that of Witgood into two: a prodigal named Wellborn, who attempts to regain his lost land, and his friend Allworth, who is in love with Overreach's daughter. In doing so, Massinger is able to separate finances from love and to develop fully the romance of Allworth and Margaret and thus avoid the problems present in Middleton's portrayal of his young lovers. At the same time, Massinger makes almost all of the characters more respectable than they are in Middleton's play: he transforms the Creditors into good-natured and well-meaning individuals, he alters the female lead from a courtesan to a rich widow, and he implies that Wellborn's prodigality is really a case of being too generous toward friends. Wellborn is therefore more a victim of ingratitude than a spendthrift gallant. Significantly, Massinger also includes a figure of goodness and probity who easily dominates the evil characters. Lovell is so noble and so wise that the outcome of the action, despite Overreach's apparent enormity, is never really in doubt. There is nothing comparable to the Dampit scenes here, and Massinger does not convey the terrifying aspects of evil. We never take Overreach's threats seriously and can easily dismiss him from our minds at the conclusion of the drama. Even more important, Overreach does not, as the usurers in *A Trick* do, represent

the world of the play. He is an aberration. We know that as soon as Overreach is inevitably overthrown, things will return to normal, and so we can heartily participate in the festivity with which the comedy concludes. In contrast to Middleton's play, the young protagonists' triumph brings with it the renewal of the society they inhabit.

40. Some critics have attempted to resolve the ambiguity for Middleton, either by stating that the play's central characters are not very superior to their society (Watson, *A Trick*, pp. xxii–xxiv), or by arguing that their triumph does indeed constitute a rebirth of the world around them (Covatta, *City Comedies*, p. 104).

41. Levin, *Multiple Plot*, p. 16. David Riggs, " 'Plot' and 'Episode' in Early Neoclassical Criticism," *Renaissance Drama* n.s 6 (1973): 149–75, comes closer to describing Middleton's technique when he argues that, in Renaissance drama, secondary plots "remind us that other versions of this story are conceivable, that other outcomes might have been possible" (p. 175). Riggs, however, does not speculate on the consequences of including episodes that directly contradict and question the values and judgments of the main plot.

42. Michel de Montaigne, "Of Friendship," *The Essayes of Michael, Lord of Montaigne*, trans. John Florio, 3 vols. (London: J. M. Dent and Son, 1928), 1:195.

Chapter 4

1. Follywit, of course, does owe some aspects of his characterization to the tradition of prodigal son plays. Leanore Lieblein, "Thomas Middleton's Prodigal Play," *Comparative Drama* 10 (1976): 54–60, argues that Middleton's drama "questions generally the assumptions of prodigal plays" (p. 59) because Follywit does not repent and is not condemned for his foolishness. But the parable is not central in *A Mad World*. The play does not concentrate on the young gallant's denial of familial ties but on his wit. As we will see, Middleton's interests clearly lie elsewhere.

2. William W. Slights, "The Trickster-Hero and Middleton's *A Mad World, My Masters*," *Comparative Drama* 3 (1969): 87–98, has noted the relation of madness to extreme behavior in the play.

3. Quotations from *A Mad World, My Masters, No Wit, No Help Like a Woman's,* and *A Chaste Maid in Cheapside* are taken from *A Mad World, My Masters*, ed. Standish Henning, Regents Renaissance Drama Series (Lincoln: University of Nebraska Press, 1965); *No Wit, No Help Like a Woman's*, ed. Lowell E. Johnson, Regents Renaissance Drama Series (Lincoln: University of Nebraska Press, 1976); and *A Chaste Maid in Cheapside*, ed. R. B. Parker, The Revels Plays (London: Methuen, 1969).

4. For a discussion of Penitent as presenter-satirist, see Charles

Hallett, "Penitent Brothel, the Succubus and Parson's *Resolution:* A Reappraisal of Penitent's Position in Middleton's Canon," *SP* 69 (1972): 72–86.

5. Cf. Richard Levin, *The Multiple Plot in English Renaissance Drama* (Chicago: University of Chicago Press, 1971), p. 172.

6. Henning, *A Mad World*, p. xii; Levin, *Multiple Plot*, p. 173; Alexander Leggatt, *Citizen Comedy in the Age of Shakespeare* (Toronto: University of Toronto Press, 1973), p. 138; Anthony Covatta, *Thomas Middleton's City Comedies* (Lewisburg, Pa.: Bucknell University Press, 1973), pp. 121–23. At the opposite extreme, Hallett, "Reappraisal," pp. 72–86, and Brian Gibbons, *Jacobean City Comedy: A Study of Satiric Plays by Jonson, Marston and Middleton* (Cambridge, Mass.: Harvard University Press, 1968), p. 110, both stress the scene's importance in establishing a conventional moral outlook. Slights, "Trickster-Hero," p. 95, comes closer to a true account of Middleton's technique: "The very madness, the excess of this world argues for an enlarged view of the 'comic framework' which can include extreme statements of traditional piety as part of the play's comic madness."

7. The juxtaposition of contrary qualities and the rapid reversals of personality are related to what Richard Barker, *Thomas Middleton* (New York: Columbia University Press, 1958), p. 53, calls Middleton's ironic farce: "[In Middleton's plays] sinners invariably misunderstand the world in which they live, invariably set in motion the forces that bring about their own downfall." Cf. Arthur Marotti, "The Method in the Madness of *A Mad World, My Masters*," *Tennessee Studies in Literature* 15 (1970): 101. Marotti goes on to argue that the extremes in the drama are gradually brought into balance to form a *concordia discors* (pp. 100–101). Both views are, I think, overly moralistic and make Middleton's play more conventional than it is.

8. Henning, *A Mad World*, p. xi. Slights, "Trickster-Hero," pp. 87–90, comments on Follywit's relationship to Roman comedy and discusses his role as trickster-hero.

9. Northrop Frye, *Anatomy of Criticism: Four Essays* (Princeton, N.J.: Princeton University Press, 1957), p. 175.

10. It is precisely this kind of attitude that Bounteous Progress finds so admirable in Lord Owemuch's reaction to being robbed (5.1.46–50). The praise is ironically misplaced, but it nevertheless indicates what for Sir Bounteous are essential values. Covatta, *City Comedies*, p. 130, also stresses the knight's liberality and notes that he "is the play's strongest force for acceptance." He does not, however, examine closely the knight's relationship to comic values.

11. Marotti, "Method in the Madness," p. 101.

12. Henning, *A Mad World*, p. x.

13. See Levin, *Multiple Plot*, 172.

14. Arthur Kirsch, *Jacobean Dramatic Perspectives* (Charlottesville: University Press of Virginia, 1972), pp. 86–89, points out that during

the course of *A Mad World* Follywit is both an actor in and director of several plays. Marotti, "Method in the Madness," pp. 104–5, also analyzes in detail the play-within-the-play, but his emphasis is different from mine. According to Marotti, the function of Follywit's playlet is to make the audience "recognize a certain arbitrariness about the designations 'illusion' and 'reality' " (p. 105).

15. This in itself is not unusual. As Harry Berger has shown in "Renaissance Imagination: Second World and Green World," *Centennial Review* 9 (1965): 36–78, Renaissance writers generally conceived of their works as "temporarily self-sufficient" creations (p. 75) which the reader must recognize as idealized versions of reality, not reality itself: "The reader . . . is enjoined not to lose himself in the work but to interpret and move on" (p. 75). For Middleton, however, the hypothetical "might be" of comedy does not represent a golden ideal which we must strive to imitate as best we can. Rather, it is a foolish misconception.

16. Marotti, "Method in the Madness," p. 106, similarly argues that this reversal affirms the audience's "lack of control over their experience of the play."

17. Slights, "Trickster-Hero," p. 97.

18. On the dating of the play see David George, "Weather-Wise's Almanac and the Date of Middleton's *No Wit, No Help Like a Woman's*, *N&Q* 13 (1966): 297–301; David J. Lake, *The Canon of Thomas Middleton's Plays: Internal Evidence for the Major Problems of Authorship* (Cambridge: Cambridge University Press, 1975), p. 20; and Johnson, *No Wit*, p. xii. R. C. Bald supports the later date in "The Chronology of Thomas Middleton's Plays," *MLR* 32 (1937): 33–43.

19. On *La Sorella*, see D. J. Gordon, "Middleton's *No Wit, No Help Like a Woman's* and Della Porta's *La Sorella*," *RES* 17 (1941): 400–414; and Louise Clubb, *Giambattista Della Porta, Dramatist* (Princeton, N.J.: Princeton University Press, 1965), pp. 289–93. On Fletcherian romance, see Johnson, *No Wit*, pp. xix–xx; cf. Barker, *Thomas Middleton*, p. 87. Both critics find the experiment an unfortunate one. In Johnson's words, "Middleton was not confident enough to develop Fletcher's conventions, nor willing to give up the techniques of his successful city comedies" (p. xx).

20. Indeed, Muriel Bradbrook, *The Growth and Structure of Elizabethan Comedy* (London: Chatto and Windus, 1955), p. 158, suggests that the central plot draws on Plautus's *Captivi*.

21. David Holmes, *The Art of Thomas Middleton* (Oxford: Oxford University Press, Clarendon Press, 1970), p. 88, calls Philip "a complete moral idiot."

22. The fact that the main features of this episode are taken from *La Sorella* does not alter the import of the scene. Middleton's indebtedness is not in itself significant. What is significant is that out of the vast number of possible sources open to him, he selected a play so

amenable to his characteristic treatment of comedy. Moreover, Middleton makes Della Porta's play even more problematic. He adds an entirely new level of themes and motifs with the Lady Goldenfleece–Mistress Low-water plot and, as Gordon notes, makes Philip's encounter with his mother "even more unpalatable" ("Middleton's *No Wit*," p. 409). Clubb likewise points out that "The heartlessness in *No Wit* . . . is . . . native to Middleton; Della Porta's characters, on the contrary, manifest the tenderest of Counter-Reformation sensibilities" (*Giambattista Della Porta*, p. 292). She goes on to state that *La Sorella* is one of Della Porta's first experiments "at injecting semi-tragic elements into the form of neoclassical farce he had perfected" (p. 293). Middleton obviously found the mixture to his liking.

23. For other examples of Savorwit's peculiar sense of humor see 4.1.110–12, 270. Cynicism of this sort pervades *No Wit* to a greater degree than it does any of Middleton's other comedies, with the possible exception of *A Chaste Maid in Cheapside*. Its presence qualifies the effect of the play's more romantic elements.

24. Enid Welsford, *The Court Masque: A Study in the Relationship Between Poetry and Revels* (1927; reprint ed., New York: Russell and Russell, 1962), p. 397.

25. See Stephen Orgel, *The Jonsonian Masque* (Cambridge, Mass.: Harvard University Press, 1965), p. 73. His comments on the relationship of masque to antimasque clarify what the gallants (and Middleton) are doing: "The antimasque world was a world of particularity and mutability—of accidents; the masque world was one of ideal abstractions and eternal verities."

26. Wilbur Dunkel, *The Dramatic Technique of Thomas Middleton in His Comedies of London Life* (Chicago: University of Chicago Libraries, 1925), p. 76. Parker, *A Chaste Maid*, pp. lviii–lix. Like all readers of the play, I am greatly indebted to Parker's excellent edition.

27. See Levin, *Multiple Plot*, 198–99. Parker, *A Chaste Maid*, p.xlii, downplays the importance of the New Comedy structure of the drama. As I hope to show, Middleton's handling of the comedy's form is such that each view is partially correct.

28. Frye, *Anatomy of Criticism*, p. 170.

29. On the play's discordant elements, see especially Samuel Schoenbaum, "*A Chaste Maid in Cheapside* and Middleton's City Comedies," in *Studies in the English Renaissance Drama: In Memory of Karl Julius Holzknecht*, ed. Josephine Waters Bennett, Oscar Cargill, and Vernon Hall, Jr. (New York: New York University Press, 1959), pp. 298–308. Robert I. Williams, "Machiavelli's *Mandragola*, Touchwood Senior, and the Comedy of Middleton's *A Chaste Maid in Cheapside*," *SEL* 20 (1970): 396, extends Schoenbaum's insights and notes that "Middleton in his way quickens us to the incongruities of Cheapside by engaging us in a theatrical experience whose conflicting romance

and cynicism evoke a strong sense of perplexity." Gibbons, *Jacobean City Comedy*, pp. 165–66, approaches my reading of the play when he suggests that Middleton is satirizing Dekkeresque popular comedy.
30. On prostitutes, see, for instance, Parker, *A Chaste Maid*, p. xlvii. On family, see Schoenbaum, "Middleton's City Comedies," p. 292. He argues that Middleton, more than other contemporary dramatists, "is concerned with the effects of the competitive struggle on family relationships—on ties of blood or marriage." Cf. Ruby Chatterji, "Theme, Imagery and Unity in *A Chaste Maid in Cheapside*," *Renaissance Drama* 8 (1965): 106–16; and Parker, *A Chaste Maid*, pp. l–li.
31. On the relationship of comedy to seasonal patterns and rituals intended to celebrate or control those patterns see, for example, Francis Macdonald Cornford, *The Origin of Attic Comedy*, ed. Theodor H. Gaster (1914; reprint ed., Gloucester, Mass.: Peter Smith, 1968); Theodor H. Gaster, *Thespis: Ritual, Myth, and Drama in the Ancient Near East* (New York: Harper and Row, 1966); Northrop Frye, *Anatomy of Criticism*, pp. 163–86, and *A Natural Perspective: The Development of Shakespearean Comedy and Romance* (New York: Columbia University Press, 1965); E. K. Chambers, *The Medieval Stage*, 2 vols. (London: Oxford University Press, Clarendon Press, 1903); and C. L. Barber, *Shakespeare's Festive Comedy: A Study of Dramatic Form and its Relation to Social Custom* (Princeton, N.J.: Princeton University Press, 1959).
32. On the relationship of medieval and Renaissance drama to Christian liturgy, see Chambers, *Medieval Stage*; Karl Young, *The Drama of the Medieval Church*, 2 vols. (Oxford: Oxford University Press, Clarendon Press, 1933); and O. B. Hardison, *Christian Rite and Christian Drama in the Middle Ages: Essays in the Origin and Early History of Modern Drama* (Baltimore, Md.: Johns Hopkins University Press, 1965).
33. Hardison, *Christian Rite*, pp. 83, 284. Cf. Frye, *Natural Perspective*, pp. 73, 133. Although he overlooks the relation of the Easter season to comic structure, Parker, *A Chaste Maid*, pp. li–lvi, discusses contemporary English Lenten practices and restrictions and argues that the paradoxes of this season are a key to understanding the paradoxes of the play. My comments on the Lenten–Easter liturgy are based upon the 1551 Anglican prayer book. References will be made parenthetically to the version contained in F. E. Brightman, *The English Rite: Being a Synopsis of the Sources and Revisions of the Book of Common Prayer*, 2 vols. (London: Rivingtons, 1915). As far as is known, Middleton, if he was a Christian, was a member of the Church of England. See Bertil Johansson, *Religion and Superstition in the Plays of Ben Jonson and Thomas Middleton*, Essays and Studies on English Language and Literature, vol. 7 (New York: Haskell House, 1966), p. 51.
34. Brightman, *English Rite*, 1:303, 309; 2:731.
35. Ibid., 1:288.

36. Ibid., 2:735.

37. Chatterji, "Theme, Imagery and Unity," pp. 111–12.

38. Alan Brissenden compares this episode to the episode of Mak the shepherd in the *Second Shepherd's Play* of the Towneley Cycle, in his New Mermaids edition of *A Chaste Maid in Cheapside* (London: Ernest Benn, 1968), p. xxi.

39. This commitment to the flesh should be distinguished from a similar tendency on the part of the characters in *The Family of Love*. In the earlier drama, the individuals' literal-mindedness reinforces the play's overall (and typically comic) development away from opposing extremes and idealized abstractions and toward a more moderate middle ground which emphasizes the homogeneous nature of the play-society and accommodates as large a cross section of that society as possible. Likewise, their almost amoral obsession with physical matters results from their involvement with another comic good—the sexual love which enables the community to renew itself. In *A Chaste Maid*, on the other hand, the characters' lack of interest in things spiritual is a mark of their alienation from all forms of rebirth. Their commitment to the flesh does not signal a commitment to fertility and procreation, nor does it reinforce a general comic movement within the play toward moderation and inclusiveness. As we will see, the characters' disdain for the renewal of the spirit is matched by their inability to find any hope of regeneration in human sexuality.

40. Arthur F. Marotti, "Fertility and Comic Form in *A Chaste Maid in Cheapside*," *Comparative Drama* 3 (1969): 67. He basically interprets the comedy as if it were totally conventional. Cf. Covatta, *City Comedies*, pp. 158–62.

41. Parker, *A Chaste Maid*, p. 1, notes the ambiguous relationship between parents and children in the play and finds that the drama's attitude toward fertility is not "unqualified approval," but he does not develop the point.

42. For an excellent account of the manner in which Middleton "seems at pains to give full value to both levels of significance, the comic and the near tragic, on which the scene is built," see Dorothy M. Farr, *Thomas Middleton and the Drama of Realism: A Study of Some Representative Plays* (Edinburgh: Oliver and Boyd, 1973), p. 30. She goes on to state that "comedy is concerned with the immediate and familiar, the transitory and the odd, but the diabolic character carries us into universals which are not easily reconciled with the commonplace" (p. 32). This is exactly what occurs in Whorehound's repentance scene and in the Lethe and Dampit subplots of *Michaelmas Term* and *A Trick*, respectively. But despite the import of her own comments, Farr surprisingly argues also that *A Chaste Maid* affirms marriage and procreation (p. 22).

43. See Samuel Schoenbaum's discussion of Middleton's attitude toward sexuality in relation to the views of other dramatists in "*Hen-*

gist, King of Kent and Sexual Preoccupation in Jacobean Drama," *PQ* 29 (1950): 182–98.

44. Levin, *Multiple Plot*, p. 202.

45. Of course, we may wish to discover a difference, and some critics do. For example, Williams, "Machiavelli's *Mandragola*," p. 393, argues that Middleton persuades "us to feel that this redirection of wealth [Kix to Touchwood Senior] is just, tending as it does toward something like planned parenthood." Parker, *A Chaste Maid*, judges the episode correctly, I believe, when he finds that the parallelism "raises certain problems" and "undercuts any simple moral interpretation of the play" (pp. xliv–xlv).

46. On the other hand, both Parker, *A Chaste Maid*, p. 1, and Chatterji, "Theme, Imagery and Unity," p. 115, argue for a qualified approval of marriage at the end of the play and attempt to show that it is fitting that only Whorehound is punished.

47. Johan Huizinga, *Homo Ludens: A Study of the Play Element in Culture* (Boston: Beacon Press, 1950), pp. 1, 10, 17.

48. Frye, *A Natural Perspective*, pp. 75–76. The appropriateness of closely linking comedy and play is further demonstrated by the fact that medieval playwrights and audiences conceived of the great Corpus Christi cycles—themselves comic in form—as significant play. See V. A. Kolve, *The Play Called Corpus Christi* (Stanford, Calif.: Stanford University Press, 1966), pp. 8–32.

49. See Baxter Hathaway, *The Age of Criticism: The Late Renaissance in Italy* (Ithaca, N.Y.: Cornell University Press, 1962), pp. 129–143; and *Marvels and Commonplaces: Renaissance Literary Criticism* (New York: Random House, 1968), esp. pp. 88–132; William Nelson, *Fact or Fiction: The Dilemma of the Renaissance Storyteller* (Cambridge, Mass.: Harvard University Press, 1973), pp. 56–91; and Berger, "Renaissance Imagination." Nelson, pp. 56–72, discusses the tendency of Renaissance writers to view fiction as a kind of play.

50. Huizinga, *Homo Ludens*, p. 11.

51. Cf. Leo Salingar, *Shakespeare and the Traditions of Comedy* (Cambridge: Cambridge University Press, 1974), p. 127; and A. N. Kaul's comments on "vital intelligence" in *The Action of English Comedy: Studies in the Encounter of Abstraction and Experience from Shakespeare to Shaw* (New Haven, Conn.: Yale University Press, 1970), pp. 47–48.

Chapter 5

1. Richard Barker, *Thomas Middleton* (New York: Columbia University Press, 1958), pp. 90–91; Samuel Schoenbaum, "Middleton's Tragicomedies," *MP* 54 (1956): 8. But Schoenbaum does go on to argue that Middleton's moral stance remains constant, and that this consistency lies "in the intellectual passion which led him to envision the ironic order that gives coherence to his individual works" (p. 19).

Arthur Kirsch, *Jacobean Dramatic Perspectives* (Charlottesville: University Press of Virginia, 1972), p. 96. For an exception to the tendency to downgrade Middleton's tragicomedies, see Carolyn Asp, *A Study of Thomas Middleton's Tragicomedies*, Jacobean Drama Studies, no. 28 (Salzburg: Institut für Englische Sprache und Literatur, 1974).

2. This transitional quality may have resulted from Middleton's attempts to adapt his talents to the demands of adult companies and their audiences after the closing of the children's theaters, as well as his desire to respond to the popularity of Fletcher's plays. See Michael Shapiro, *Children of the Revels: The Boy Companies of Shakespeare's Time and Their Plays* (New York: Columbia University Press, 1977), pp. 225–27. Yet we must be careful not to overemphasize the importance of Middleton's new dependence on adult troupes. After all, both *Women Beware Women* and *The Changeling* were written for adult companies, and the two tragedies describe a world totally consistent with that of the early comedies (see Chapter 6).

3. The same is true of the romantic comedies written during the later stages of Middleton's career. By contrasting the triumph of a foolish young man of confidence named Ricardo—a character who recalls Tharsalio in Chapman's *The Widow's Tears*—with the difficulties of ostensibly clever and intelligent individuals (Valeria, Phillipa, the two Suitors), *The Widow* continues the analysis of wit found in the city comedies. *Anything for a Quiet Life* ends with a series of amazing reconciliations which are blessed, ironically, by a hypocritical and immoral nobleman, Lord Beaufort, a man scarcely fitted to the role of peacemaker and host of a traditional comic feast. Both plays, however, lack the intensity and interest of Middleton's earlier comedies.

4. See John F. McElroy's *Parody and Burlesque in the Tragicomedies of Thomas Middleton*, Jacobean Drama Studies, no. 19 (Salzburg: Institut für Englische Sprache und Literatur, 1972), a study which argues that Middleton's tragicomedies "attack romantic illusion by demonstrating the absurdity of one of its main vehicles in the Jacobean period—Fletcher's tragicomedy" (p. 26). McElroy's approach in many ways complements my own, but in light of the playwright's entire career it seems that Middleton's examination of comic values is both prior to and a cause of any parodic use he may make of Fletcher's techniques. For further discussion of McElroy's thesis see Chapter 1, note 32.

5. See Chapter 1; Bernard Weinberg, *A History of Literary Criticism in the Italian Renaissance*, 2 vols. (Chicago: University of Chicago Press, 1961), 2:1080–81; and Cyrus Hoy, "Renaissance and Restoration Dramatic Plotting," *Renaissance Drama* 9 (1966): 250: "One must not be blind to the essentially comic design of Jacobean tragicomedy, with its intrigue-ridden plots and with romantic love—the time honored subject of comedy—the ground of all its arguments."

6. Hoy, "Renaissance and Restoration Dramatic Plotting," p.

250; Jackson I. Cope, *The Theater and the Dream: From Metaphor to Form in Renaissance Drama* (Baltimore, Md.: Johns Hopkins University Press, 1973), p. 89.

7. All quotations from *More Dissemblers Besides Women* and *The Old Law* are taken from *The Works of Thomas Middleton*, ed. Arthur Henry Bullen, 8 vols. (1885–86; reprint ed., New York: AMS Press, 1965).

8. Critics have described the nature of this fallen existence in various ways. For David Holmes, *The Art of Thomas Middleton* (Oxford: Oxford University Press, Clarendon Press, 1970), p. 76, the play is Middleton's culminating treatment of the "idea that virtue can only be real and effective when it has been tempered by experience." Charles A. Hallett, *Middleton's Cynics: A Study of Middleton's Insight into the Moral Psychology of the Mediocre Mind*, Jacobean Drama Studies, no. 47 (Salzburg: Institut für Englische Sprache und Literatur, 1975), approaches the play in a similar fashion, arguing that the drama's central "technique is to thwart the natural expectations of the individual [character]" and thus cause his true self to "come out of hiding to handle the deteriorating situation" (p. 158). McElroy, on the other hand, argues that the play shows "the inherent limitations of reason" (p. 139).

9. Caroline Lockett Cherry, *The Most Unvaluedst Purchase: Women in the Plays of Thomas Middleton*, Jacobean Drama Studies, no. 34 (Salzburg: Institut für Englische Sprache und Literatur, 1973), p. 85, states that the "opposition of sterile chastity and lasciviousness and their reconciliation in a synthesis runs throughout the play."

10. Cherry, *Most Unvaluedst Purchase*, p. 58, and McElroy, *Parody and Burlesque*, p. 129, both note the *topos* in passing.

11. Barker, *Thomas Middleton*, p. 99, argues that the play portrays a "world of weak or despicable characters who, in their blindness, undo themselves for ends they can never attain." Similarly, Schoenbaum, "Tragicomedies," p. 13, finds the central characters "hypocrites who resort to devious intrigues to gain their ends." Andrugio seems to be the only upright character in the play, because he is relatively constant throughout. Yet his very constancy makes him appear pitiable and foolish.

12. Schoenbaum, "Tragicomedies," p. 15, notes this. McElroy, *Parody and Burlesque*, p. 124, likewise states that nothing changes in the play, and stresses a parallel irony in the scene, "the complacency with which the two chief characters [the Cardinal and the Duchess] respond to the saving of their reputations."

13. On the various *topoi* concerned with the relationship of love and war, see Edgar Wind, *Pagan Mysteries in the Renaissance* (New Haven, Conn.: Yale University Press, 1958), pp. 81–88. Because Andrugio is both a warrior and a lover, he literally is concerned with both martial and amatory struggles. In fact, his war-caused deformity may

be a sign of an association with the demonic power of love (as I hope to show). Thus there is a great deal of irony in Aurelia's rejection of Andrugio because she likes "not him that has two mistresses, / War and his sweetheart; he can ne'er please both" (2.3.98–99). The distance between war and love is clearly not as great as she assumes.

14. For exemplary comments on the relation of deformity to extraordinary powers and behavior, see William Willeford, *The Fool and His Scepter: A Study in Clowns and Jesters and their Audience* (Chicago: Northwestern University Press, 1969), pp. 13–23, and the many general comments scattered throughout Mikhail Bakhtin, *Rabelais and His World*, trans. Helene Iswolsky (Cambridge, Mass.: MIT Press, 1968).

15. Willeford, *The Fool and His Scepter*, p. 86.

16. The *OED* does not cite *crotchet* used precisely in this sense until 1750, although an analogous definition (a hooklike instrument) goes back as far as 1430. But Middleton's pun is too appropriate to be false and must constitute an earlier usage than the editors of the dictionary were aware of.

17. The great exception is McElroy, *Parody and Burlesque*, who argues that the play is a "systematic demolition of the idea of law" (p. 223) and "travesties not merely Beaumont and Fletcher but, intentionally or unintentionally, the basic moral and aesthetic orientation of the greatest plays of the period" (p. 262).

18. Barker, *Thomas Middleton*, pp. 184–89, summarizes the findings of earlier critics, and notes that the manuscript is so confusing that "what now looks like Rowley may sometimes be corrupt Middleton or even corrupt Massinger" (p. 186). The best accounts of the text are those of George R. Price, "The Authorship and the Manuscript of *The Old Law*," *Huntington Library Quarterly* 16 (1953): 117–39; and David J. Lake, *The Canon of Thomas Middleton's Plays: Internal Evidence for the Major Problems of Authorship* (Cambridge: Cambridge University Press, 1975), 206–14. For an evaluation of the talents of the play's initial publisher, Edward Archer, see Samuel Schoenbaum, *Internal Evidence and Elizabethan Authorship: An Essay in Literary History and Method* (Evanston, Ill.: Northwestern University Press, 1966), p. 157.

The seminal study of the Middleton–Rowley collaboration is Pauline G. Wiggin's *An Inquiry into the Authorship of the Middleton-Rowley Plays*, Radcliff College Monographs, no. 9 (Boston: Ginn and Co.; 1897). Wiggin declines to consider *The Old Law* because of its text, concluding: "Evidently, any opinion as to the authorship of this play must be advanced with extreme caution" (p. 1). The rather neat distinctions she draws between Middleton and Rowley were first questioned by Wilbur Dunkel in "Did not Rowley Merely Revise Middleton?" *PMLA*, 48 (1933): 800–805. He plausibly suggests that Rowley was simply "a reviser, skilled in acting, according to tradition, comic roles" (p. 805). Recently, Holmes, *Art of Thomas Middleton*, p. 216, has reemphasized Dunkel's argument: "It has been conjectured that

Middleton needed Rowley the comedian to write 'comic underplots,' but this idea overlooks the fact that in the preceding sixteen years Middleton had written plays that contain comic action of the same kind." Charles Barber, "A Rare Use of the Word *Honour* as a Criterion of Middleton's Authorship," *ES* 38 (1957): pp. 161–68, further demonstrates the difficulty of separating Middleton's writing from Rowley's.

Massinger may have revised some of the play, but his revisions (if they exist) are certainly very minor ones. See A. H. Cruickshank, *Philip Massinger* (New York: Frederick A. Stokes Co., 1920), pp. 21, 141–42; T. A. Dunn, *Philip Massinger: The Man and the Playwright* (London: Thomas Nelson and Sons, 1957), p. 267; and especially Lake, *Canon*, p. 207: "Massinger cannot be a substantial contributor to any section except V.i.a (the 'trial scene'), and even here the hypothesis of his authorship poses difficulties." The drama's bitterly ironic theme is completely alien to Massinger's work. For example, as noted in Chapter 3, Massinger romanticizes and idealizes *A Trick to Catch the Old One* in his *A New Way to Pay Old Debts*—a play which is essentially a revision of Middleton's earlier comedy.

On scene and line apportionment, see Edgar Morris, "On the Date and Composition of *The Old Law*," *PMLA* 17 (1902): p. 67; Holmes, *Art of Thomas Middleton*, p. 219. Schoenbaum, *Internal Evidence*, p. 162, states the moral: "It is risky to attempt the allocation of scenes in collaborations, even when all the partners are known—Middleton, Rowley, and Massinger's *The Old Law*, for example, which has come down in a wretched text."

19. Dewar Robb, "The Canon of William Rowley's Plays," *MLR* 45 (1950): 136.

20. Middleton, *Works*, 2:119.

21. Northrop Frye, *A Natural Perspective: The Development of Shakespearean Comedy and Romance* (New York: Columbia University Press, 1965), pp. 75–76.

22. They judge Hippolita in the same way. After she enters and pleads for her husband's release, the Second Courtier advises: "You are fresh and fair; practise young women's ends" (5.1.79).

23. In contrast, Asp, *Tragicomedies*, pp. 149–53, argues that the audience is never taken in by the play's extraordinary premise, a reading in keeping with her generally optimistic interpretation of the drama.

24. As McElroy notes, "Gnotho takes over Sim's role of irreverent chorus," and is "an even more emphatic voice of perversity and cynicism than his predecessor had been" (*Parody and Burlesque*, p. 246).

25. Leonides' lodge is also an Edenic retreat (1.1.434–41). These peaceful sanctuaries in turn symbolize the wisdom and stoicism which should accompany old age:

> For what is age
> But the holy place of life, chapel of ease
> For all men's wearied miseries?

[3.2.250–52]

And so, Lysander's reformation is marked by a peaceful acceptance of whatever life brings (5.1.111–24). He no longer wishes to alter the course of nature.

Chapter 6

1. Quotations from *The Changeling* and *Women Beware Women* are taken from *The Changeling*, ed. N. W. Bawcutt, The Revels Plays (London: Methuen, 1958); and *Women Beware Women*, ed. J. R. Mulryne, The Revels Plays (London: Methuen, 1975).

2. Una Ellis-Fermor, *The Jacobean Drama: An Interpretation* (1935; reprint ed., New York: Random House, Inc., 1961), pp. 139–44. See also Thomas M. Parrott and Robert H. Ball, *A Short View of Elizabethan Drama* (New York: Charles Scribner's Sons, 1943), p. 237; Samuel Schoenbaum, *Middleton's Tragedies: A Critical Study* (New York: Columbia University Press, 1955), pp. 103–32; T. B. Tomlinson, *A Study of Elizabethan and Jacobean Tragedy* (Cambridge: Cambridge University Press, 1964), pp. 158–84; Robert Ornstein, *The Moral Vision of Jacobean Tragedy* (Madison: University of Wisconsin Press, 1965), pp. 191–99; R. B. Parker, "Middleton's Experiments with Comedy and Judgement," *Jacobean Theater*, Stratford-upon-Avon Studies, no. 1 (New York: St. Martin's Press, 1960), pp. 192–98. Middleton's use of comic and tragic elements is related to the morality play tradition by both Arthur Kirsch, *Jacobean Dramatic Perspectives* (Charlottesville: University Press of Virginia, 1972), p. 95; and Penelope B. R. Doob, "A Reading of *The Changeling*," *ELR* 3 (1973): 199–201.

3. Dorothy Farr, *Thomas Middleton and the Drama of Realism: A Study of Some Representative Plays* (Edinburgh: Oliver and Boyd, 1973), pp. 7, 96. See also especially pp. 50–63, 94–96. Charles Hallett, *Middleton's Cynics: A Study of Middleton's Insight into the Moral Psychology of the Mediocre Mind*, Jacobean Drama Studies, no. 47 (Salzburg: Institut für Englische Sprache und Literatur, 1975), p. 210. As the title of Hallett's study implies, he, like Farr, stresses the unheroic stature of Middleton's tragic figures.

4. For analyses of the play as a commentary on Petrarchan love, see Ornstein, *Moral Vision*, pp. 179–90, and Thomas L. Berger, "The Petrarchan Fortress of *The Changeling*," *Renaissance Papers, 1969* (Southeastern Renaissance Conference, 1970), pp. 37–46. Robert Jordan interprets the play as an ironic version of the beauty and the beast fable in "Myth and Psychology in *The Changeling*," *Renaissance Drama* n.s. 3 (1970): 157–65. For the relationship of the main plot to traditional comic conflicts, see Farr, *Drama of Realism*, p. 50. Richard

Levin comments on the thwarting of audience expectations in the subplot in *The Multiple Plot in English Renaissance Drama* (Chicago: University of Chicago Press, 1971), p. 37. As a "tonal thrill-show," see Raymond J. Pentzell, "*The Changeling*: Notes on Mannerism in Dramatic Form," *Comparative Drama* 9 (1975): 7–8. Pentzell goes on to argue that "we should see in Middleton and Rowley's work . . . not the intention of mystifying the spectators nor solely of exciting them, but rather a refusal (or inability) to force their commitment to a single kind of stage reality" (p. 14).

5. Two of the most influential statements of this view can be found in Parker, "Middleton's Experiments," pp. 198–199, and G. R. Hibbard, "The Tragedies of Thomas Middleton and the Decadence of the Drama," *Renaissance and Modern Studies* 1 (1957): 35–64.

6. Cf. Pentzell, "Notes on Mannerism," pp. 3–28.

7. See Bawcutt, *The Changeling*, pp. xxvi–xxviii; and *Hengist, King of Kent; or, The Mayor of Queenborough*, ed. R. C. Bald (New York: Charles Scribner's Sons, 1938), p. xxvi.

8. See the accounts of Schoenbaum, Tomlinson, Ornstein, Parrott and Ball, Parker, and Farr cited above in note 2.

9. See Christopher Ricks, "Word-Play in *Women Beware Women*," *RES* 12 (1966): 238–50. Ricks finds some of the same characteristics in *The Changeling* as well in "The Moral and Poetical Structure of *The Changeling*," *Essays in Criticism* 10 (1960): 290–306.

10. Parrott and Ball, *A Short View*, p. 238. Cf. Ellis-Fermor, *Jacobean Drama*, pp. 140–44; and Ornstein, *Moral Vision*, p. 198. J. B. Batchelor traces our changing responses to Livia in "The Pattern of *Women Beware Women*," *Yearbook of English Studies* 2 (1972): 78–88.

11. Mulryne, *Women Beware Women*, p. lxix, notes that Livia's house "ostensibly symbolizes hospitality but in fact serves the opportunism of this society's values."

Index